What is a Fair International Society?

Today's world is postcolonial and post-Cold War. These twin characteristics explain why international society is also riddled with the two major forms of injustice that Nancy Fraser identified as afflicting national societies. First, the economic and social disparities between states caused outcry in the 1950s when the first steps were taken towards decolonisation. These inequalities, to which a number of emerging states now contribute, are still glaring and still pose the problem of the gap between formal equality and true equality. Second, international society is increasingly confronted with culture- and identity-related claims, stretching the dividing line between equality and difference. The less-favoured states, those that feel stigmatised, but also native peoples, ethnic groups, minorities and women, now aspire to both legal recognition of their equal dignity and the protection of their identities and cultures. Some even seek reparation for injustices arising from the past violation of their identities and the confiscation of their property or land.

In response to these two forms of claim, the subjects of international society have come up with two types of remedy encapsulated in legal rules: the law of development and the law of recognition. These two sets of rights are neither wholly autonomous and individualised branches of law nor formalised sets of rules. They are imperfect and have their dark sides. Yet, they can be seen as the first milestones towards what might become a fairer international society; one that is both equitable (as an answer to socio-economic injustice) and decent (as an answer to cultural injustice).

This book explores this evolution in international society, setting it in a historical perspective and critically examining its presuppositions and implications.

Volume 5 in the series French Studies in International Law

French Studies in International Law

General Editor: Emmanuelle Tourme-Jouannet (Sorbonne Law School)

French Studies in International Law is a unique new series which aims to bring to the attention of an English-speaking audience the most important modern works by leading French and French-speaking scholars of international law. The books which appear in this series have been selected by Professor Emmanuelle Tourme-Jouannet of the University of Paris 1 (Sorbonne Law School). French Studies in International Law is a book collection of the IREDIES Paris 1 Sorbonne Law School (The Centre for Studies and Research in International Law). The IREDIES is the largest French research centre for international law comprising 11 professors, 3 lecturers, 21 research professors and researchers, and 188 PhD students. IREDIES follows an active policy of collective work in several key fields of research, including general international law, law of the United Nations, international disputes, international economic and finance law (in particular WTO), international human rights law, theory, philosophy and history of international law and foreign doctrines, international air space law, and the law of the sea.

Volume 1: Ordering Pluralism: A Conceptual Framework for Understanding the Transnational Legal World *Mireille Delmas-Marty translated by Naomi Norberg*

Volume 2: International Law, Power, Security and Justice: Essays on International Law and Relations *Serge Sur*

Volume 3: The Advancement of International Law *Charles Leben*

Volume 4: The Law against War: The Prohibition on the Use of Force in Contemporary International Law *Olivier Corten*

What is a Fair International Society?

International Law Between Development and Recognition

Emmanuelle Tourme-Jouannet

·HART·
PUBLISHING
OXFORD AND PORTLAND, OREGON
2013

Published in the United Kingdom by Hart Publishing Ltd
16C Worcester Place, Oxford, OX1 2JW
Telephone: +44 (0)1865 517530
Fax: +44 (0)1865 510710
E-mail: mail@hartpub.co.uk
Website: http://www.hartpub.co.uk

Published in North America (US and Canada) by
Hart Publishing
c/o International Specialized Book Services
920 NE 58th Avenue, Suite 300
Portland, OR 97213-3786
USA
Tel: +1 503 287 3093 or toll-free: (1) 800 944 6190
Fax: +1 503 280 8832
E-mail: orders@isbs.com
Website: http://www.isbs.com

British Library Cataloguing in Publication Data
Data Available

ISBN: 978-1-84113-430-7

Typeset by Hope Services, Abingdon
Printed and bound in Great Britain by
Lightning Source UK Ltd

For Stéphane, Vincent, Marion and Suzanne

Series Editor's Preface

This Series aims to contribute to the dissemination in English of the works of the most eminent international law scholars writing in French. Because these works have not yet been published in English, this scholarship is inaccessible to a great number of potential readers who, due to the language barrier, cannot become acquainted with or discuss it. This is highly regrettable, as it limits the debate on international law to works in English – the *lingua franca* of our contemporary world – and thus primarily to Anglophone scholars.

The publication of these works in English therefore seeks to create the conditions for genuine debate among Francophone and Anglophone international law scholars across the globe, a debate that should ideally be based on the work of both. *Learning* of the others' theories through translation is in fact the first essential step towards *acknowledging* the contributions and differences of each. Knowledge and acknowledgement lead to understanding the core of irreducibility, as well as truth, in each legal culture's international law doctrine, its traditions and distinct ideas, as well as each author's way of thinking. They should make it possible to avoid the all-too-frequent misunderstanding of each other's position on international law that results from simple ignorance of each other's work. Between the Francophone and Anglophone worlds, the rule is still too often mutual, even courteous indifference or ignorance, dialogue the exception.

Emmanuelle Tourme-Jouannet
Professor, University of Paris I (*Sorbonne Law School*)

A Cautionary Note About This Edition

This is a translation of a French book first written in 2010 and published in 2011 by Editions Pedone.[1] It is based on international reports of the time. I have updated references to those reports that provide new insights, notably the 2012 UN report on the Millennium Objectives, but in other instances this was not necessary because the more recent reports merely confirm, alas, the initial diagnosis.

Moreover, this book is based on a French understanding of 'development law' and so on an understanding that is not widely shared in the English-speaking world. The expression 'international law of development' is often thought of as a creation of the French-speaking world, although it has been used elsewhere.[2] In the years following the first United Nations Conference on Trade and Development, under the impetus of André Philip and Michel Virally,[3] several French international lawyers grouped together and systematised rules pertaining to this concept which was new at the time. They attempted to show that a new form of law had emerged for the benefit of developing countries and to separate it from the usual frameworks of analysis to which legal rules were attached such as the law of cooperation, economic and commercial law, or the law of international organisations.[4] The aim was also to show that two sets of standards had emerged, corresponding to the concrete differences between states: some pertaining to relations among developed countries and others to relations between developed and developing countries. It was this specific law of development that arose in the 1960s

[1] Emmanuelle Jouannet, *Qu'est-ce qu'une société internationale juste ? Le droit international entre développement et reconnaissance* (Paris, Pedone, 2011).

[2] See Guy Feuer, 'Le droit international du développement. Une création de la pensée francophone'; www.gemdev.org/publications/publications_en_ligne/etatdessavoirsdev/IV_feuer.PDF.

[3] It seems that the principle of international development law was introduced in France by André Philip at a Conference in Nice, 27–29 May 1965: *L'adaptation de l'ONU au monde d'aujourd'hui* (Paris, Pedone, 1965) 129 *ff*. It was taken up in Michel Virally, 'Vers un droit international du développement' (1965) *Annuaire Francais de Droit International* 3–12.

[4] For French scholarship, see especially Mohamed Bennouna, *Droit international du développement* (Paris, Berger-Levrault, 1983); Mario Bettati, *Le nouvel ordre économique international* (Paris, Presses Universitaires de France, Que sais-je?, 1985); Maurice Flory, *Droit international du développement* (Paris, Thémis, 1977); Edmond Jouve, *Le tiers-monde dans la vie internationale* (Paris, Berger-Levrault, 1986); Alain Pellet, *Droit international du développement* (Paris, Presses Universitaires de France, Que sais-je?, 1987); Guy Feuer and Hervé Cassan, *Droit international du développement* (Paris, Dalloz, 1990); Guy Ladreit de Lacharrière, *Commerce extérieur et sous-développement* (Paris, PUF, 1964).

and 1970s, which is called classical international development law here. It is important to specify this since many English-speakers, for example, do not identify in this way a *law of development* that is distinct from international economic law and they group together all legal and economic practices relating to development under the heading of *law and development*. However, in doing so, they fail to distinguish a law that reflects aspirations for reform, equity and social justice (the social law of nations) and a law based solely on the rules of liberal, financial and market capitalism. The fact of the matter is, however, that through classical development law an attempt was made to replace the liberal model of development, embodied in the legal and economic rules of the General Agreement on Tariffs and Trade, International Monetary Fund and World Bank, with a liberal-social model of development.

Contents

Introduction

THIS BOOK ENQUIRES into the changes in classical liberal international law and examines to what extent and in what ways it has readjusted in recent decades.[1] More specifically, it looks at the way in which international law has changed following decolonisation and the end of the Cold War. These episodes led to major re-alignments of some of the branches of international law and they are closely associated with the paradigms of development and recognition. We shall ask how this change relates to the growing demand for justice within international society and how it begs the question of what a fair international society might be.

The world today is a postcolonial and post-Cold War society.[2] Accordingly, it is beset by the same two forms of injustice that Nancy Fraser identifies in individual countries.[3] First, economic and social disparities among states caused outcry from the 1950s onwards with the first stages of decolonisation. These inequalities, to which a number of emerging states now contribute, are still glaring and still pose the problem of the gap between formal equality and true equality. Second, international society is increasingly confronted with cultural and identity-related claims, distorting the dividing line between equality and difference.[4] The less-favoured states, those which feel stigmatised, but also native peoples, ethnic groups, minorities and women now aspire to a legal recognition of their equal dignity and to the protection of their identities and cultures. Some even seek reparation for the injustice arising from the violation of their identities and the confiscation of their property or land. While this phenomenon of the demand for recognition has been examined at length in relation to national societies, crucial as it is, it has so far been very inadequately investigated in international society.

[1] This book pursues a line of thought first begun in Emmanuelle Jouannet, *The Liberal-Welfarist Law of Nations. A History of International Law* (Cambridge, Cambridge University Press, 2012).

[2] The UN identifies 16 'non-self-governing territories' that may be decolonised, including the Western Sahara, New Caledonia and Gibraltar. They are supervised by the UN Special Committee on Decolonisation. While mindful of their limits and ambiguities, we shall not go into the involved discussions of the terms 'colonialism' and 'postcolonialism'. See also John McLeod, *Beginning Postcolonialism* (Manchester, Manchester University Press, 2000) 4 *ff* and Robert JC Young, *Postcolonialism. An Historical Introduction* (Oxford, Blackwell, 2008) 13 *ff*. On the introduction of this little used term for the French-speaking world, see Marie-Claude Smouts, 'Le post-colonial pour quoi faire?' in Marie-Claude Smouts (ed), *La situation post-coloniale* (Paris, Ed Sciences Po, 2007) 25 *ff*.

[3] A selection of the American philosopher's work is published in French: Nancy Fraser, *Qu'est-ce que la justice sociale? Reconnaissance et redistribution* (Paris, La Découverte, 2005).

[4] See Sophie Guérard de Latour, *La société juste. Egalité et différence* (Paris, A Colin, 2001) 6 *ff*.

In answer to these two forms of claim, the subjects of international society have come up with two kinds of remedy encapsulated in the legal rights of development and recognition. Claims relating to socio-economic inequalities have led to the formulation of an international law relative to *development* – and not redistribution – as the solution to those inequalities; what Alain Pellet in 1987 called a 'social law of nations'.[5] This body of law has been thriving for some years and it has shifted from being a law of economic development to a much more complex law encompassing human, social and sustainable development. The second type of claim, about culture and identity, is currently giving rise to what we shall call an international law of *recognition*. It brings together a set of legal practices relating to recognition in the international arena that had not previously been theorised in that way, nor indeed collated. This is what is illustrated, for example, by the enshrinement in treaty of the principle of diversity of cultural expressions in 2005, by the reappearance of minority rights, by the emergence of rights of indigenous peoples, or again by legal issues relating to the World Conference against Racism (2001–2009), the mission of which was to symbolically re-establish the international community by putting an end to racism as a pre-eminently humiliating state of affairs.

A change of this kind reflects the similarity of concerns found in both internal and international law. This can come as no surprise since international law has always been the product of values and concerns that dominate within national societies, and in addition since international law is called upon to govern many internal states of affairs. When they are transposed into the international arena, domestic issues are rearranged in a way that is dependent on international society and on the specific circumstances of justice as it relates to the characteristics of contemporary international society. And yet, such a change is not self-evident; for not only is there nothing straightforward about it, as can readily be agreed, but moreover its content and its implications may appear particularly problematic. International law may well prove as much of a problem as a possible solution to inequalities, for it itself engenders rules that create injustice.[6] Besides, the concepts of recognition and of development are far from new; they are constructs that have become unreliable now that the intensive use that has been made of them has rendered them problematic, and they have come in for some very forceful criticism, to which we shall return in the course of the study, along with criticism levelled at the idea of a law of development or a law of recognition.[7] So

[5] Alain Pellet, *Le droit international du développement*, 2nd edn (Paris, PUF, 1987) 4.

[6] See David Kennedy, *Nouvelles approches de droit international* (Paris, Pedone, 2009) and Martti Koskenniemi, *La politique du droit international* (Paris, Pedone, 2007) and the present author's critique of that work (especially 33 *ff*).

[7] See, for example, on development, Serge Latouche, *L'occidentalisation du monde* (Paris, La découverte, 2005) or Gilbert Rist, *The History of Development: From Western Origins to Global Faith* (London and New York, Zed Books, 2002); on recognition, Axel Honneth, *La société du mépris. Vers une nouvelle théorie critique* (Paris, La découverte, 2006) 257 *ff*.

this change calls for an exploration of the facts and legal data that have led us to formulate it in these terms. But there is also need for a critical discussion of the presuppositions on which the change is based as much as of its actual or supposed effects. It is with a view to successfully conducting this double investigation that the two main lines of the evolution described here have been studied. The endeavour is to ascertain and question the way in which international law has responded to the calls for development (Part I) and for recognition (Part II).

It ought to be said from the outset that what is to be addressed here are not contemporary theories of justice and the philosophical questions that the topic raises – the issues covered by Fraser, but on the international stage. Many highly interesting studies have already sprung from these questions in recent years and accordingly it is the aim to address them here from a different angle: from within legal practice, as it were. Instead of discussing the great principles of justice in the international arena and their ultimate theoretical foundation, and subsequently seeking out concrete manifestations of them, I have opted for an approach based on existing legal practice, with a view to conceptualising and questioning it. It is not a matter of adhering to this legal practice but of adopting a point of view that might be described as 'moderately external' to international law; a half-way house between the external viewpoint and the strictly internal viewpoint so that, by a reasoned exposition of what it represents from the inside, one can think about the fundamental principles underlying the contemporary international legal order.[8] While no attempt has been made to take up any a priori definition of international justice, my hope is, through this examination of legal practice, to empirically identify the contours of what a fair international society might be in this day and age; and in doing so, to fuel a contemporary debate on justice which sometimes seems to completely ignore existing international practice in normative and institutional terms and is therefore unaware of the actual conditions in which the problem arises empirically.[9]

But it is not my aim to make a detailed analysis of the legal rules at issue, nor a study of their mandatory character; two points that shall be necessary later on. I have attempted simply to begin by identifying the principles and legal practices relating to development and recognition and by setting aside past legal struggles and the fundamental ethical and economic challenges involved. However vital it may be for jurists to conduct more technical future research into the legal nature of the principles, texts and practices that are

[8] These are methodological distinctions set out by Michel van de Kerchove and François Ost, *Le système juridique entre ordre et désordre* (Paris, PUF, 1988) 9 *ff.*

[9] Leaving one to wonder about the perception some commentators may have of the state of international society. See, for example, John Rawls, 'The Law of Peoples' (1993) 20 *Critical Inquiry* 36–68 and the series of debates it prompted, which often seem poorly informed about international realities: Philip N Pettit, 'Rawls's Peoples' in Rex Martin and David Reidy (eds), *Rawl's Law of Peoples: A Realistic Utopia* (Oxford, Blackwell, 2006) and David Reidy, 'On Global Economic Justice: in Defense of Rawls' (2007) 11(2) *Journal of Ethics* 193–236.

to be expounded, that research will depend on each researcher's conception of law and of their amenability to law in general, as no conception can make any claim to absolute truth in this domain. Moreover, evoking the question of justice in a book on international law does not have any polemical purpose as might sometimes be thought within the discipline in French-speaking countries. I have simply sought to show how questions that cannot be reduced to their legal and technical aspects are envisaged ethically and how they can be discussed without necessarily falling into the arbitrariness of ideology or the moralisation of law.[10]

Finally, it should be pointed out that precedence has been given to the historical perspective inasmuch as it challenges any idea of a radical break between past and present and provides an understanding of the current persistence of a certain ambivalence and of past contradictions of international society and of its law on these issues. To act as if the past were no longer relevant can only lead us to endlessly reproduce legal practices and techniques that are no more than heedless repetitions of a past that has been forgotten or that we have sought to repress.[11] For example, for some commentators the latest episode of globalisation has supposedly rendered obsolete any reading based on colonial and postcolonial concepts and replaced it by one using transnational and global concepts. I see this as a curious misreading of history and its effects. Admittedly, the current phase of globalisation has renewed some terms of the debate, a point that will be taken up later and which should certainly not be underestimated, for the world is changing. However, contemporary international law and postcolonial society cannot easily shrug off a past that continues to haunt them and that all too often leads them to reproduce discursive structures and practices of the colonial/postcolonial legacy even in what seem to be the most emancipating of present day legal techniques.[12]

[10] See Alain Boyer, 'Justice et égalité' in Denis Kambouchner (ed), *Notions de philosophie, III* (Paris, Gallimard, 1995) 10.

[11] See the convincing analyses in Nathaniel Berman, *Passion and Ambivalence. Colonialism, Nationalism and International Law* (Leiden, Brill, 2011) but also Ania Loomba, *Colonialism/Postcolonialism*, 2nd edn (New York, Routledge, 2005) 213 *ff.*

[12] Nathaniel Berman, 'Les ambivalences impériales' in Emmanuelle Jouannet and Hélène Ruiz-Fabri (eds), *Droit international et impérialisme en Europe et aux Etats-Unis* (Paris, Société de législation comparée, 2007) 137 *ff.*

Part I

International Law and Development: An Equitable International Society?

Ever since the end of the Second World War, development has been viewed as the way for poor states to catch up with rich states and thereby narrow the socio-economic gap between countries. Rules of international law have been drawn up along these lines, the United Nations has launched several 'development decades' (10 year periods over which to promote and measure improvement in living standards in the poorer countries), multiple plans and strategies have been implemented, and numerous international and regional organisations have been set up to this end. But more than 60 years after the earliest international texts were first adopted, there is no readily discernible result.[1]

For one thing, history seems to be accelerating, and what was the Third World is experiencing such upheavals that some of the old mindsets need to be reconfigured. We are witnessing the spectacular success of big emerging nations like India, Brazil, South-East Asian countries and most of all China, which became the world's second largest economy in 2010. The Organisation for Economic Cooperation and Development (OECD) predicts a 'shift of wealth' towards the South in the coming years.[2] Not only might the world be becoming post-Western, but the Third World has fragmented, broken up and reformed, with some states having hived off from it for good. We now need to speak of North(s) and South(s) when referring to sets of countries that are ever more composite and divided, and comparisons that were previously confined to North–South relations now need to cover South–South and South–North relations.[3] The success story of former Third World countries is a new factor: the gap with the North was bridged and the facts of the problem as some commentators had posited them for decades

[1] The results of development are controversial anyway, teeming with untruths and fuelled by the recurrent battle of statistics and yardsticks. Figures on poverty, for example, differ according to the measuring instruments and underlying representations. See Odile Castel, *Le Sud dans la mondialisation. Quelles alternatives?* (Paris, La découverte, 2002) 25 *ff*. The same goes for the gap between South and North: see Jacques Brasseul, *Introduction à l'économie du développement* (Paris, A Colin, 2008) 11 *ff*.

[2] OECD, Report 2010, 'Perspectives on Global Development: Shifting Wealth'; www.oecd.org/document/42/0,3343,en_2649_33959_42032170_1_1_1_1,00.html.

[3] Sylvie Brunel, *Le Sud dans la nouvelle économie mondiale* (Paris, PUF, 1995) 245 *ff*.

were changed, because the economic model of development that had been imported from the North truly seemed to have borne fruit in the South. A degree of material equality among states was restored by the rise in the living standards of hundreds of millions of people and it is astonishing that some observers should fail to acknowledge this fact.[4]

But poverty, hunger and economic and social inequalities between states persist in terrifying and unacceptable proportions, ruling out any idea that the Third World has disappeared entirely, as Robert Zoellick recently suggested.[5] The Third World is still with us, along with its hunger, its destitution and its poverty, and it is wholly dependent on international aid. The figures prove it. The 2010 United Nations Conference on Trade and Development (UNCTAD) report on the least developed countries is particularly gloomy and calls for a wholesale reform of development.[6] Hunger reached its highest level worldwide in 2009 and declined only slightly in 2010 since 925 million people still suffer from chronic undernourishment.[7] Although progress had been made in recent years, 64 million more people slipped into poverty in 2010 due to the world financial and economic system crisis.[8] The fact of the matter is that the recent financial crisis further dashed the hopes for successful globalisation because it showed just how fragile the whole system was and how it was liable to repeatedly lead to widespread social tragedy engendering unemployment, job insecurity, hunger and poverty in the South and North alike.

Confronted with this very disturbing change, which is every bit as paradoxical as it is problematic, it has to be asked what part international law has played and is playing with respect to development. Can development law still be seen as a possible solution for poor countries and the world's inequalities? Or has it merely contributed to what Sophie Bessis calls the 'great post-colonial illusion'?[9] Or is development law merely one legal tool among many,

[4] On the facts, see for example La Documentation française, *Pays émergents: vers un nouvel équilibre mondial?* Problèmes économiques, April 2010, 2993. For a denial that the North–South divide is being narrowed by the economic development of the South, see for example Gilbert Rist, *The History of Development: From Western Origins to Global Faith* (London and New York, Zed Books, 2002).

[5] Robert Zoellick is President of the World Bank Group. See his speech in Washington on 14 April 2010, web.worldbank.org/WBSITE/EXTERNAL/NEWS/0,,contentMDK:22541126~pagePK:34370~piPK:42770~theSitePK:4607,00.html.

[6] UNCTAD, 'The Least Developed Countries Report 2010. Towards a New International Development Architecture for LDCs';www.unctad.org/Templates/webflyer.asp?docid=14129&intItemID=1397&lang=1.

[7] See the Food and Agriculture Organization of the United Nations (FAO) figures for 2010. The hungry make up 16% of the population in developing countries and 30% in Sub-Saharan Africa, but numbers are growing in the developed world, too. See the FAO website; www.fao.org/hunger/hunger-home/en/.

[8] That is, living on less than $1.25 a day. See the World Bank figures quoted in *Le Monde*, 16 September 2010; www.lemonde.fr/idees/article/2010/09/16c-est-la-croissance-qui-eradiquera-la-pauvrete_1411907_3232.html.

[9] Sophie Bessis, *L'Occident et les autres. Histoire d'une suprématie* (Paris, La découverte, 2003) 121.

and one which has been overestimated all round, while, in keeping with the ultraliberal credo, only the rules of international economic law are of any relevance?

Actually, the existence of an international law specifically on development now seems to have been completely forgotten by the new generations of jurists. Indeed the subject is no longer taught at all in universities, which is a stark contrast to the impassioned debates and prolific research it once spawned. Around the 1970s, development law had come to be pretty much a subject in itself in university law departments, but having since been subsumed under various branches of law within which it enjoys no special standing, it is now only a marginal and piecemeal topic. This change is related to the ideological revisions brought about by the collapse of Marxism and the new phase of globalisation after 1989. These changed circumstances have brought about far-reaching transformations that must be appraised in order to examine anew the very idea of a branch of law that is specific to development, the demand for equity that such law contains and the possibility of such a law surviving in the new, globalised, post-Cold War context.

To achieve this objective, it is proposed that the changing legal practice is studied so as to ascertain the historical context in which development law arose and the forms it has taken on to date. The intention is to move beyond the model for which international economic law serves as a vector (chapters one and two). Questions must also be asked about the dark side and the dead-ends of development law, by making an overall assessment of it, by showing in particular the gaping divide between the legal principles it vaunts and their very limited effectiveness, and the fact that it serves at one and the same time to challenge but also to legitimise the international economic law of neoliberal globalisation that has prevailed since the end of the Cold War (chapter three). While the subject is under discussion, questions shall then be asked about the possible alternatives to the existing law by reformulating the terms of the social justice/economic efficiency equation (chapter four).

1

Classical International Law and Development

AFTER THE SECOND World War and, above all, after decolonisation, a worldwide consensus was to form around development as a key value for reconstructing post-war and postcolonial society, with the shared conviction that all countries would finally enjoy prosperity and well-being. In an age when it seemed everything was still possible, the 'darker nations',[1] which had at long last emerged into the light, proposed a project for the world, the high point of which was indisputably the proclamation of a New International Economic Order. It was designed, by means of a general reform of the international order, to re-introduce the legal principles and practices of a development law that some wanted to bring in to offset the extreme economic and social imbalance of postcolonial society. But that historical impetus was halted in the decolonised countries for internal and external reasons, leaving the way open to the post-Cold War neoliberal model.

I The Development Paradigm

As attested by the many declarations and practices of international law from the post-war period to the present day, development is one of the most important intellectual and social matrices of contemporary times, reflecting as it does an imagination that draws on the old Western belief in progress and that feeds on the different economic and social theories of the day. This new paradigm was firmly established through an agreement that was broadly shared between South and North in the aftermath of independence, although the project was never fully accomplished. It was the tragic paradox of development during the Cold War years that it was constantly announced and endlessly postponed. The general reconciliation of the postcolonial world around development was superficial anyway insofar as the crucial debate about the causes of under-development, and the ways to escape it, emerged at the time of independence, marking out what was to become one of the keenest and most tenacious confrontations between North and South.

[1] Vijay Prashad, *The Darker Nations. A People's History of the Third World* (New York, The New Press, 2007).

A The Development Era

Articles 1(3) and 55(a) of the UN Charter clearly include development among the aims of the post-war international legal order, with Article 55(a) using the term 'development' itself:[2]

> With a view to the creation of conditions of stability and well-being which are necessary for peaceful and friendly relations among nations based on respect for the principle of equal rights and self-determination of peoples, the United Nations shall promote:
>
> a. higher standards of living, full employment, and conditions of economic and social progress and development;

And yet the idea of making development a UN objective was controversial at the time. The USSR was strongly opposed to any UN intervention in the economic and social domains, probably out of fear of seeing any model being imposed, and was therefore lukewarm about any provision going beyond matters of security. However, it was the American and British position in favour of intervention in the economic and social spheres that won out, with the idea of getting to the root causes of peace, in other words, of making development a means to ensure peace. Such subordination of development to peace was criticised on the grounds that it should be the other way around; but the fact of the matter is that the principle of development was established and was to be more successful certainly than the drafters of the Charter had imagined. With decolonisation and the massive influx of newly independent states to the UN, Article 55(a) was to become the legal basis for what was called the 'development ideology' of the 1960s–1970s and the driving force behind considerable UN activity.

That being so, the principle of specific aid for Third World development and the decisive impetus in this field came about with post-war US policy. On 20 January 1949, President Harry S Truman told the world it was divided into developed and underdeveloped nations and the US was to provide financial, economic and technological assistance to all the world's 'underdeveloped' nations:[3] 'Fourth, we must embark on a bold new program for making the benefits of our scientific advances and industrial progress available for the improvement and growth of *underdeveloped* areas.'[4]

[2] See Alain Pellet, 'Commentaire de l'article 55, alinéas a et b' in Jean-Pierre Cot, Alain Pellet and Mathias Forteau (eds), *La Charte des Nations Unies. Commentaires article par article* (Paris, Economica, 2005) 1453.

[3] See Firouzeh Nahavandi, *Du développement à la globalisation. Histoire d'une stigmatisation* (Brussels, Bruylant, 2009) 30 *ff.*

[4] President Truman's Inaugural address of 20 January 1949; teachingamericanhistory.org/library/index.asp?document=1453. Emphasis added. Truman's speech led to the signing of the Act for International Development in June 1950.

Truman's address had a decisive influence since it heralded the dawn of the development era that was to break with the old system of the past. In his 1949 address, Truman immediately sought to draw a sharp distinction, differentiating the new world objective of development and aid to the 'under-developed' nations from the old European colonial and imperialist system: 'The old imperialism – exploitation for foreign profit – has no place in our plans. What we envisage is a program of development based on the concepts of democratic fair-dealing.'[5]

Being strongly anti-colonial by tradition because of its own struggle for independence, the US in 1949 had every interest in dismantling the great European colonial empires since that would afford it access to new markets, but it would also prevent poor countries from siding with the communist camp. Truman therefore proposed to replace the old imperialist system by a new global vision in which all states were equal and all of humankind was involved in the new 'development' paradigm. Against colonialism, which placed the colonised peoples in a hierarchical relationship with the colonial power, he brandished a world in which all the nations of the 'development era' were on an equal footing and enjoyed the same rights. He replaced unilateral constraint and the system of colonial exploitation with the idea of international cooperation to bring about a change in the circumstances of the 'underdeveloped' nations and their transition to a developed condition. This economic and technological development was also presented as a solution that went beyond the ideological divide, as it could be evaluated on the basis of economic and scientific statistics that were neutral and objective rather than in terms of the arguable subjective values of any particular civilisation.

However, development is far from being a neutral concept but conveys one of the most fundamental of Western beliefs.[6] Development merely perpetuates under another name the old idea of progress that had been largely discredited after 1945 and it restored the certainties of an age that had been badly shaken by the Second World War. The very principle of economic development had been invented in nineteenth-century Europe initially to compare the standings of different European states with each other and to evaluate that standing with respect to an optimum level of economic prosperity calculated on the basis of European economic data alone. It was then generalised, interpreted more extensively and applied to colonised territories. Article 22 of the Covenant of the League of Nations, establishing the system of mandates over colonised peoples, states that 'the well-being and *development* of such peoples form a sacred trust of civilisation' and that 'The best method for giving practical effect to this principle is that the tutelage of such peoples should be entrusted to the advanced nations'.[7] This was the first

[5] ibid.

[6] Gilbert Rist, *The History of Development: From Western Origins to Global Faith* (London and New York, Zed Books, 2002).

[7] Emphasis added.

time that development had been used as a criterion with which to classify the world's nations on a scale ranging from least to most developed.

The issue of development was therefore not the result of decolonisation but was foremost the result of concerns of the nineteenth-century industrialised nations that had gone on to colonise half the world. Development was initially a concern of rich, not poor countries, of colonial countries, not colonised or decolonised countries; and the development of the colonised was measured by the condition of the colonisers. This is why decolonised states soon came to be known as 'underdeveloped' and then, more diplomatically, as 'developing' countries. This gives rise to an inevitable but odd continuity between the discourse and practice of international law before 1945 and of contemporary international law. States are arranged on a scale according to their degree of development and the 'underdeveloped/developed' categorisation of nations maintains a divide in South–North relations based on the difference in circumstances between the two, with the same persistent idea that the one that is lagging behind should catch up with the one that is ahead and which serves as a model to be imitated.[8] Just like the work of colonisation and civilisation before it, development was presented as highly positive, desirable and necessary, and justifies ahead of time all the legal rules adopted for this purpose.[9] In short, development has therefore been from the outset the continuation of the policy of Western colonial domination by other means and this has made it intrinsically ambivalent right down to the present day.

In addition, the first development model to emerge with the Americans reflected the attachment to an economic model of liberal capitalism that they would have readily extended to the entire planet. It was defined as a state of abundance secured through ever-increasing wealth, whereas underdevelopment was, quite the contrary, a state of low output. Hope lay, then, in an increase in wealth worldwide which, by itself and through the simple multiplication of goods and of world output, was to close the gap between nations. This conception of development presupposed certain economic postulates, which were those of the international economic law that began to emerge at the same period via the International Monetary Fund (IMF) and the World Bank, set up by the 1944 Bretton Woods Agreements, and the General Agreement on Tariffs and Trade (GATT) adopted in Geneva in 1947: growth, the necessary increase in output based on investment and foreign

[8] See David F Greenberg, 'Law and Development in Light of Dependency Theory' (1980) 3 *Research in Law and Sociology* 129 *ff*.

[9] Uma Kothari, 'From Colonial Administration to Development Studies: A Post-Colonial Critique of the History of Development Studies' in Uma Kothari (ed), *A Radical History of Development Studies* (London, Zed Books, 2005) 47–66. The way the colonial past continues to haunt this new development paradigm is also evident from the fact that development studies are the direct continuation of colonial law studies. In France, for example, the *Précis Dalloz de droit colonial* was superseded by the *Précis du droit d'outre-mer et de la coopération* and then by G Feuer and H Cassan's *Précis du droit international du développement*. See Yves Daudet, 'Propos introductifs' to Emmanuelle Jouannet, Hélène Ruiz-Fabri and Mark Toufayan (eds), *Le droit international et les nouvelles approches sur le tiers monde* (Paris, Société de législation comparée, 2012).

aid, the principle of free trade and the existence of a multilateral commercial and monetary system, with the human goals of full employment and prosperity for all as its objective. Those Keynesian objectives, which are all too often forgotten nowadays, and which are included in the preamble to the GATT in particular, clearly indicate that the liberal and multilateral economic model of the post-war period, free trade or growth policies were not considered at the time as ends in themselves but as mere means to achieve greater social objectives. What was firmly being put in place was a Western liberal type of economic international law that was clearly different from today's dominant neoliberal model.[10] In point of fact, even though these humanistic ends were announced at the time as essential all round, the new economic and financial institutions were still initially designed to serve the interests of the rich nations alone and were denounced by the poor states at the conferences of Bretton Woods, Havana and at the Geneva and London preparatory conferences. The 1947 GATT was decried as it did not provide for any preferential tariffs that could help the Third World and it remained off-limits to non-Westerners. The contempt that Western economists displayed for the Third World delegates at the various conferences at the time was as plain as it was appalling. Keynes himself regretted that countries like Colombia, Venezuela and Liberia were invited to the Bretton Woods talks as they would merely 'encumber the ground' turning it into 'the most monstrous monkey-house assembled for years'.[11]

That said, the Western origin of development by means of the continuation of a neo-colonial policy of domination must not make us forget that all the world's states largely subscribed to it immediately. The decolonised or formerly dominated countries, which came together in the non-aligned movement (NAM) and met at the emblematic Bandung, Belgrade and Cairo conferences, were also firm believers in economic development, so much so that development was presented as a fundamental objective even in the final text of the 1955 Bandung Conference. No-one at the time contested the principle and it is only today that arguments are emerging (in the North) that all development should be abandoned. There was none of that in the 1950s and 1960s. Most Third World states were poor or very poor and lived in the hope that they could escape from poverty in time through the development of their economies and through anything that promoted economic growth. They all aspired to evolve into modern, industrial societies so as to eradicate destitution and secure higher living standards for their populations but also to equal the rich countries which were their former 'guardians'. Development, as a key factor in the reconstruction of postcolonial society, therefore became one

[10] See Emmanuelle Jouannet, *The Liberal-Welfarist Law of Nations. A History of International Law* (Cambridge, Cambridge University Press, 2012).

[11] John Maynard Keynes to David Yales, 30 May 1944, Donald Moggridge (ed), *The Collected Writings of John Maynard Keynes* (Cambridge, Cambridge University Press, 1980) vol 26, 42. See also Prashad, *The Darker Nations* (n 1) 68.

of the most important paradigms in international law after the Second World War and the intellectual and social matrix that guided behaviour at the time. The economic context was also particularly favourable and so optimism was the order of the day. There was even concern as to how the developed countries would cope with the accelerated development of the underdeveloped nations. As experts from the League of Nations remarked in 1943:

> It may be that after the war, given the expansion of engineering industries and the simplification of manufacturing processes, the industrial development of the backward regions will be so fast that it will make it extremely difficult and painful for other countries to adapt to the new conditions of competition.[12]

They could not have been more wrong. But it is easier to understand how, after the war, the belief in rapid economic development was to underpin the whole world view. The same optimism was to be found in the United Nations. The UN became the main centre for help to underdeveloped countries and put in place the first technical assistance programme in 1949. In 1951 it published a report describing the differences between states owing to their level of national income. It dubbed the 1960s the 'Decade of Development', suggesting that Third World countries would have achieved development in 10 years' time thanks to the legal and economic policies and rules on development.[13] The first legal rules on technical assistance, transfer of resources and aid were put in place through international organisations and through bilateral treaties. Apart from situations of particular conflict relating to certain independence movements, former colonial nations stated that they were ready to aid the new states, as were the two post-war great powers, which were clearly anti-colonialist. From the 1950s onwards the countries of the North constantly proclaimed their willingness to help with the development of the countries of the South. Although the rich countries above all were eager to safeguard their own interests by limiting concessions made to the poor countries to what they themselves though acceptable, they constantly repeated their promises and conceded certain dispensatory or compensatory legal measures in favour of the South. This attitude was both hegemonic and paternalistic, for while the shock of decolonisation engendered a very profound moral, political and economic crisis in the North, the Western World still saw itself as the centre of the new postcolonial society whose destiny was in its charge. The aspirations of the newly independent states to development were encouraged as they implied, initially, acceptance of the Western model of development and were therefore not a challenge to Western supremacy. Besides, at the time, the enemy was certainly not the emerging South but each

[12] Quoted by Jean-Jacques Friboulet, 'Développement économique et social. Histoire' in *Encyclopedia Universalis* 13; www.universalis.fr/encyclopedie/developpement-econmique-et-social-histoire/. (Our translation.)

[13] UN General Assembly Resolution 1715 (XVI) (19 December 1961) declaring the period 1961–1970 United Nations Development Decade: A programme for international economic co-operation.

of the two blocs, and it was only if a country fully rallied to either that the other bloc punished and ostracised it. The political and humanistic aspect of development was relegated behind the question of economic development. The possible spread of democracy and of human rights was not a concern of the West as the mere fact of having rallied to it was proof of good conduct. South-East Asia, South Korea and Taiwan were particularly well thought of and so received far more aid than other countries. As for the East and the USSR, as might be imagined, they were not concerned with pluralistic liberal democracy, and while they advocated adhesion to the principles of socialist planning, it was likewise allegiance to their camp that mattered above all. The two major powers thus separated the economic side of development from its political side, which suited the aspirations of the young Third World nations, which were above all eager to maintain their domestic sovereignty. This was to become one of the characteristic features of classical international development law.

B Disagreements over Development. Theories of 'Underdevelopment'

Although development became the new paradigm, disagreement soon arose over the conception of underdevelopment and therefore over the legal and economic rules by which to escape from it. Economists and then politicians and jurists argued over whether underdevelopment should be thought of as simply lagging behind the development of the richest states because of economic, political and social shortcomings endogenous to Third World countries or, on the contrary, as a product of that development, as the outcome of a political and economic world system established at the expense of the Third World.

The prevailing view of Americans and West Europeans was that underdevelopment was a lagging behind. This was propounded quite systematically by US economist Walt W Rostow. A fierce anti-communist and believer in the effectiveness of capitalism and free enterprise, Rostow was President Johnson's special adviser for national security in the 1960s. He embodied what were to be called 'modernisation theories'. In his 1958 book significantly entitled *The Stages of Economic Growth: A Non-Communist Manifesto*,[14] he sought to show that all countries develop in accordance with the same linear pattern and that the situation of the underdeveloped poor countries can be explained by their structural lag in the world process of economic development, which ultimately leads to a liberal society of prosperity and plenty (none other than the model of the United States).[15] He thought that underdevelopment was due essentially to natural, internal conditions of underdeveloped societies. They were 'backward'

[14] Walt Whitman Rostow, *The Stages of Economic Growth: A Non-Communist Manifesto* (Cambridge, Cambridge University Press, 1960).

[15] ibid, ch 2.

because of their run-away demography, their archaic social and political structures and their lack of economic policy. Hence the need to break 'the mould of traditional cultures' and apply the US and European pattern of economic development to all. No responsibility for the situation of poor countries was ascribed to colonialism and to past Western domination or to the existing international economic system. Rostow barely speaks of European colonisation and domination that were the past lot of underdeveloped countries. He dedicates a mere handful of pages[16] to the subject and at no point does he consider that they could have been the cause, even in part, of the state of poverty of the formerly colonised countries, resulting in a situation where the solutions proposed are the application of the rules of existing liberal economic international law with the integration of the new states in the world market governed by the GATT and the internal transformation of those states. Rostow even went so far as to suggest that underdeveloped countries should aid developed countries in the event of a crisis, and not vice versa, considering that the economic 'fall-out' would be beneficial all round:

> In the event of a crisis, precedence must be given to the well-off countries. It is in the interest of underdeveloped countries to help them through, for their own development is dependent on the positive fallout from the well-off countries being better off. Underdeveloped countries must know how to wait: the fallout will occur automatically.[17]

Depending on one's frame of mind, this may bring a wry smile or leave one dumbfounded because the obstinate reasoning leads to untenable conclusions in view of the situation of extreme indigence of certain decolonised countries at the time. Besides, the refusal to accept any responsibility was clearly anathema to many Third World politicians and intellectuals whose countries were emerging from two centuries of Western domination and found themselves caught up in a legal and economic system that they had not wanted and in which they were once again dominated. They were to come up with a counter-theory to underdevelopment. Some of the theories produced were characterised as 'dependency theories' as opposed to 'modernisation theories'.[18] These Marxist or structuralist theories saw underdevelopment not as backwardness or failure, but as the result of the economic development of wealthy states. Underdevelopment did not arise from natural factors endogenous to the decolonised nations, but it was primarily the result of past colonialism, of capitalist imperialism, of the exploitation of dominated countries and of unfair trade that affluent countries perpetuated through the new international economic law. In support of their thesis, dependency theorists developed

[16] ibid, ch 8.

[17] Text of 1940 cited by Mohammed Bedjaoui, 'L'humanité en quête de paix et de développement', vol II (2006) 325 *RCADI* 394 (our translation).

[18] For an overview of the many theories of the time, see Gerald M Meier and Dudley Seers (eds), *Pioneers in Development* (London, World Bank Publication, Oxford University Press, 1984).

historical studies showing how the acceleration of economic growth and the technological and military development of nineteenth-century Europeans led them to enslave three-quarters of the globe, thereby breaking with a situation of near homogeneity across the continents in the eighteenth century. That domination meant Europeans could grab land and wealth, extend their lead and keep the dominated and colonised peoples in a state of dependence and of underdevelopment that could not be papered over by the colonial measures taken with regard to infrastructure, health or education. The subservience of all those peoples made them structurally dependent on a colonial and imperial system that oppressed them for centuries. Since the Western nations had plundered the wealth of the colonised countries and exploited them for several centuries, the dependency theorists considered that they ought to face up to their responsibility for the wrongdoing and provide reparations in the form of unconditional subsidies to the former colonised peoples. Likewise, they thought it unacceptable that newly decolonised states should continue to be sacrificed in the name of a conception of development that perpetuated their dependence. They argued that the underdeveloped condition was maintained after decolonisation by an economic system that continued to make the periphery (the underdeveloped countries) dependent on the centre (the developed nations), with the result that the development of the core continued to produce the underdevelopment of the fringe. The legal and economic solution they advocated to underdevelopment was obviously not the same as in the dominant legal and political discourse of the Europeans and North Americans, for while they too wanted to see the Third World changed, they called for a no less far-reaching change in the structures of the international economic and political system.

Emblematically of dependency theorists, the South-American Raul Prebisch published a paper in 1949 on 'The Economic Development of America and its Principal Problems'.[19] It raised a simple question: how could development strategies that really benefited the populations there be put in place in Third World countries that were so impoverished? To answer this, Prebisch developed his own conception of 'development economics'. Since the development of the North was dependent on the underdevelopment of the South, the bonds of dependency between developed and underdeveloped countries had to be severed and a national economic system brought in that could ensure their independence. The new nations had to make national investments and introduce import/export legislation to protect themselves. On becoming United Nations Conference on Trade and Development (UNCTAD) Secretary General in 1964, Prebisch reiterated in his introductory report his views on

[19] Raul Prebisch, 'The Economic Development of America and its Principal Problems' (1962) 7(1) *Economic Bulletin for Latin America* 1–12. See also HW Singer, 'US Foreign Investment in Under-Developed Areas: The Distribution of Gains between Investing and Borrowing Countries' (1950) 40 *American Economic Review* 473–85. The two gave rise to what came to be known as the Singer-Prebisch thesis.

underdevelopment and proposed that a preferential legal regime should be extended to developing countries to help them to cope with their unequal status compared with developed countries.[20] This proposal was completely at loggerheads with the two fundamental principles of GATT 47, which was built on non-discrimination and reciprocity among Member States, and it departed from the principle of formal equality of classical international law. Adopting Prebisch's structuralist theories of underdevelopment, UNCTAD soon came to be thought of as anti-GATT. Accordingly, the North–South divide at the time was directly reflected institutionally through the moves and counter-moves of these two organisations.[21]

II The Emergence and Evolution of International Development Law – NIEO

Prebisch and many Third World countries demanded new international obligations specific to the new postcolonial society.

Their calls for two standards that might reform the existing economic order, which was denounced as unfair, were partly heard in the end and gave rise to classical international development law. From that time on, the question of development moved on to a whole new level from that of cooperation or aid; it became a demand for social justice from the Third World. The development law that emerged was one of its manifestations and took on a critical function with respect to the existing international economic law.

A Classical International Development Law

The expression 'international law of development' is often thought of as a creation of the French-speaking world, although it has been used elsewhere.[22] In the years following the first UNCTAD conference, under the impetus of André Philip and Michel Virally,[23] several French international lawyers grouped together and systematised rules pertaining to this concept which was new at the time. They attempted to show the emergence of a new

[20] Raul Prebisch, *Towards a New Trade Policy for Development* (New York, UNCTAD, 1964).

[21] UNCTAD led calls for an economic order based on equitable relations between developing countries and industrialised nations. Being entirely independent of GATT, it could make many recommendations that went against GATT's liberal rules but which could only become effective if adopted in the GATT rounds of trade talks. Hence the constant tension between the two organisations until the end of the Cold War.

[22] See Guy Feuer, 'Le droit international du développement. Une création de la pensée francophone'; www.gemdev.org/publications/publications_en_ligne/etatdessavoirsdev/IV_feuer.PDF.

[23] It seems that the principle of international development law was introduced in France by André Philip at a Conference in Nice, 27–29 May 1965: *L'adaptation de l'ONU au monde d'aujourd'hui* (Paris, Pedone, 1965) 129 *ff*. It was taken up in Michel Virally, 'Vers un droit international du développement' (1965) *Annuaire Francais de Droit International* 3–12.

law for the benefit of developing countries and to separate it from the usual frameworks of analysis to which legal rules were attached, such as the law of cooperation, economic and commercial law, or the law of international organisations.[24] The aim was also to show the emergence of two standards, depending on the concrete differences between states: some pertaining to relations among developed countries and others to relations between developed and developing countries. This international development law was from the outset subject to criticism from the two opposing sides. It was excoriated by the proponents of orthodox continental-type law, who denied its specificity or its legal nature and denounced the ideology underpinning it;[25] and it was also denounced by some representatives of the Third World who thought that neither the interests nor the conceptions of the Third World were taken into account by such law, which merely prolonged Western hegemony.[26]

There is little point returning to these quarrels, which have been largely abandoned today, other than to pick up on the new picture of law that emerged at the time. Even though its coherence, true legal character and the specificity of some of its norms might be criticised, for all its ambivalence and the unfair effects it might cause, international development law still emerged as a set of legal rules and practices designed to meet the aspirations of many developing countries, to address their development problems and to attempt to remedy the huge socio-economic inequalities between states in the aftermath of decolonisation. Notwithstanding the particular positions of some jurists, and despite the fact that it was not a formalised whole and that it gave rise to its own specific difficulties, it was considered a possible legal solution to those inequalities, a palliative for what international economic law alone could not bring about. It is important to highlight this as it clarified the legal options on development that emerged in practice, but it also meant that a score could be kept of those different options and possible legal alternatives. The economic development of new states was thought of as the eventual solution to inequalities among states but, in line with the differing conceptions of underdevelopment, it could be considered achievable in two different ways:

[24] For French scholarship see especially Mohamed Bennouna, *Droit international du développement* (Paris, Berger-Levrault, 1983); Mario Bettati, *Le nouvel ordre économique international* (Paris, PUF, Que sais-je?, 1985); Maurice Flory, *Droit international du développement* (Paris, Thémis, 1977); Edmond Jouve, *Le tiers-monde dans la vie internationale* (Paris, Berger-Levrault, 1986); Alain Pellet, *Droit international du développement* (Paris, PUF, Que sais-je?, 1987); Feuer and Cassan, *Droit international du développement* (n 9); Guy Ladreit de Lacharrière, *Commerce extérieur et sous-développement* (Paris, PUF, 1964).

[25] See the two conferences of the Société française de droit international, *Le droit international économique, Orléans, 1971* (Paris, Pedone, 1972) and *Pays en voie de développement et transformations du droit, Aix, 1973* (Paris, Pedone, 1974).

[26] See especially Mohammed Bedjaoui, *Pour un nouvel ordre économique international* (Paris, Unesco, 1979) / *Towards a New International Economic Order* (Holmes and Meier, 1979) and Madjid Benchikh, *Droit international et sous-développement. Nouvel ordre dans la dépendance* (Paris, Berger-Levrault, 1983).

either as the outcome of the interplay of ordinary rules of existing international economic law, in which case the new states, if they agreed, were simply subjected indiscriminately to the rules of the GATT, IMF and World Bank; or, on the contrary, as unachievable other than by specific rules that derogated from ordinary economic law and that were adapted to the situation of developing countries. It was this specific law of development that arose in the 1960s and 1970s which is called classical international development law, here. It is important to specify this since many English-speakers, for example, do not identify a *law of development* in this way that is distinct from international economic law and group together all legal and economic practices relating to development under the heading of *law and development*. However, in doing so, they fail to distinguish a law that reflects aspirations for reform, equity and social justice (the social law of nations) and a law based solely on the rules of liberal, financial and market capitalism. The fact of the matter is, however, that through classical development law an attempt was made to replace the liberal model of development, embodied in the legal and economic rules of the GATT, IMF and World Bank, with a liberal-social model of development.

Institutionally, what is sometimes called the 'United Nations system for development' was put in place, eliciting a considerable deployment of international bureaucracy and expertise in the field of technical assistance operations, with financial aid falling, in contrast, to the IMF and the World Bank. In normative terms, this international law of development rested on a small group of fundamental principles such as permanent sovereignty over natural resources, freedom of choice of economic system and the principle of equity. It also corresponded to a more technical set of legal rules that were interventionist, discriminatory or preferential in character and which differed from the ordinary rules of international law applicable to other states in that they were devised to correct the failings of the existing liberal legal and economic system by closing the material gap between developed and developing countries. This set of principles and rules led to the formulation of a New International Economic Order (NIEO) in the 1960s and 1970s with which the Third World countries wanted to replace the existing legal and economic system and which, for the sake of understanding, should be resituated within the great movement of Third World legal reform which preceded and prepared it.

B The Third World: A Reformist Project for the World

Although all the decolonised or formerly dominated countries accepted the principle that they were underdeveloped, this idea was plainly devaluing as it placed them once again at the back of the field of the world's countries, bringing up the rear. It did not allow the decolonised nations to express their difference and their dignity, at a time when they had just shaken off the European domination of the world that had maintained the cult of Western supremacy for centuries.[27] Conversely it was clear enough that the term 'Third World', coined by the French demographer Alfred Sauvy in 1952, could impart to 'underdeveloped' countries some feeling of worth and identity. In fact, Sauvy had alluded almost incidentally to the Third World at the end of a column he wrote for *L'Observateur*. He had no inkling how successful the term would prove and wanted primarily to discuss the Third World as what was at stake for the major powers as the Korean War unfolded.[28] But the idea caught on. It was taken up by Mehdi Ben Barka and then by Frantz Fanon in his *Les damnés de la Terre* (*The Wretched of the Earth*) in 1961 and was popularised in the English-speaking world by Peter Worsley in 1967.[29] While being much criticised for its ambiguity, it became a generic term that lost its French connotation and became more specific among those who adopted it. It signified the historical existence of a common destiny of a group of states making up two-thirds of the world's population but which had long been completely ignored and continued to be ignored by the other two dominant worlds that at the time formed the Eastern and Western blocs. It therefore encapsulated the newly emancipated nations' desire for dignity and recognition of their independence and their yearning for justice and equality.[30] This ambition was that much greater as at the beginning of the Cold War the two blocs that formed did not properly gauge the scope of the upheaval that was underway. For the First World, the Western bloc, the decolonised or decolonising nations were plainly still backward. The same was true for the Second World, the Eastern bloc, which adopted the same attitude initially, although the egalitarianism advocated in the East was an obvious draw for those countries which, having recently won their political independence, aspired to true equality. At the conference to inaugurate the Kominform in Poland in 1947, the Soviets also adopted the vision of a world divided into just two blocs and restricted themselves to speaking of national liberation movements alone. It was only when, in reaction to the Truman Plan, the USSR adopted a foreign-

[27] This was Raymond Aron's observation at the time. He was highly sceptical about the idea of underdevelopment as it is a comparative idea characterising societies by what they are not and not by what they are. Raymond Aron, 'Développement, rationalité et raison' (July 1963) *Preuves* 4.

[28] Sauvy wrote: 'We readily speak of the two worlds present, of their possible war, of their co-existence, etc., forgetting too quickly that there is a third, the largest, and all in all the first chronologically. It is the set of those that in United Nations style are called: the underdeveloped countries [. . .] this third-world that is ignored, exploited, scorned, like the third estate, it too wants to be something', Alfred Sauvy, 'Trois mondes, une planète' (14 August 1952) 118 *L'Observateur* 5.

[29] Peter Worsley, *The Three Worlds. Culture and Development* (London, Weidenfeld and Nicholson, 1967).

[30] The term 'Third World' has now been largely abandoned because of the change in the international situation since the end of the Cold War. However, the term is still used for its heuristic value by some highly dynamic, second-generation, English-speaking commentators in the TWAIL (Third World Approaches to International Law) project. See for example Makau Mutua, 'What is TWAIL' (2003) 31 *American Society of International Law Proceedings* 31 *ff* and Balakrishnan Rajagopal, 'Locating the Third World in Cultural Geography' (1998–99) 1 *The Third World Studies* 1 *ff*.

aid policy for the Third World that the Third World became an important feature in the Cold War and a bone of contention between East and West.[31]

However, the new nations now known as the Third World sought to organise themselves so as to be autonomous and united with respect to the two blocs and to express their own view of the world and of international law. They hoped above all to achieve equal dignity with other peoples, to recover their economic independence and to combat colonialism. Their leaders were all great names in the international arena, although some of them subsequently saw their image considerably tarnished. They included India's Jawaharlal Nehru, Egypt's Gamal Abdel Nasser, Ghana's Kwame Nkrumah, Indonesia's Ahmed Sukarno, Algeria's Ahmed Ben Bella, Cuba's Fidel Castro and so many others.[32] They organised the memorable first great conferences of Bandung in 1955, Belgrade in 1961 and Cairo in 1964, which were extraordinary moments of enthusiasm, euphoria and rediscovered pride for millions of people. The Brioni Declaration of 19 July 1956, initiated by Nasser, Tito, Nehru and Sihanouk, was the beginning of the Non-Aligned Movement (NAM), that is, aligned neither against nor with a major world power and supportive of each other. In 1958 Nehru announced: '[T]he essential cleavage in the world of today lies not so much between Communist and non-Communist states as between the nations enjoying a highly developed industrial economy and the underdeveloped nations struggling to survive.'[33]

The joint declaration of the 77 developing countries of 15 June 1964 was the founding act of the Group of 77 which was to defend the economic interests of the Third World in the United Nations. For at the time, as Vijay Prashad superbly relates, the Third World was also a project riddled by contractions but replete with immense hope.[34] This Third World project was the first real legal and political counter-narrative influential enough to challenge the representation of the world that the West had imposed until then.[35] The countries that were already independent like Japan, China, Turkey or those of South America were too concerned about joining in the international game to try to redefine the representation of the world and the rules governing it. This time round, the newly decolonised countries wanted to change the rules of the game and impose their vision of international society and of its law. In this they were behind an unprecedented movement for legal reform within international society, the impetus of which is all too often underestimated today by pointing out only its legal shortcomings or economic dead-ends.

This was a very unusual moment in the history of decolonisation when the new nations engaged in state nationalism but which was directed at the

[31] Henry Trofimenko, 'The Third World and US/Soviet Competition' (1981) 59(5) *Foreign Affairs* 1021–40.

[32] Prashad, *The Darker Nations* (n 1) 9 *ff*.

[33] Cited by Bedjaoui, *Towards a New International Economic Order* (n 26) 34.

[34] Prashad, *The Darker Nations* (n 1) 9 *ff*.

[35] Karoline Postel-Vinay, *L'Occident et sa bonne parole. Nos représentations du monde de l'Europe coloniale à l'Amérique hégémonique* (Paris, Flammarion, 2005) 119 *ff*.

outside world, at internationalism. The issue of postcolonial reconstruction of the world was just arising for these newly independent nations with a question mark that hung over them: how to live and think after colonialism and domination? Contrary to what is often remembered, the Third World was not driven solely by anticolonial resentment, although it was extremely strong, but also aspired to a far-reaching reform of international society and of its law. These aspirations were borne by a number of political leaders but also by great figures of international law. It was a longing for peace, freedom and justice. The Indonesian President, Ahmed Sukarno, who was also a staunch anti-colonialist, declared at Bandung in 1955:

> Let us not be bitter about the past, but let us keep our eyes firmly on the future. [. . .] Let us remember that the highest purpose of man is the liberation of man from his bonds of fear, his bonds of poverty, the liberation of man from the physical, spiritual and intellectual bonds which have for long stunted the development of humanity's majority. And let us remember, Sisters and Brothers, that for the sake of all that, we Asians and Africans must be united.[36]

Many initiatives were taken as countries became independent. Jawaharlal Nehru, Prime Minister of the Republic of India of 1947, feared the Third World might suggest a third military force and spoke out for peace and justice. He constantly emphasised the principles of political independence, non-violence in international relations and recourse to the United Nations as a fundamental institution for world justice.[37] It was at India's instigation that it was decided to create a UN Sub-Committee on Disarmament[38] in 1953 while the Statute of the International Atomic Energy Agency (IAEA), adopted in 1956, took up the text of the final Bandung communiqué on the subject.[39] Before that, the 29 Latin American countries played a central part for human rights in San Francisco in 1945. All these countries fought at the time for a broad definition of human rights and made numerous declarations about education, work, health and social security.[40] At the United Nations Educational, Scientific and Cultural Organization (UNESCO) conference in London in 1945 the Indian delegate Rajkumari Amrit Kaur observed that neither of the two blocs had a programme to meet the Third World's expectations. She called for 'true freedom', for a world rid of exploitation and injustice which required more than just 'pious expressions of good intentions and high-sounding policies'.[41] Ten years later at the celebrated Bandung

[36] Cited by Prashad, *The Darker Nations* (n 1) xvii.

[37] Jawaharlal Nehru, *India's Foreign Policy: Selected Speeches, September 1946–April 1961* (Delhi, Publications Division, 1961) 77–78.

[38] UN General Assembly Resolution 502 (VI) (11 January 1952).

[39] UN General Assembly Resolution 914 (X) (16 December 1974).

[40] See Mary Ann Glendon, 'The Forgotten Crucible: The Latin American Influence on the Universal Human Rights Idea' (2003) 16 *Harvard Human Rights Journal* 27–39.

[41] Conference for the Establishment of the UNESCO, Insitute of Civil Engineers, London, 1–16 November 1945 (Paris, Archives de l'UNESCO, No 1G41, 33); unesdoc.unesco.org/images/0011/001176/117626e.pdf.

Conference of 1955, the final communiqué called for 'economic cooperation', the establishment of a Special UN Fund for Economic Development (SUNFED), an International Finance Corporation to regulate speculative capital flows and a UN Permanent Advisory Commission on International Commodities Trade. Two years later, in 1957, Third-World delegates were behind the Federation of Afro-Asian Women to promote their rights.[42]

This desire for reform was to be taken straight to the heart of the international instances. Between 1955 and 1960 41 new states joined the UN; between 1960 and 1970 another 27 joined. The UN became truly universal and the General Assembly became the focus for new demands. In 1961 Burma's U-Thant became UN Secretary General, the first Third-World candidate to hold the position. He was re-elected in 1966. In 1967 Malta, which was then a member of the Non-Aligned Movement, instigated the General Assembly Resolution on Common Heritage designed to prevent one group of states from taking control of the deep-sea bed.[43] In 1960 the International Development Association (IDA) was set up. In 1961 the first United Nations Development Decade was proclaimed and the United Nations Conference for Trade and Development (UNCTAD), the United Nations Development Programme (UNDP) and the United Nations Industrial Development Organisation (UNIDO) were established in its wake.

All the proposals of that time were a sort of 'legal new deal'[44] that the Third-World representatives were to try to guide through the international instances by means of their new majority, particularly via UN General Assembly resolutions. The most emblematic of those proposals was indisputably the New International Economic Order (NIEO), which was the spearhead of classical international development law which the NIEO both integrated and extended, proposing a wholesale reform of the international order. The call for a fairer and more equitable world order that no longer bore the stamp of domination of the rich and former colonising countries thus took up a central position in the South's alternative discourse.

C The New International Economic Order (NIEO)

On 12 December 1974 the UN General Assembly proclaimed a Charter of Economic Rights and Duties of States designed to establish a NIEO. This came at the height of the oil crisis as it was in the aftermath of the OPEC embargo. OPEC had been established on 14 September 1960 at the Bagdad

[42] *The First Afro-Asian Women's Conference, Cairo, 14–23 January 1961* (Cairo, Amalgamated Press of Egypt, 1961).

[43] Malta's *note verbale* of 18 August 1967 (UN Doc A/6695) about a 'declaration and treaty concerning the reservation exclusively for peaceful purposes of the sea-bed and the ocean floor, underlying the seas beyond the limits of present national jurisdiction, and the use of their resources in the interests of mankind'.

[44] Bedjaoui, *Towards a New International Economic Order* (n 26) 140.

Conference in reaction to foreign oil companies (the seven sisters) imposing their prices on producing countries for their own petroleum resources.[45] In October 1973, during the Yom Kippur War, the Arab OPEC member countries announced an embargo on oil supplies to states supporting Israel. OPEC's boldness had a huge effect in the Third World, but also triggered the first oil crisis and it was against this particularly tense background that the NIEO was proclaimed the next year.

Plans for a new economic order had been under discussion for some time, especially with the UNCTAD through the Group of 77. They were adopted by the NAM at its 1973 Algiers summit. At the end of that Fourth NAM Conference, the heads of state and government asked the UN Secretary-General, through the Algerian President Boumediene, to convene an extraordinary session of the United Nations. This was held from 9 April to 2 May 1974 and the General Assembly adopted the Declaration on the Establishment of a New International Economic Order and an action programme. On 1 May 1974 the UN members, having adopted Resolution 3201, undertook to:

> [W]ork urgently for the establishment of a New International Economic Order based on equity, sovereign equality, interdependence, common interest and cooperation among all States, irrespective of their economic and social systems which shall correct inequalities and redress existing injustices, make it possible to eliminate the widening gap between the developed and developing countries and ensure steadily accelerating economic and social development and peace and justice for present and future generations [. . .][46]

Then on 12 December 1974 the first two resolutions were supplemented by the adoption of the Charter of Economic Rights and Duties of States (Resolution 3281). The proponents of the NIEO announced the recasting of the rules of economic international law after centuries of domination, exploitation and colonisation of the South and the end of an international economic system that still prevented them from developing properly.

The NIEO did not take the form of the adoption of an international convention or the revision of the GATT, but it did entail several General Assembly resolutions that in principle were not mandatory. At the time, the mandatory character of the resolutions was discussed at length and heatedly so among jurists because it was an essential question as to whether the provisions in the 1974 Charter were binding on UN Member States or not. A quarrel arose, which has become recurrent in international law, as to the ways in which to contemplate international law and its binding character in general, with some commentators narrowing its character and scope and others widening it to less formalistic criteria. The matter was decided in part by arbitral case law

[45] For an understanding of the background, see Anthony Sampson, *The Seven Sisters: The Great Oil Companies and the World They Made* (London, Hodder and Stoughton, 1975).

[46] UN General Assembly Resolution 3201 (S.VI) (1 May 1974) UN Doc A/RES/3201, Declaration on the Establishment of a New International Economic Order.

and then finally abandoned along with the NIEO itself. This celebrated 'soft law', consisting solely of resolutions, was often presented as one of the characteristics and shortcomings of the NIEO at the time and as a feature of the ideology underpinning it. Even so, several of its provisions were taken up in treaties and by custom, thereby indisputably conferring on them the mandatory character that had been in dispute theretofore. The debate contributed to stamping out, consciously or not, the Third World spirit of legal reform of the time that was reflected by these resolutions and the aspirations to more justice in the international order that lay beneath it. Not that the vision of a fairer international order proposed was without its own contradictions and weaknesses, far from it; it was beset with ideological ambiguities with unforeseeable effects, but at least it introduced an alternative discourse to the legal discourse that had prevailed until then, and in that alone it counterbalanced the overarching might of the international powers-that-be of the time in the way law was formulated and in its content. That is why the NIEO contained within it points of economic and social justice that is particularly interesting to bring out. In this respect, the efforts of the Working Group tasked with establishing the NIEO[47] show how difficult the exercise of drafting a proposal was because of the extremely deep divergences between developed countries with market economies and the developing countries with planned economies, but also among the developing countries themselves depending on their level of economic development or their political orientation. All the same, the NIEO that was finally adopted by Resolution 3281 went much further than the existing principles with respect to development law, as it attempted to completely redefine relations among states. It reaffirmed the principles of freedom and equality among states (a and b) and the principle of the right of peoples to self-determination (g), observance of human rights and fundamental freedoms (k), the promotion of international social justice (m) and general and complete disarmament (Article 15) and the duty to eliminate imperialism, colonialism and apartheid (Article 16).

But it was the economic issues that were to prevail in the legal battle underway in the UN and in the texts adopted. As the preamble to the 1974 Charter very plainly stated, the NIEO required the establishment of true international social justice by introducing 'a just and equitable economic and social order'.[48] The NIEO therefore introduced the principles of justice for postcolonial society, taking account of the 'circumstances of justice' of this postcolonial society, that is, a new world shared by very poor, former colonised or dominated peoples who had united and joined together against dominant states, most of which were very affluent, a world in which the profoundly unequal distribution of wealth and of power resulted in part from the colonial past and in which the more powerful continued to hold an unfair

[47] By Resolution 45 (III) of 18 May 1972, UNCTAD had decided to set up a working group of government representatives to draft a Charter of Economic Rights and Duties of States.
[48] UN General Assembly Resolution 3201 (S.VI) (n 46).

advantage over the poor because of the existing system. These circumstances explained the need for a new world justice and the confrontation between these two worlds led them to rethink the fundamental principles of the existing legal and economic order.

In fact, apart from a few very radical provisions, the NIEO appeared to be less of a wholesale break with the older order than a re-direction of the old pluralistic liberal law in favour of a new equilibrium in economic relations between North and South. Not only was it clearly in compliance with the UN Charter (Article 33) and the GATT objectives (Article 14), but it was particularly significant that the first major legal principle proclaimed by the NIEO was not about equality or equity but about the sovereign freedom of states (Article 1). While presented as fundamental, this legal principle was above all to reinforce the sovereign independence of decolonised states and their free choice as to their own model of development. But it was far from new at the time. International economic law in its entirety has been founded on the freedom of states to make their own economic and social choices. What has been termed the liberalism of classical international law[49] resided in the fact that international law was founded on complete observance of each state's domestic sovereignty. This principle of sovereign freedom, called for by the new states, nonetheless took on a new dimension that was fundamental for the Third World in the context of development law, as it oriented that law in such a way that it was a law of '*economic independence*' and not just a '*law of aid*',[50] which was its main form of existence until then. This resulted in a new and decisive principle of development law, which had first been proclaimed in 1962, that of permanent sovereignty over natural resources, which in the 1974 Charter included the right to nationalise foreign property and economic activities (Article 2). From the assertion of the sovereignty of states by the 1974 Charter followed the principle of necessary cooperation among equal partners that was constantly reiterated and which had to replace the earlier unilateral policies of assistance or aid (Articles 3, 8, 9, 11, 12(1), 13, 14, 17, 23, 28). Lastly, the economic sovereignty of states was reflected externally by the state's right to freely order its foreign trade relations as it chose and not as some alien economic model required (Article 4).

After the principle of state sovereignty, which was enshrined both internally and externally, the principle of legal equality among states was also asserted (Article 10). However, it was adjusted to make equitable correction for socio-economic inequalities. Many of the Charter's provisions were based on equity, as they were a constant reminder that allowances had to be made for the specific circumstances of developing countries in applying the measures referred to. It was no longer simply a matter of recognising that states had equal rights but, where necessary, by transgressing formal equality, of

[49] Jouannet, *The Liberal-Welfarist Law of Nations* (n 10) 28 *ff*.

[50] The distinction is proposed by Guy Feueur, 'Réflexions sur la Charte des droits et devoirs économique des Etats' (1974) *Annuaire Francais de Droit International* 276.

taking account of the socio-economic inequalities between rich and poor so as to introduce affirmative measures for the poor states and so restore the possibility of materially equitable conditions. The NIEO also included several specific provisions designed to correct the situation for the South and which in some instances were to anger the West. These included more equitable involvement of developing countries in decision-making within international organisations (Article 10), the transfer of resources, technology and know-how from rich to poor countries (Article 13), preference schemes (Articles 14 and 18), agreements on commodities (Article 6), commodity producer cartels (Article 5) or the principle of common responsibilities differentiated in the domains of the sea bed (Article 29) and the environment (Article 30).

Of the leading provisions of the NIEO some were accepted in practice and others discarded – a point we shall return to when reviewing classical development law in its entirety. The adoption of a trade preference scheme under the GATT was particularly emblematic of what the NIEO and international development law of the 1970s attempted to introduce.[51] It is used here by way of example. There was therefore a two-stage change that led to the creation of exceptions to the cardinal rules of the GATT and of the liberal model underpinning them. First, before the NIEO, through the influence of UNCTAD, Third World countries secured a legal principle of non-reciprocity for their benefit under the revision of GATT 47 of 27 June 1966. A Part IV was added to the General Agreement, significantly entitled 'Trade and Development'. The new Article XXXVI of Part IV laid down a principle of non-reciprocity in negotiating the reduction of customs duties and impediments to trade between 'developed' and 'less-developed contracting parties' because of their unequal material circumstances. This principle of non-reciprocity in North–South trade relations was to be considered a major feature of international development law. However, some commentators have pointed out the adverse effect of the exception, for some of the 'less developed' parties were ousted from the main trade talk rounds of the GATT. This sidelining meant that for a time they were unable to make their views known in multilateral discussions.

Secondly, after the NIEO, a more positive advance came with the 'enabling clause' introduced in the Tokyo Round of talks in the 1970s. These new talks brought together twice as many nations as had been involved theretofore in the rounds of negotiations and were characterised by the new and intense involvement of developing countries among which Brazil played a major part. However, representing as they did some 60 per cent of world trade, the United States, the EEC and Japan were in an unassailable position and weighed on the outcome. Although it failed to meet the very high expectations of the developing countries, the enabling clause was successfully adopted on 28 November

[51] On the significance of the 'preferential revolution' at the time, see Guy De Lacharrière, *La stratégie commerciale du développement* (Paris, PUF, 1973).

1979 by a legally mandatory decision which this time provided a full derogation from the most-favoured nation clause and the principle of equal treatment of all the GATT contracting parties. It was no longer a purely negative measure, like the absence of reciprocity that had been granted before, but a positive measure entitling states to extend preferential arrangements to developing countries. It might be a generalised system of preferences (GSP) or 'differential and more favourable' treatment accorded by some developed states to other states because of their less favourable economic position. Special treatment was also planned for a new category of least-developed countries (LDCs), which were the poorest in the world.[52]

'Special and differential' treatment is commonly used today and is found as an enabling clause in many multilateral trade agreements such as the Agreement on Agriculture (Article 15) or the Agreement on Sanitary and Phytosanitary Measures (Article 10).[53] However, the enabling clause for preferential treatment remains limited in its scope on three points. It provides a simple option for states to grant such preferential treatment and so does not create any obligation to do so. It is defined as an exception and not a general principle applicable to poor countries.[54] It is considered transitory and may evolve ('evolutionary clause') and therefore vanish if the developing country's situation evolves favourably, which is justified by the very principle of development, since it is an evolving situation as shown by the circumstances of some former developing countries that have now become emerging states and can vie with developed nations.

III Ultraliberal Reaction and the Impact of Economic Globalisation

In spite of the hope that had been placed in it, the NIEO was to remain contested for many years before it was finally abandoned. Admittedly, classical international development law was to survive through legal mechanisms like the enabling clause in matters of trade, but the very idea of instituting a fairer and more equitable worldwide new economic order was gradually abandoned because of the new post-Cold War ultraliberal consensus. The new phase of globalisation that was ushered in by the fall of the Berlin Wall certainly created new prospects for development that were far brighter than before. In addition, the threat that the Cold War and its ideological erring

[52] There is still no precise criterion for determining what makes a least-developed country. It is usually determined by per capita gross domestic product of less than $1000 per year (example of Multilateral Agreement on Subsidies, Annex VIIb) and by reference to the list drawn up by the UN.

[53] See the full list in Dominique Carreau and Patrick Julliard, *Droit international économique*, 4th edn (Paris, Dalloz, 2010) 117.

[54] Appellate Body Report 7 April 2004, WT/DS/246/AB/R, *European Communities – Conditions for the Granting of Tariff Preferences to Developing Countries*, paras 89 *ff*.

had held over Third World issues was finally removed. Even so, it has to be recognised that all of this came about only at the price of economic, legal and political rearrangements that swept away any idea of reform and of equity and which, although having furthered the spectacular development of some states, nonetheless exposed the new post-Cold War international society to substantial difficulties with respect to law, development and social justice.

A The NIEO Abandoned and the Neoliberal Model Triumphant

On 21 December 1990 the General Assembly launched the Fourth Development Decade via a resolution that for the first time no longer mentioned the NIEO and enshrined the neoliberal model of development.[55] On 22 December 1992 a new resolution was adopted, significantly on 'Privatization in the context of economic restructuring, economic growth and sustainable development' and committed the UN 'organs, organizations and bodies' to support countries so requesting in 'privatizing enterprises, demonopolizing and deregulating their economic activities and implementing other relevant policies' (para 1, b).[56] Ten years later, in December 2002, almost to the day, it passed another resolution for 'promoting development in the context of globalization and interdependence' as they 'are opening new opportunities through trade, investment and capital flows and advances in technology, including information technology, for the growth of the world economy, development and the improvement of living standards around the world' (Preamble).[57] Similarly, UNCTAD VIII confirmed the neoliberal swing in development with the 1992 Cartagena Commitment.[58]

The crisis of the 1980s and then the economic globalisation that kicked in from the 1990s made a crucial impact on development and on the spirit of reform and equity of the NIEO. The crises related to the massive Third World debt in the 1980s slammed the brakes on development. But it was also the time when a small corpus of economic principles was elaborated, known as the Washington Consensus and put in place by the Washington institutions, the IMF and the World Bank, and which reflected the ambition to have an ultraliberal model of development prevail everywhere.[59] The Washington Consensus was encapsulated by a movement for deregulation in the three

[55] UN General Assembly Resolution 45/199 (21 December 1990) UN Doc A/RES/45/199.

[56] Un General Assembly Resolution 47/171 (22 December 1992) UN Doc A/RES/47/171. See also the Resolution of 21 December 1990, Entrepreneurship, UN Doc A/RES/45/188 and the Resolution of 22 December 1999, Business and Development, UN Doc A/RES/54/204.

[57] UN General Assembly Resolution 57/274 (20 December 2002) UN Doc A/RES/57/274, Role of the United Nations in promoting development in the context of globalization and interdependence.

[58] The 1992 Cartagena Conference marked a historical change in UNCTAD policy with the acceptance of liberal principles, of market operation, of the withdrawal of the state, of the role of private actors and of good governance and human rights as requirements for proper development.

[59] A third institution, the US Treasury, is associated with them. The three are based within a few streets of each other in Washington DC.

areas of financial flow, direct investments and trade, and by the imposition of structural adjustment programmes (SAPs) designed to radically restructure the budgets and economies of debtor countries. While states were still classified by their level of development, it was no longer feasible, as in the past, to have a truly specific analysis of developing economies. In the states of the South as in the states of the North, private initiative was to be promoted and the economic environment fully deregulated by alleviating legislation as far as possible.

The globalisation of the 1990s consolidated this neoliberal mode of economic development during a period of euphoria and renewed optimism. The new episode of globalisation engendered by the ending of the Cold War and the new entente between the two blocs was reflected by an unprecedented liberalisation of trade in all domains and by greater interdependence among states and among individuals. Many hoped to see the old liberal economic dream of the post-war period become reality: the spontaneous achievement of uninterrupted growth and the advent of prosperity for all through a world market which alone would be the instrument for new worldwide regulation leading to equilibrium and harmony. This old belief was all the more firmly held because after 1989 the collapse of the communist model was interpreted as marking the incontrovertible triumph of the market economy. In 1995, the World Trade Organisation (WTO) was formed and some hoped to introduce at last the general international regulation of trade that had eluded them in 1945. But, in fact, the prevailing international economic policy continued to reflect a particularly aggressive form of liberalism based on the refusal of any political and social intervention, including legal intervention.[60] Internally, the process of deregulation and privatisation continued with a shift from 'state control' to 'market control'. Globally, the aim was for greater growth via readier access to capital and technological resources, cheaper imports and increased exports. At the same time new normative areas detached from states and international organisations emerged, together with decentralised economic networks governed by unofficial and underground power bases that circumvented the economic policies of states and international institutions. The weakening of the nation states brought about by globalisation was perceived as beneficial as it unharnessed the positive force of private actors.[61] These thrived as did investment flows. Capital flows to developing countries grew six-fold in the six years from 1990 to 1996. Multinational firms played an increasingly decisive part in setting prices and directing strategies. They came to control between 50 and 90 per cent of world output, depending on the sector.[62] In this context it was the law of private persons and operators

[60] See Jacques Adda, *La mondialisation de l'économie: genèse et problèmes* (Paris, La découverte, 2006).

[61] Here we discuss the impact of globalisation worldwide but it is a multidimensional phenomenon acting at transnational, regional, national and local levels. See Jean-Bernard Auby, *La globalisation, le droit et l'Etat*, 2nd edn (Paris, Librairie générale de droit et de jurisprudence (LGDJ), 2008) 28 *ff.*

[62] Wladimir Andreff, *Les multinationales globales*, 2nd edn (Paris, La découverte, 2003) 6 *ff.*

that was prominent, the law of contract and private property, the pillars of economic liberalism and a more abstentionist than interventionist state legal policy. Admittedly, international institutions (the IMF and World Bank especially) were to become very decisively involved in the affairs of the countries they were aiding, but to deregulate domestic law, privatise it and promote market action alone. Accordingly, development relied primarily on the guarantee of private rights, on liberal economic international law and the integration of least-favoured states in the world market.[63] Besides, from that time on, the most significant decisions in terms of development were no longer taken by the UN but by the Bretton Woods financial institutions, the Organisation for Economic Cooperation and Development (OECD) or the G8, where developing countries had no foothold. UNCTAD, the Group of 77 and the NAM became insignificant and lost all influence.[64]

From here it can readily be seen that the triumph of the ultraliberal or neoliberal model,[65] begun in the 1980s and completed in the 1990s, ran counter to the Third World claims of the 1960s and 1970s and of classical international development law. This triumph went along with the denunciation from all directions of the NIEO, the theories of dependence and domination, to attribute underdevelopment to domestic causes only, thereby sweeping aside the effects of history and the possibility of a more balanced and more equitable approach to international relations as recommended by the NIEO. There was, besides, no need in international law to abolish the texts on the NIEO that had been drafted in the 1960s and 1970s. Their mandatory character was already challenged and they were gradually falling into disuse. Classical development law also vanished as an autonomous discipline in universities, even if it still remained in practice in the form of legal principles and practices of commercial law, the law of cooperation and aid, and was at the heart of the activity of many international organisations. It was a time when legal teaching and research were abandoned especially since it was an area which from the outset was run through with very strong, internal, ideological tensions, which ended up tearing it apart in the new context of the post-Cold War triumph of

[63] In addition, public development aid collapsed. It fell by 30% between 1990 and 2000 as it did not fit the new model in which private investment was supposed to take over. But private investment went only to emerging countries or countries with valuable raw materials. See Sylvie Brunel, *Le développement durable*, 2nd edn (Paris, PUF, Que sais-je?, 2009) 14–15.

[64] In 1983, for the first time since it was established, the UNCTAD failed to adopt a common declaration of developed and developing countries as the developed countries rejected a voluntarist agenda on development considering that the UNCTAD was no longer the relevant forum for discussing development. The only relevant organisations were now the GATT, the IMF and the World Bank. See Mehdi Abbas, 'La CNUCED XI: du consensus de Washington au consensus de Sao Paolo' (2004) 21 *La chronique des Amériques* 5 *ff.*

[65] Neoliberalism and ultraliberalism are used interchangeably here for a particular form of deregulated, financialised economic liberalism based on the most thoroughgoing liberalisation of trade. On the distinctions, see Monique Canto-Sperber and Nicolas Tenzer, *Faut-il sauver le libéralisme?* (Paris, Grasset 2006) 29 *ff.* The term 'supercapitalism' is used here to describe ultracompetitive capitalism in which the common good and welfare of society are secondary issues. See *Problèmes économiques. Le capitalisme en questions*. Special issue 2994, April 2008, 6.

liberalism.[66] It is true that development policies had prompted expectations that had had to be reduced over time because of certain economic and political disasters that had mounted up. It thus appeared that some of the measures taken in line with dependency theories or otherwise had not really had any telling result or had led to bankruptcy or serious setbacks in other domains, including the most basic of human rights, prompting doubts among some international lawyers who had been impelled by the hope of a fairer world and had fought legal battles in the name of the cause.

Apart from all the internal difficulties of the Third World project and the new post-Cold War context, it was the successful 'take-off' of the South-East Asian countries and then of the emerging states that drove the rise of neoliberalism and the decline of reformist principles. The 'East Asian miracle' as the World Bank styled it,[67] had repercussions for the Third World project, for dependency theories and for the definition of the NIEO. Along with dependency theories, the Third World's efforts to transform the world order into a more just and more equitable order, elicited far less enthusiasm. Some observers felt vindicated in their belief that there had not been and was not any injustice in the domination by the Western liberal economic legal system but, on the contrary, the liberal model was the Third World's pathway to salvation. Besides, it was perfectly natural that this line of questioning emerged at that time. If a tiny country like Singapore had become the world's second most competitive economy by applying a strictly liberal model, did that not prove that the liberal legal and economic system in place was effective and that failures were attributable solely to internal causes in the countries of the South? Singapore was not an isolated case. The same was true of Taiwan, South Korea and Hong Kong. Some inferred that the same neoliberal and modernist model could work anywhere. The idea that everyone could benefit equally from the development of worldwide trade gained currency and that the New Industrialised Countries (NIC), which were good students and succeeded because they applied neoliberal instructions for their development to the letter and did not 'violate the laws of the market economy', could be distinguished from the poor students who had not applied the market rules properly.[68] For sure, the IMF and World Bank were aware that the take-off of East Asia was achieved without their structural adjustment programmes, but they saw this 'miracle' as a sign that their neoliberal economic model was the only valid model along with the existing rules of international economic law. In addition, it is clear that the spectacular progress since the 2000s by the new major players like India, Russia, South Africa, Brazil and China

[66] See Yves Daudet, 'Propos introductifs' (n 9).

[67] World Bank Report, 'The East Asian Miracle, Economic Growth and Public Policy' (1993).

[68] Several World Bank studies argue along these lines, including the celebrated report on development aid presented at the 2002 Monterrey Conference. They have come in for harsh criticism both for the statistics employed and the way the World Bank links growth and poverty. See especially Abhijit Banerjee, *An Evaluation of World Bank Research, 1998–2005* (World Bank, Washington DC, 2006). Yet, the World Bank's basic practices remain unchanged.

supported such analysis and diagnostics, even if many endogenous factors were sometimes opportunely concealed, especially as most of these countries have become ardent defenders of advanced capitalism and economic neoliberalism. By 2020 it is expected that the gross national product (GNP) of the seven largest emerging economies, the E7, will exceed that of the G8 group of the richest nations. This incontrovertible economic success of the 'emerging' states has substantially improved the standard of living for their populations and reduced poverty for many categories of their populations. It has logically gone along with a call to have a greater say in international relations, since the new rich countries of the South intended to vie with the former industrial powers. The new expression 'emerging countries' to characterise the new major powers like Brazil, Russia, India and China (BRIC) is perfectly in keeping with the revamped theories of modernisation. The term comes from the international financial organisations, from the IMF and from the credit rating agencies. It was introduced in 1980 by the financial spheres to identify countries with emerging markets, that is, countries where growth was rapid and with investment opportunities for the businesses of rich countries. But the term 'emerging country' is intended to be congratulatory and to acknowledge the status of the new arrivals at the top table. As Jacques Gabas and Bruno Losch assert, the scope of what is left unsaid, of what is implied and of the value judgements for which the concept is still a vehicle can be immediately perceived together with the same economic development paradigm that was theorised by Rostow.[69]

B Law Devalued and the Human Ends of Economics Overlooked

It was consistent with the logic of the new neoliberal model that law and politics should be implicitly devalued since the new model was to spell the decline of all political interventionism and to end all prospects of international legal regulation. Admittedly, the 1990s saw law return to the domain of development to some extent, where it introduced the model of good governance and of the rule of law as one of the end purposes of development,[70] while the WTO without a doubt strengthened the binding character of trade rules.[71] Moreover, globalisation extended international law to new areas and

[69] Jacques Gabas and Bruno Losch, 'La fabrique en trompe-l'œil de l'émergence' in Christophe Jaffrelot (ed) *L'enjeu mondial. Les pays émergents* (Paris, Sciences Po les Presses, 2008) 25 *ff.*

[70] Leading several commentators to claim we have entered into a new era of development where the primacy of law and the rule of law are not just new means for development but are the actual purpose of development. See Amanda Perry-Kessaris, 'Introduction' in Amanda Perry-Kessaris (ed), *Law in the Pursuit of Development* (London and New York, Routledge, 2010) 2 *ff.* Law supposedly steps up a gear, but far from reflecting a decline in politics, I feel, reinforces the politicisation of development for the benefit of a Western liberal model. But see David Kennedy, 'The "Rule of Law", Political Choices and Development Common Sense' in David M Trubek and Alvaro Santos (eds), *The New Law and Economic Development. A Critical Appraisal* (Cambridge, Cambridge University Press, 2008) 95 *ff.*

[71] Hélène Ruiz-Fabri, 'La contribution de l'organisation mondiale du commerce à la gestion

brought about the emergence of a global law that had not existed as such before then.[72] But this evolution cannot disguise the economic hegemony of the model that since the 1980s and 1990s led to a process of general deregulation, which played a crucial part in transforming international finance and direct investment where the few remaining regulatory authorities were constantly outflanked. This phenomenon led to political power slipping towards private actors, a reversal in priorities between political freedom and economic freedom, and the primacy of finance over economics and of economics over social, legal and political considerations.[73] This resulted in a reversal of the principles laid down by the texts of the post-war period, which has been clearly expounded by Alain Supiot,[74] with the result that now economic choices are subject only to the financial logic of profitability and are not made for human purposes. The free trade included in GATT I and II was devised initially as a means to serve the ends stated in the preamble, which were full employment, prosperity for all and sustainable development (introduced by GATT II 1994) with their obvious social and human dimensions. It was a departure of multilateral trade practice that saw it progressively become an end in itself in GATT talks and that the human ends for which it was recommended and for which it was supposed to be constantly adapted, were forgotten. If the means, free trade, becomes an end in itself, it is logical that there are few legal limits as to the way in which it is applied and so as to the logic that everything can be bought and sold which it ultimately implies.

In actual fact, this process of deregulation or this absence of international public regulation did not prevent the parallel development of certain legal rules, for there cannot be a market without rules.[75] But outside of the existing and piecemeal regulation mechanisms,[76] the rules are essentially those of private international law, of competition to find the most attractive among domestic legislative systems and of the extension of a whole series of individual rights under domestic private law in the service of markets and invest-

de l'espace juridique mondial' in Catherine Kessadjian and Eric Loquin (eds), *La mondialisation du droit* (Paris, Litec, 2000) 347 *ff*.

[72] Auby, *La globalisation, le droit et l'Etat* (n 61) 209 *ff*. For the expansion of international law to many other areas, see Jouannet, *The Liberal-Welfarist Law of Nations* (n 10) 191 *ff*.

[73] See François Morin, *Le Nouveau Mur de l'argent: essai sur la finance globalisée* (Paris, Seuil, 2006). Financial organisations maintain close and sometimes problematic links with international organisations, see Habib Gherari and Sandra Szurek (eds), *L'émergence de la société civile internationale* (Paris, Pedone, 2003) 179–97.

[74] Alain Supiot, *L'esprit de Philadelphie. La justice sociale face au marché total* (Paris, Seuil, 2010) 91 *ff*. See also Jean-Paul Fitoussi, *La démocratie et le marché* (Paris, Grasset, 2004) 8 *ff*.

[75] See the many examples in Bhupinder Chimni, 'TWAIL, A Manifesto' in Antony Anghie et al (eds), *The Third World and International Order, Law, Politics and Globalization* (Leiden, Boston, M Nijhoff, 2003) 52 *ff*.

[76] It should not be forgotten that despite this rapid presentation there are legal regulation mechanisms, of course, but they are simple regulatory tools and are tangled up and barely serviceable for more restrictive regulation. For an overview of the law of financial markets in the current globalised context, for example, see Eilis Ferran and Charles AE Goodhart (eds), *Regulating Financial Services and Markets in the 21st Century* (London, Hart Publishing, 2011).

ments, where property rights, security rights, freedom of movement and freedom to engage in business, which have been said to be the legal pillars of economic liberalism, prevail. They regulate the majority of international economic and financial transactions which are not conducted between states but between private operators. Certain areas of the law are therefore favoured, but under no circumstances do they have a role of international public regulation, as this is thought to disrupt the spontaneous order of the world market and of international finance. Besides, there is nothing surprising in that; it is just a familiar logic that is at work and which is self-consistent since neoliberal thought aims to spare the economy any political intervention and to depoliticise international relations for the benefit of economic laws of the market which, ultimately, will benefit everyone. This logic is economistic, that is, it sets economics up as the 'final instance' and recommends eventual de-politicisation for the benefit of worldwide market laws so as to avert any return to interventionist social policies. Despite the countless criticisms levelled at it, this model continues to prevail with the result that the few attempts made to further the regulation of trade and international finance have not yet amounted to anything concrete, as is evidenced by the suspension of the Doha Round of talks or the meeting of G20 finance ministers in Paris in 2011. They show that once one economic crisis has blown over, states return to their selfish ways to combat any idea of truly restrictive international regulation, and even international economic and financial institutions now advocate as much.

The post-Cold War episode of globalisation therefore incontrovertibly tolled the bell for the NIEO by imposing a neoliberal model of development. Economic development remains the remedy for the inequalities of postcolonial international society, but the rules leading to it are those of existing international economic law to the detriment of a specific international law of development. In other words, the best international development law is the new neoliberal economic law for it is the market alone that must bring about development. Should it be thought, as Maurice Flory enquired, that 'globalisation got the better of a development law that was accused of getting involved in what was none of international law's business'?[77] Does globalisation spell the end of reformist intervention by politicians and therefore of a more equitable international law to promote the development of poor countries and remedy inequalities among states? Has the very idea of a specific law of development been abandoned along with that of a form of international social justice?

[77] Maurice Flory, 'Mondialisation et droit international du développement' (1997) 3 *Revue Generale de Droit International Public* 628.

In truth, for the new economic practices to have made their mark, they would have had to continue to be unanimously accepted and prove they were fully effective, which was far from being the case. Although the existing economic model has survived, it has come up against a barrage of criticism. New development voices have appeared, bringing in new legal principles which contribute to the same rationale that is designed to go beyond the economistic model of development and quite clearly show that the idea of a specific law of development, separate from economic law, is still very relevant. At the same time, we have become aware of the limits of globalisation, which is accused of failing to 'keep its promises' and of the difficulties or even the dead-ends to which it inevitably leads unless it is controlled in some way. We have also become aware of how globalisation becomes an instrument of unlimited abuse whereby we continually sacrifice the requirements of equity and all human purpose to the rationales of interest and the law of the market.

2

The New International Development Law

THE NEOLIBERAL DEVELOPMENT model presented as an alternative to development theories based on the New International Economic Order (NIEO) has revealed its limitations in the various crises of the last decade or so. The Asian crisis from 1997 onwards, the stagnation of a large part of South America, the Argentinian catastrophe in 2001,[1] the ever-widening gulf with the least-advanced countries, especially in Africa, but also growing inequalities and the major financial crisis of 2007 and 2008 are all factors that have prompted a rethink of development and have engendered new legal practices in this area.

Besides, whatever the real impact of globalisation and despite the disappearance of the NIEO, an international development law has continued to exist in institutional, normative and practical terms. It has also continued to exist in international and regional terms insofar as it is possible to identify and group together an impressive set of legal practices and discourses pertaining to development and encompassing practices of economic international law alone and practices concerned with aid and equity of classical development law. Institutionally, many international organisations now handle development and many of the resources and staff of the United Nations are geared to development. With regard to norms, countless international, regional and national resolutions and commitments are made each year to promote development and combat poverty, making a whole stack of unilateral declarations topped with a few multilateral conventions and several regional or bilateral treaties on cooperation or aid.

Moreover, a new international development law has progressively superseded the old one, based on a fresh understanding of development. In 1992 the UN considered it had achieved for the first time 'a shared vision of development' especially with the Agenda 21 adopted in Rio.[2] This new global vision reflects a multidimensional understanding of development that had been previously unknown since it now encompasses the social, human and

[1] For it being impossible to apply World Bank and International Monetary Fund (IMF) directives on the ground, see Phillippe d'Iribarne, *Le Tiers-Monde qui réussit. Nouveaux modèles* (Paris, O Jacob, 2003) 11 *ff*.

[2] www.un.org/en/development/devagenda/devagenda.shtml.

environmental aspects of development. The new development law is therefore itself far more diversified and more complex to comprehend, for, while it too opposes the economistic reductionism induced by ultraliberal globalisation, it extends well beyond classical development law to embrace a whole spectrum of legal practices and principles ranging from human rights to the fight against global warming via good governance. It is important to recognise that it thereby enshrines the general reorientation of development law towards new human, social and sustainable ends and that it takes on a worldwide dimension, concerning both North and South, that it did not have before. Added to this is the fact that the 2000s have been seen as a contemporary turning point in favour of the targeted fight against poverty with certain specific objectives proclaimed in September 2000 as the Millennium Development Goals. However, has this been a positive change or is it not rather a change that brings in a liberal political model which, compounded with the neoliberal economic model, greatly intensifies the social and political strains on the developing countries without actually bringing them better development?

I The Human Ends of Development

It is essential to understand that one of the major changes in development law since 1989 has been to put people back at the heart of development and of the many legal practices designed to combat the world's socio-economic inequalities. This is a decisive turning point in international law, characteristic of the new post-Cold War requirements and of the triumph of liberal humanism; but it too has its own difficulties and dark side. This sea change in development law is, on the surface at least, in striking contrast with the evolution of international economic law since not only has development law reintroduced human ends from which economic law had severed all connection, but it opposes the economistic model for which it had been the vehicle since the end of the Cold War by upgrading law (and especially human rights and the rule of law) compared with economics. International development law and international economic law therefore have rationales that apparently are constantly diverging although, for the time being, the new humanistic side of development has been taken over by financial institutions with the result that it now vindicates the same underlying neoliberal paradigm. Accordingly, the future of development law will probably depend in large part on whether the new liberal humanist practices can influence their ultraliberal economic side and also on whether they can cope with their own ambiguities.

A Human Development

The law relating to 'human development' redirects development towards the service not of states but of individuals so that people are thought of as being its ultimate beneficiaries. The internationalist discourse evolved in this direction between 1995 and 2000, at which time the first resolutions and international texts were adopted. However, there was no international convention and so it remained soft law. Even so, it was on the legal foundation of these texts that some of the international institutions justified and developed new actions and operations, their practice and the practice of the states that followed them reinforcing the legal effect of their provisions.

It all began with the United Nations Development Programme (UNDP) which launched a human development index (HDI) in 1990. This index is designed to evaluate a country's level of development not just in terms of income (per capita GDP) but also in terms of each individual's ability to make 'choices'. To do this, it includes two non-economic indicators: one for health (life expectancy at birth) and the second for education (schooling for children and adult literacy). The new HDI was designed to modify the earlier development paradigm and go beyond a narrow economic vision of development. As Pakistani economist Mahbub ul Haq, father of the HDI, said, the objective of development should no longer be growth as such but to 'create an enabling environment for people to enjoy long, healthy and creative lives'.[3] This involves ensuring that people have a greater range of choices for it is the capacity to choose in line with their own preferences and values, thanks to the opportunities available to them, that ensures their well-being and not the increase in income or the accumulation of wealth. For sure, these opportunities depend in part on the individual's income but they also lie in better access to knowledge, food, water, better health services, physical safety and social security but also political and cultural freedom and involvement in the activities of their community.[4] All these factors are essential to people, for even if they did have equal incomes, they do not have the same opportunities to choose their way of life and develop their potential (capacities or capabilities).

However, the UNDP does not relinquish the credo of the market and growth and considers that a real development cannot occur without an open market and strong economic growth. But the introduction of international indicators and actions focused on individuals' life choices shows at any rate that the market model or frenetic growth are no longer a panacea since the new model for human development enhances the role of social support of government and international policies when those policies seek to enhance people's lives and to create real opportunities for choice through public regulations on health, education, security and freedom. By the same token, legal practices related to human development act implicitly as a safety catch on the market vision of the world purveyed by the rules of what has become ultraliberal international economic law and has lost sight of the human ends

[3] Cited on the UNDP website: hdr.undp.org/eng/humandev/. Mahbub ul Haq's work is related to that of Amartya Sen, *Development as Freedom* (Oxford, Oxford University Press, 1999) 13 *ff.*

[4] See the 2010 UNDP Human Development Report, 'The Real Wealth of Nations: Pathways to Human Development'; hdr.undp.org/en/media/HDR_2010_EN_Overview_reprint.pdf.

for which it had been introduced. Those practices are indicative of the need to invest anew in those human ends so that those ends might guide development law and prevail over the exclusive market and financial rationale of today's international economic law. However, it remains to be seen whether they will have any real impact on international economic law for, if not, they will paradoxically simply put up a smokescreen and therefore consolidate it.

B Human Rights and Development: Two Converging Objectives

It is easier to understand, in light of this re-centring on human development, how the question of human rights finally came to be asked in direct connection with development law, for the conception of people as free beings with their own wills, which lies at the heart of this vision, is also the conception of human rights.[5] The idea underlying the new model of human development is highly ambitious while being culturally situated since it derives directly from Enlightenment philosophy. As seen, the idea is to leave people as much 'free choice' as possible, as a sign of their flourishing. This is based on an individualistic definition of people through their freedom and their rational capacity to make decisions, which is a representation of people that is typical of modern humanistic Western liberal thought found in the economic theories of social choice. It is also what accounts for the essential importance assigned to education and literacy, for they have always been thought of, according to this perspective, as the key principles of any possible transformation of the individual into a fully rational human being, freed from any bond of servitude or community bond that might condition him; a free being, emancipated, with his own will and aware of his choices. This conception of development based on human choice also aims to ensure that people are no longer the simple passive recipients of development programmes drawn up by experts in international organisations and non-governmental organisations. They are to be entrusted with their own destinies and acknowledged to be free agents, who make and assume their own life choices, including with respect to the aid to be provided to others.

Human development and human rights naturally converge, then, which is why among the essential opportunities of human development that people should enjoy are the basic civil, economic and social rights and freedoms that concretely mean an individual can make choices. Right from the first UNDP report in 1999, it is stated that human development necessarily presupposes the observance of human rights:

> Human development shares a common vision with human rights. The purpose is human freedom. This freedom is crucially important in the pursuit of capabilities

[5] Since I do not wish to take sides in the semantic quarrel on this, different terms are used here for human rights especially when speaking of the rights of persons, individuals or human beings. See Danièle Lochak, *Les droits de l'homme*, 2nd edn (Paris, La découverte, 2005) 4–6.

> and in the materialisation of rights. People must be free to make their own choices and to participate in making decisions that affect their lives. Human development and human rights are mutually reinforcing, in contributing to ensure the well-being and dignity of all, in developing self-esteem and respect for others.[6]

Gradually, there came about a far greater movement of convergence which exceeded human development alone when all the international texts, the acts of international organisations, the General Assembly resolutions and declarations by states associated development with human rights in a way that enabled the UN to return to the Charter's original objectives. In Article 1(3), the drafters of the Charter had grouped together development and human rights as the main goals of the UN almost by chance, it seems,[7] but the two had subsequently been dissociated and conferred on separate organs. At the same time, a programme began within the UN to give greater binding force to fundamental rights on development, like the right to food, water or health.

A series of spectacular shifts occurred within development law. Where classical international development law and the NIEO were entirely contained within the classical framework of international law and the observance of states' sovereign freedom, where they advocated the principle of neutrality with respect to developing states' political regimes, current development law imposes on sovereign states a particular non-neutral model of development to be achieved, based on human rights and respect for the individual.[8] While classical international development law is directed entirely at the free choice of sovereign states (NIEO Article 1), the new international development law is directed at the free choice of individuals. So classical and new development laws are still today vehicles for legal rules and practices that are based on profoundly different conceptions of the role of the state and the nature of sovereignty; and sovereignty becomes functional in the context of the new model as it is subordinate to the achievement of the human ends of development. But the outcome is that human rights become more specifically both the means and the end of development, which is an aspect that is less often perceived.[9]

[6] hdr.undp.org/en/media/hdr_1999_fr_contenu.pdf. (our translation).

[7] Olivier de Frouville, 'Commentaire Article 1, paragraphe 3' in Jean-Pierre Cot, Alain Pellet and Mathias Forteau (eds), *La Charte des Nations-Unies*, (Paris, Economica, 2005) 358–59.

[8] Although the human rights approach differs and sometimes runs counter to the fundamental needs approach. See Patrice Meyer-Bisch, 'Les violations des droits culturels, facteur d'appauvrissement durable: pour une observation des pauvretés culturelles' in Emmanuel Decaux and Alice Yotopoulos-Marangpoulos (eds), *La pauvreté, un défi pour les droits de l'homme* (Paris, Pedone, 2009) 185 *ff*.

[9] Here we find the influence of the work of Amartya Sen, including that on the World Bank, via its former President James Wolfensohn. See Sen, *Development as Freedom* (n 3) 3 *ff*. Sen argues for 'development as freedom' or more specifically development as 'a process of expanding the real freedoms that people enjoy'. His work on famine underpins his argument: Amartya Sen, *Poverty and Famines: An Essay on Entitlement and Deprivation* (Oxford, Clarendon Press, 1981). The fact that famine, the absolute deprivation of food, could still occur in the 20th century was a real puzzle and a study of the great famines led him to conclude that they occurred only under authoritarian or tyrannical regimes and never in states where people had basic rights such as the possibility of having sufficient income, work, or the right to sell or trade foodstuffs

On the one hand, they are considered as having to contribute significantly to the country's economic development by reinforcing free choice and potential for the initiative of people, who are seen as the true driving force behind development as 'development agents', with the result that human development and human rights become a necessary condition for economic development; and on the other hand they are considered to be the ultimate objective of the new development model that is ordered entirely around the person and no longer around the state.

By going back a little we can gain a better understanding of the scope of these major shifts, the strains that may subsist and the difficulties they may engender. As Olivier de Frouville records,[10] the UN General Assembly was, for a long time, the theatre of a stand-off between North and South over human rights. Third World countries long sought to shirk any responsibility in this area, rejecting any new western diktat and raising arguments of national sovereignty, non-interference in their domestic affairs, and the difficulty of implementing development. They repeatedly suggested that the establishment of civil and political rights was not a priority with respect to the conditions of material impoverishment of their populations and, with the support of the eastern bloc, they emphasised the importance of economic and social rights. Alongside this, they constantly sought to highlight the responsibility of the former colonising countries with respect to their present difficulties and the need to establish the NIEO in order for human rights to be implemented. This was materialised by Resolution 32/130 of 16 December 1977, adopted by the General Assembly under the impetus of the Non-Aligned Movement (NAM). But support for oppressive and dictatorial regimes from Third World states meant that their own discourse progressively lost credibility and prevented any placid discussion of the inseparable connections between political, economic and social rights and the NIEO. This resulted in a strained dialogue between the two camps, which was reflected for several years by the General Assembly adopting two competing resolutions. One resolution was adopted under the influence of the NAM reasserting the requirements of a NIEO and the other by the 'Western' camp reaffirming the need to comply with human rights; the former emphasising the principle of non-interference in the domestic affairs of states, including with regard to human rights; the latter considering that any violation of human rights was a matter for the UN.

The post-Cold War evolution left this quarrel behind along with the human rights issue that had become bogged down with it. Development and human rights came to be associated and what is probably the most fundamental

and access to food and where individuals had civil rights that allowed them to participate in public life and influence political decisions. For Sen, democracies prove to be the best bulwark against famine because elected politicians, who are subject to changes in opinion, are compelled to put effective prevention mechanisms in place.

[10] De Frouville, 'Commentaire Article 1, paragaphe 3' (n 7) 362 *ff.*

challenge of all these shifts came about: development came to be conceived as the flourishing of the individual. And while one might think what one likes of this very emphatic reference to human rights in relation to development which raises its own specific difficulties, to which we shall return, one should not underestimate the scope of the change involved. This new understanding of development makes it possible, in principle at least, to avoid the abuse and contradictions that strictly characterised inter-state classical development law and the way it went soft on particularly liberticidal regimes. This classical law, which had once freed new states and protected their sovereignty, had finally become an accomplice to the particularly repressive ways of some of them, to the point that not only were populations deprived of their fundamental rights but the states were foundering economically and socially. Once again, historical hindsight allows us to gauge this more accurately.

C States' Responsibility for Inadequate Development of their Populations

After the good years of the 1960s and the early 1970s, the economic and social disillusions were extremely intense. One budgetary crisis followed another; the problem of debt became crucial and completely stifled the poorest countries. The international institutions gradually began to impose unbearable constraints with devastating social effects (Structural Adjustment Programmes (SAPs)). But the new countries bore their own share of responsibility in the disaster as some had sunk into contradictory criminal and authoritarian policies. By the 1970s and 1980s many young independent nations had accumulated social, political and economic failures. Tanzania, among so many others, is the damning example of the establishment of unprepared and unthinking socialism that led to the displacement of a fifth of the population to 'development villages' with no water, no schools, no dispensaries and which drifted towards an authoritarian regime, appalling bureaucratic state interventionism, destruction of the environment and total disregard for individuals.[11] The country had been the leading African producer of cereals for food in 1960. By 1974 it was forced to import $180 million's worth.[12] True, Tanzania's problems were also due to fluctuations in world prices, but even so the political and economic regime that was in place was an unmitigated disaster and could not, under any circumstances, achieve the economic development of the country, let alone the human and social development of its population. Nor did these problems affect socialist countries alone. The non-socialist states of national liberation fared no better, as attested by the dictatorships in Latin America or Asia in the same period.

[11] Especially the ujamaa programme. See RR Matango, 'Operation Mara: The Paradox of Democracy' (1975) 20 *Maji, Maji* 17 *ff.*

[12] Alan Rake, 'Collapse of African Agriculture' (1975) 9 *African Development* 18.

The international development law at the time supported this state of affairs. It was a time when, as seen, the new nations relied on their sovereignty and independence to adopt the political, economic and social models of their choice, clamoured for with the NIEO. It was also the period when the new nations made much in the UN General Assembly of their unfavourable economic and social situation and the absence of NIEO to avoid introducing civil and political freedoms. It was a lose-lose game all round. The Third World, which had set before the international community a project for justice and freedom, which had initiated major international legal reforms, found itself prey to its own economic and political waywardness. From India to Egypt, from Ghana to Indonesia, the great Third World liberation movements were to successfully mobilise whole peoples in order to win their freedom; but no postcolonial state then authorised its people to truly play the part of a free people in implementing the national project. Even if important measures were introduced for social change in some countries after colonialism, there was no equal and democratic participation of the people in the elaboration of the national plan and states with a single leader and a single party were imposed everywhere, whether the countries had market economies or were socialist states. As Fanon had foretold, the introduction of true social democracy was to fail and, in his own terms, the people would be sent back 'into its cave'.[13] The fall of some of the great figures of Bandung like Indonesia's Sukarno, Ghana's Nkrumah or Burma's U Nu, who had all played a fundamental part in designing the Third World political project, was emblematic of the difficulties that befell the newly independent states as they became entangled in their own internal contradictions.

Some reaction was inevitable eventually. This took the form of a worldwide ultraliberal economic order. But it also took on the appearance of democracy and of human rights enshrined by the 1993 Vienna World Conference. One can better measure the scope of the shifts that occurred since then and that have been confirmed by the end of the Cold War for, as Mohammed Bedjaiou,[14] one of the most fervent supporters of the NIEO in its time, emphasises, the human rights approach to development virtually has revolutionary consequences for development law and for development itself in that it is not just one more new approach to development but now seems to make the individual the horizon of development as a whole. The way in which this new legal discourse on development is used still remains problematic, for it is essential to know whether it is the populations concerned, that had been forced to return to their 'caves', that will be able to take control of it or if it will serve only to establish new hegemonic control by donor states and international institutions.

[13] Frantz Fanon, *Pour la révolution africaine: écrits politiques (1964)* (Paris, La Découverte, 2001) 145.

[14] Mohammed Bedjaoui, 'Faim et pauvreté aux assises du droit international' in *Mélanges en l'honneur de Madjid Benchikh* (Paris, Pedone, 2011) 395 *ff*.

Besides, this re-enhancement of the legal discourse on freedom and human rights within the context of development does not go unchallenged by states themselves and the old North–South rivalries continue to have effects. The consensus over human development and the reference to human rights is undoubtedly a major advance for classical development law which was perilously forgetful of individuals and failed to make any connection between human freedoms and development. But even so it does not solve all the difficulties and especially the difficulty of achieving effective rights in socially and economically impoverished states that are dependent on an inequitable global system. There is hardly any need to point out that the experience of human rights is more difficult to imagine in economically impoverished countries than in rich or emerging countries. Of course, such situations do not justify a suspension of human rights as in the past, but they do prompt reflection about the difficulties in ensuring them in unfavourable economic and social conditions which, moreover, are considered by those who live in them as the outcome of a global system that continues to operate at their expense. Hence the continuation by other means of the NIEO/human rights quarrel as is attested to by the debates over the proclamation of a *right to development* and the content of that right.

D The Right to Development

In the 1980s the right to development was established as a new right by the General Assembly resolutions and in particular by the Declaration on the Right to Development of 4 December 1986. This Resolution was the subject of very wide international consensus as it was adopted by 146 votes out of 155 countries voting, with eight abstentions and one vote against by the United States. Moreover, the right to development was officially newly enshrined as a 'universal and inalienable right' with the 1993 Vienna Declaration and, in the new post-Cold War context, it seemed to consolidate that other approach in favour of 'human' and not 'state' development, via the recognition of human rights and not by the rights of states alone. This was clearly set out in the Preamble to the 1986 Declaration: 'Recognizing that the human person is the central subject of the development process and that development policy should therefore make the human being the main participant and beneficiary of development.'[15]

A distinction was drawn, then, between the *law of development*, which is an interstate law and the *right to development* as a new human right. But it has to be acknowledged that, as many commentators have pointed out, despite the efforts of the Human Rights Commission, this right to development, which is the outcome of hard-won compromise, has never been sufficiently specific as to its content, and as to who is entitled to it and who owes it, to become

[15] Reasserted in Article 2(1); www.cetim.ch/fr/documents/bro6-develop-A4-fr.pdf.

legally binding and potentially justiciable; and that it raises more questions than it answers.[16] For sure, the right to development is affirmed as an 'inalienable right' by virtue of which any human individual and all peoples have the right to participate in and contribute to 'economic, social and cultural development' (Article 1(1)). For sure, states are presented as owing this right as 'States have the primary responsibility for the creation of national and international conditions favourable to the realization of the right to development' (Article 3(1)), with a specially reasserted obligation for access to basic resources, housing, education, health, fair distribution of income and encouragement for popular participation in decision making (Article 8). But reading the text of the Declaration elicits uncertainty as to who is entitled to this right as it is also presented as a right of peoples. Confusion also arises when it also emphasises that the right of peoples must be fully realised for human rights to be secured (Article 1(2)). Accordingly, from one provision to the next, the right to development appears to be an indeterminate right that may have several recipients and several facets. It seems to have an individual (human individuals) and a collective dimension (peoples) as well as a national (state) and international (international system) dimension which overlap each other, cloud the issue and inevitably create ambiguity.

This ambiguity seemed to have been dissipated somewhat with the 1993 Vienna Declaration which expressly recognised the new right to development as a 'universal and inalienable right and an integral part of fundamental human rights' (Point 10). However, the difficulties it raises in interpretation have been crystallised again in subsequent works on it. The Human Rights Commission set up working groups to monitor its application and to promote the right but, as the latest open-ended working group report, adopted in 2010, showed, this merely revived the old opposition between North and South.[17] On one side the countries of the South consider the application of right to development involves above all good governance internationally and a reform of the economic and financial system towards more just and more equitable redistribution. On the other side, the countries of the North consider that it is the internal transformation of states that is required to bring about a right to development and not the transformation of the international system. We see the resurgence of the ambition of one side to reintroduce the question in the context of a general transformation of the world economic system they consider detrimental to them, while the other side wishes to restrict the problem to internal societies alone. And it has to be acknowledged that if there is still opposition over the issue, it is because it raises the crucial problem of the material possibility of achieving human rights but also development, and therefore the problem of what necessary material conditions are required for human

[16] Georges Abi-Saab, 'Droits de l'homme et développement: quelques éléments de réflexion' (1996) *African Yearbook of International Law* 5 *ff*.

[17] Report of the Working Group on the Right to Development on its eleventh session (Geneva, 26–30 April 2010) A/HRC/15/23.

rights to be viable. Moreover, the debates on the right to development again fire up an old controversy as to responsibility, which is closely correlated with development and which has not been resolved since the theories of underdevelopment: is it the poor country or is it the international system and the group of most powerful states that are responsible for underdevelopment?[18] The answer to this question becomes decisive if it can be imagined that it involves a legally binding right to development. The countries of the North fear that this right to development may mean the countries of the South have a new indeterminate claim on them and elude their own responsibility with respect to their own populations. Interestingly, this fear extends to the new emerging countries. Maurice Kamto summarised it recently:

> In the name of what should the new rich nations which have made more effort than other developing countries to escape poverty be bound by some obligation to develop their former fellow travellers in underdevelopment who supposedly opt for the 'easy way out'?[19]

All these factors suggest how far these questions are from being settled and they cast doubt on the possibility of settling them via this right to development which, being unclear in its meaning, makes it particularly difficult to come to any agreement and reflects the ambiguities that underlie development. It is therefore hardly surprising that the debate is not advancing nor is legally binding force being attributed to a right whose hybrid character, at the crossroads of the right of peoples and of human rights, seems to call for much more general reflection on the factors and causes of development but also seems to demand a degree of agreement on the subject worldwide. Such agreement, it will be agreed, is far from being forthcoming and probably remains unachievable. While it is an indication that there are fundamental issues involved, this approach is therefore perhaps just a misguided solution to a real problem and is not the only one that can be contemplated. Alongside the right to development and in line with the dynamics it suggests, the UN has undertaken what is probably more satisfactory work to render mandatory and to ensure certain fundamental economic and social rights are materialised, like the right to water, to health or to adequate nourishment so as to put them back at the heart of development policies. As they are already recognised in several treaties, the application of these rights are conferred on controlling bodies and are more clearly identified as human rights than the

[18] The issue of the responsibility of postcolonial countries is not developed here but it remains a controversial subject among states and the source of many doctrinal discussions. Some commentators argue that postcolonial nations cannot be held responsible for the situation as, since colonisation, they have been deprived of their 'original economic capacity' and therefore of all responsibility in this respect. See Charles Beitz, *Political Theory and International Relations* (Princeton, Princeton University Press, 1999) and Thomas W Pogge, *World Poverty and Human Rights: Cosmopolitan Responsibilities and Reforms* (Cambridge, Polity Press, 2007). But see Stéphane Chauvier, *Justice et droits à l'échelle globale* (Paris, Vrin, 2006) 110 *ff.*

[19] Maurice Kamto, 'Retour sur le "droit au développement" au plan international: droit au développement des Etats' (1999) 13 *Revue Universelle des Droits de l'Homme* 5.

right to development is and therefore plainly comply with a different rationale to the rights of states.[20]

E Social Development

Human development law is often associated with and sometimes confused with social development law which also emerged in the 1990s. Social development law is similarly focused on individuals and not on states and likewise looks to go beyond the reductive economistic paradigm of the Washington Consensus. The actual principle of social development is far from being a new idea since the UN has always associated economic development with the prospect of social well-being, as demonstrated by Resolution 642 of 20 December 1952, which is one of the earliest resolutions on development.[21]

But the considerations on the social well-being of populations did not give rise to any concrete legal proposals or to any specific action programmes insofar as any intervention in this area was viewed by the South as an encroachment on its sovereignty. The classical and therefore interstate framework of development law still prevailed. Besides, the first attempts at social development by international institutions and certain Western states were already perceived as self-interested and as imposing additional constraints on the impoverished countries. So when the US Secretary of Labor suggested at the 1981 International Labour Organisation (ILO) conference that a minimum international standard should be imposed on all states, the proposal was met with a wave of protest from Third World countries which doubted the good intentions of the Americans and saw in this, on the contrary, a self-serving manoeuvre to introduce disguised protectionism.[22]

It was with the 1995 Copenhagen World Summit for Social Development that social development, now conceived of as an autonomous phenomenon, truly began to feature in the worldwide legal discourse, that is, at a time when new considerations on human development were being introduced. The Declaration and Programme of Action of 12 March 1995 focused social development on the demand for social justice, concern for human individuals, on the reduction of poverty, job creation and social integration.[23] The Programme of Action invited development banks, including of course the World Bank, to take into account access to social services, the possibility for

[20] Although they may be reconciled, see Pierre-Marie Dupuy, 'Le droit à l'eau, un droit international?' (2006) 6 *EUI Working Papers, Law* 1–12.

[21] UN General Assembly Resolution 642 (VII) (20 December 1952), Integrated Economic and Social Development. See also, a decade later, General Assembly Resolution 2542 (XXIV) (11 December 1969), Declaration on Social Progress and Development.

[22] Francis Blanchard, *L'Organisation international du travail. De la guerre froide à un nouvel ordre modial* (Paris, Seuil, 2004) 224.

[23] Copenhagen Declaration on Social Development and Programme of Action of the World Summit on Social Development (12 March 1995) A/CONF.166/9; www.un.org/documents/ga/conf166/aconf166-9.htm.

each individual to secure the means of subsistence, and the promotion of systems for social protection. It contained several fundamental principles such as the 'fair share' of the gains of globalisation which aimed to modify national policies by bolstering economic and social rights, introducing a minimum income or pursuing policies to counter unemployment. The ILO found itself at the forefront of thinking in this area and worked on recasting the legal principles that extend this social dimension of development. In June 1998 it adopted the Declaration on Fundamental Principles and Rights at Work that gave new impetus to the question of social minima on a worldwide scale. On 10 June 2008 it unanimously adopted the Declaration on Social Justice for a Fair Globalisation which is a leading text, rightly acclaimed as a return to the forgotten human purposes of the post-war period and as a reassertion of the principles of social justice in the new post-Cold War environment that seems to entrust development to the principles of international economic law alone, forsaking any principle of equity and justice.[24] Besides, the 2008 Declaration is not conflated with the NIEO as it has neither the same object nor scope. The Declaration takes on a dimension that runs across all countries and, in line with the ILO's mission, it is mainly about work. It enshrines the principle of 'decent work' for all and recommends that the 182 ILO Member States implement policies aimed at employment, social protection, social dialogue and rights in the workplace.

This emergence of a post-Cold War legal discourse on social development comes as no surprise as it too is part of a reaction against ultraliberal globalisation. As in any internal system where capital is left to roam wild, unregulated and highly competitive capitalism on a world scale has hit vulnerable populations hard and prompted the need to put in place human and social safeguards in rich and poor countries alike. Accordingly, the specific idea of 'social' development reflects an awareness that however positive the economic globalisation of the 1990s might be in terms of economic development, it remains untenable in some of its social effects and shall be unacceptable unless it involves social protection for individuals. Again it means that the increased wealth of states from globalisation does not mean better social development of individuals unless states have some incentive to redistribute that wealth equitably among their populations and to combat social inequalities and unemployment.[25]

F Good Governance: Democracy and Human Rights

It is particularly interesting to see that the human ends of development were to be finally taken into account by international financial institutions through

[24] See Supiot, *L'esprit de Philadelphie: la justice sociale face au marché total* (Paris, Seuil/La République des Idées, 2010).

[25] See in particular the 2006 World Bank Report, 'Equity and Development'; siteresources.worldbank.org/INTWDR2006/Resources/WDR_on_Equity_FinalOutline_July_public.pdf.

the concept of 'good governance', thereby intensifying the international movement of convergence between development and human rights. And yet the effects are profoundly ambivalent for the good governance imposed by financial institutions remains associated with the post-Cold War neoliberal economic paradigm which has nothing to do with any human purpose of development and which increases the strain on developing countries terribly.

Initially, good governance was not associated in any way with democracy and human rights. The concept of 'governance' comes from the business world and was introduced by the World Bank in the 1990s to alleviate the unwanted effects of the SAPs which it, along with the IMF, had imposed since the 1980s. In 1992 it published a report on 'Governance and Development' in which it tried to learn the lessons of the failures of the SAPs. Amid the tide of criticism, the major economic institutions had begun to realise the limits of the neoliberal economic model of the Washington Consensus in which the importance and role of state institutions were pushed into the background, while the market took centre stage. But the questions relating to how effective the aid was also lay behind this change. In its 1998 report on aid, the World Bank made a particularly critical appraisal of the use of aid and provided the example of several governments, such as in Zambia and Indonesia, that had dilapidated or totally misappropriated aid.[26] The World Bank observed that aid is only effective in the fight against poverty in states with non-corrupt, stable and relatively transparent institutions practising 'good governance'. This idea was taken up in the 2002 Monterrey Consensus on Financing for Development that redefined the criteria for aid to developing countries so as to include good governance (Point II, 11).[27]

The principle of good governance amounts to introducing a new type of condition that was not provided for by the statutes of the World Bank and the IMF and which sometimes seems incompatible with those statutes. The idea of conditions being placed on the intervention of the international financial institutions had been expressly rejected in the preparatory works for Bretton Woods. Article V of the IMF Articles of Agreement provides that a country may have access to resources upon a simple declaration of the need for financing. Article 4–10 of the International Bank for Reconstruction and Development (IBRD) Articles of Agreement prohibits any interference by the World Bank in a country's political activities. But the principle of reserving aid to those most able to use it was introduced in practice. This was done above all in response to technical and financial considerations, although polit-

[26] 1998 World Bank Report, 'Assessing Aid – What Works, What Doesn't, and Why'. By way of example, Sylvie Brunel makes enlightening and uncompromising observations about France's public aid to Africa and also shows the complicity of a rich state in the waste of aid by corrupt poor states. Sylvie Brunel, *Le gaspillage de l'aide publique* (Paris, Seuil, 1993).

[27] Final Declaration of 22 March 2002 (Mexico), Monterrey Consensus on Financing for Development; www.un.org/esa/ffd/monterrey/MonterreyConsensus.pdf. The same criteria were taken up in the Paris Declaration on Aid Effectiveness of 2 March 2005 and imposed on beneficiaries in the Accra Agenda for Action (AAA) in 2008.

ical considerations were obviously not absent, since the aim was to impose a liberal model of development including all the legal principles of economic liberalism. The list of conditions then grew longer until the World Bank and IMF engaged in permanent talks with the countries in which they intervened to reconstruct the state both politically and economically. These conditions are officially negotiated and never imposed, although there is little room for manoeuvre for the applicant countries. The direct consequence of these conditions is that certain countries are selected as suitable recipients of aid, with the result that, so as not to be left out, other countries have to comply with the conditions, at least superficially. In 2009 almost half of the structural conditions required by the IMF related to better governance in the countries in question.

In accordance with its original meaning, the principle of good governance imposed by the World Bank and IMF is a set of legal principles of an administrative and institutional order in the broad sense and not a reform of the political system of developing countries in a democratic direction. For example, according to its 1997 guidelines on its role in matters of good governance, the IMF works essentially to fight corruption and not to impose human rights and democracy. However, the control it thereby exerts over the fight against corruption requires it to resort to an independent judge or administrative transparency, which are features of regimes where the rule of law prevails and which correspond to a specific type of society subject to the legal system typical of the 'rule of law' model. More offensively still, the World Bank, without saying as much, tends to impose a political and social model that is increasingly democratic, humanistic and legalistic. The tests of good governance that many developing countries now have to pass to secure the Bank's aid are evaluated via several criteria that encompass the characteristic features of democracies, of countries where the rule of law prevails, including the observance of certain human rights: primacy of law, independence of the judiciary, quality of public services, observance of property rights, equality of the sexes, freedom of the press, freedom of thought and association, participation of citizens in civic life and politics, transparency and the fight against corruption. The World Bank's website provides the list of global governance indicators that has become the benchmark used by many operators.[28] The direct inclusion of certain basic human rights, like those on the physical integrity of people, further intensifies the strong, new trend. One striking example is the first three-year arrangement between Burkina Faso, the IMF and the World Bank, where aid was made conditional, among other things, on the reduction in the number of excisions.[29] At this extremely concrete and specific stage, things have obviously come a long way since the official neutrality posted by the two Bretton Woods institutions and

[28] info.worldbank.org/governance/wgi/index.asp.

[29] See Christian Chavagneux and Laurence Tubiana, *Gouvernance mondiale (Rapport du CAE, n° 37)* (Paris, La documentation française, 2002) 50.

we can no longer speak of them being apolitical, or of a strictly economic approach, but we speak rather of convergence with the general movement begun by the UN and the 'developmentalist' institutions in favour of the rule of law, democracy and human rights. There is also an unmarked shift in all areas from 'good governance' to 'democratic governance'.[30] Interestingly, the Bretton Woods institutions are moving closer to the UN institutions on this point after decades of being symbols of opposing sides.

G The Contemporary Dominance of the Liberal Model

It is more generally unsurprising, then, that many international texts associate development, good governance, democracy, human rights and the rule of law. This is attested to by the Plan of Implementation of the 2002 Johannesburg Summit:

> Good governance within each country and at the international level is essential for sustainable development. At the domestic level, sound environmental, social and economic policies, democratic institutions responsive to the needs of the people, the rule of law, anti-corruption measures, gender equality [. . .] are the basis for sustainable development.[31]

In truth, the notions used in international texts are so vague that it is terribly difficult to derive a precise standard from them and any common legal principle even less. They are a very mixed bag and practice is very varied with no truly consistent model appearing. But this is a sign of the convergence of legal models and practices with respect to development and there is nothing surprising about it given the way the idea of development based on the rights of human individuals and not of states has gradually come to the fore. It can also be seen how the liberal and democratic model gradually spreads to all levels of intervention with respect to development. This results in the enshrinement of true dominance of liberal thinking with the defence of the democratic rule of law and human rights in political terms and with the mobilisation of the same economic development model in economic terms. The situation can be explained by the post-Cold War context and the new consensus, by default built on the collapse of the communist regimes and of discredited Marxist thought. But the situation still poses considerable difficulties related mostly to the neoliberal economic side which relate in part, too, to the way good governance and human rights can be imposed in a particularly invasive fashion for states and by differentiating again between the good pupils (with good governance) and the poor pupils engaging in bad governance. We shall

[30] See UNPD and democratic governance; www.beta.undp.org/content/undp/en/home/ourwork/democraticgovernance/overview.html.

[31] Plan of Implementation of the World Summit on Sustainable Development (4 September 2002, point 4, A:CONF. 199/20; daccess-dds-ny.un.org/doc/UNDOC/GEN/N02/636/93/PDF/N0263693.pdf?OpenElement.

return to this point about the social and political control that is now exercised over developing countries in chapter three. It can be observed that it prolongs the imposition of a specific model of development from Western countries and therefore the ever greater reliance of the more vulnerable developing countries on that model and on the states and international institutions that impose it, and that its use in the context of the policy of good governance of international financial institutions has often been denounced as serving only to render more acceptable a neoliberal economic model whose harmful social consequences are unchanged.[32]

Notwithstanding this joint use and the potential manipulations it reveals, it must also be seen that the two sides of the global liberal model are not necessarily compatible. The requirements associated with the democratic rule of law or human rights are not necessarily compatible with what has become a neoliberal economic model that is heedless of human purposes. This is the focus of the very intense, intrinsic strain between the ultraliberal economic side and the humanistic and social, human rights oriented, liberal political side. It is hard to imagine how the strain can be eased when democracy and human rights reintroduce human purposes from which neoliberal international economic law has become dissociated.[33] It is no small paradox to realise that, far from reflecting the triumph of a unified vision of development, the post-Cold War liberal impetus has engendered contradictory forces and rationales that may well end up breaking it apart.[34]

II Sustainable Development

The re-enhancement of the human ends of development with which the last two decades can be credited has also been driven by another evolution of international law, relating this time to the environment. The denunciation of the economistic model of development and of its harmful effects has come in the form of sustainable development, which has without contest become the ultimate benchmark of all development today. In its current form, sustainable development is, as it were, the culmination and the synthesis of all the earlier changes bound up in a critical version that seeks to satisfy the economic and social purposes of development, along with the concern for the environment and for future generations. Will the new model of sustainable development make its mark as the new development paradigm? And can it be the ultimate remedy for the inequalities and disequilibria affecting all of postcolonial

[32] On these questions, see Antony Anghie, *Imperialism, Sovereignty and the Making of International Law* (Cambridge, Cambridge University Press, 2004) 245 *ff.*

[33] See Jean-François Flauss, 'Le droit international des droits de l'homme face à la globalisation économique' in *Commerce mondial et protection des droits de l'homme*, Publications de l'Institut international des droit de l'homme (Brussels, Bruylant, 2001) 217 *ff.*

[34] Unless the ultraliberal order is itself reformed. See ch 4.

world society? Or might it even be the paradigm of a new outlook for all of humanity in general?

A A New Development Paradigm?

'Sustainable development' is the name given to the third model of development that arose with the celebrated Brundtland Report in 1987 and has become ubiquitous in the practice, texts and discourse of contemporary international law. It is called 'sustainable' development since, according to one famous formulation, it must meet 'the needs of the present without compromising the ability of future generations to meet their own needs'.[35] More specifically, it refers to a form of development that is environmentally friendly, that allows the renewal of natural resources and their reasoned exploitation so as to preserve the planet for future generations, but that which also integrates the fight against disparities in wealth and against poverty. It is of particular interest insofar as it attempts to act politically, economically and legally, too, against the two great contemporary worldwide imbalances:[36] the major disequilibrium resulting from the massive inequality in the distribution of the world's wealth and the environmental disequilibrium due to the accelerated deterioration of the biosphere. These two imbalances are considered to be related to economic development itself and to contemporary instrumental rationality. It is the economic model of development, all-out growth and the need for frantic consumption that are exhausting the world's resources, causing the first worldwide ecological threats and exacerbating social inequalities on all levels. However, as with human and social development, the advocates of sustainable development do not deny the liberal economic model of development, but seek to control it to prevent it from destroying our environment and to allow it to remedy poverty and social inequalities around the world. Hence the multidimensional character of the new model and the fact that it encompasses all other aspects of development, of which it seeks to produce a synthesis.

Can such a challenge be met? And does such a model really lead to a rethink of the development model? Some observers see in it the way for humankind to escape from an alienating technological development for which humanity is itself responsible and the end of the domination of instrumental rationality in which human problems are thought about only in terms of computations, efficiency and profitability.[37] Therefore, it is supposedly the best response to the crisis of a neoliberal model of economic development and a far-reaching contemporary political, social and moral disarray over a model of unlimited

[35] Report of the World Commission on Environment and Development, 'Our Common Future' (Bruntland Report) (I.3.27); www.un-documents.net/ocf-ov.htm.

[36] Dominique Bourg, 'Le développement durable' *Encyclopedia universalis* 1; www.universalis.fr/encyclopedie/developpement-durable/.

[37] Jean-Philippe Pierron, *Penser le développement durable* (Paris, Ellipses, 2009) 7.

growth based on the progress of science and technology, on an economistic vision of social life and on indefinite consumption of resources that may seriously endanger the planet and the internal cultural and social equilibria of many societies. But others, on the contrary, see it as a useless rag-bag of contradictory features, or even a roundabout way of legitimising the dominant economic paradigm. Serge Latouche, for example, sees it as a masterpiece in the art of revamping what is old hat, arguing that 'sustainable' means whatever enables development to prolong its final moments indefinitely.[38]

Sustainable development, however, does appear to want to be the critical version of previous development and of the human, social and environmental development that it generates ever more irremediably. The concept of 'sustainability' shows that development, as introduced in 1945, is no longer sustainable. In this sense, the concept of sustainable development is no longer synonymous with progress, at least not with the old dogmatic idea of progress and of historical optimism that underpinned unfailing faith in the future. That is what almost all international lawyers from the eighteenth century through to the mid-twentieth century believed in. The Western belief in progress underlay the practices and discourses of international law throughout the colonial period through belief in the values of Western civilisation, then during the postcolonial period through the post-1945 development paradigm.[39] The post-war model of economic development continued to nurture hope for a better future through the idea that continued growth would eventually result in a 'fallout' that would benefit all and would lead to a state of worldwide prosperity. But such optimism was only an illusion, which has been fully revealed by Gilbert Rist.[40] The illusion consisted of believing that such development was harmless for people and the environment, whereas consumers have incessantly enjoyed an ever greater excess of goods and a system is being maintained that intrinsically worsens poverty and harms the environment. The point that such development can only be achieved by the constant use of natural resources which are not inexhaustible has also been ignored, so that far from securing the promised abundance, economic growth can but lead to generalised shortage if nothing is done about it.[41]

Confronted with this illusion of economic development, sustainable development reflects the fundamental idea that infinite growth cannot be defended in a finite world, and therefore we must break with the old dogma of progress to make an alternative model of development legally binding, a model to cope not with guaranteed progress but, on the contrary, with an uncertain future. The 1992 Agenda 21 in Rio began by asserting that 'Humanity stands at a

[38] Serge Latouche, *Survivre au développement* (Paris, Mille et une nuits, 2004) 22–23.

[39] See Thomas Skouteris, *The Notion of Progress in International Law Discourse* (The Hague, TMC Asser press, 2010).

[40] Gilbert Rist, *The History of Development: From Western Origins to Global Faith* (London and New York, Zed Books, 2002), 439 *ff*.

[41] ibid 440.

defining moment in history' (Preamble, 1.1) and then, 10 years later in 2002, the Johannesburg World Earth Summit Final Report (III.14) announced that 'Fundamental changes in the way societies produce and consume are indispensable for achieving global sustainable development'. The sustainable development model seems to really reflect the awareness of the global threat to humanity from its model of economic development and therefore the need for a global and intergenerational response to confront that threat. That is also why sustainable development, although it is aimed primarily at developing countries, has a global scope of application that extends beyond the poor countries alone. This is true of the environmental issues but also of the social ones. The 'shared risks' associated with environmental damage mean that the question of social and sustainable development and the related legal practices concern all societies in the North and South alike.

And so the association of the two seemingly contradictory meanings of 'sustainable development' is perhaps not necessarily the outcome of this ideological manipulation so vehemently decried by post-developmentalists today, but the naming of a reality by which an attempt is made to reconcile development in space with its sustainability over time at the price of a renewal of the concept itself. Post-developmentalists constantly reduce development, whatever its new guises, to its economic dimension, which they identify with the same undefined underlying structure of accumulation of capital and production of new needs. In doing so, they materialistically presuppose that development is unlimited and indefinite as a matter of principle, it cannot be controlled, and so they criticise the principle of this economistic and de-humanising spiral. But by the same token, they reject any other possible meanings of the term 'development' and the fact that it may represent different realities, and in so doing reject any possible alternative to the development crisis starting from development itself. But the point is that we can abandon the principle of unlimited economic growth and of international economic law built entirely on this dogma by subjecting it to the ecological and human limits set out by sustainable development and moving towards a 'sustainable economy'.[42] Even so, sustainable development would have to kick in, in keeping with the rationale of its three dimensions, which is far from being the case at present. The risks associated with this new model relate to the way in which ecological or economic challenges may quite simply force out challenges associated with socio-economic inequalities among states and with the human ends of development. It is a very real problem that faces us today which can be better perceived when we analyse the different legal practices associated with it.

[42] See Tim Jackson, *Prosperity without Growth. Economics for a Finite Planet* (London, Routledge, 2009). He does not speak of negative growth since it would be unstable and would generate mass unemployment and a spiral of recession. He speaks instead of a 'growth dilemma' and the need to limit growth by reforming the existing economic system.

B The Law Relating to Sustainable Development

The law relating to sustainable development is the legal reflection of this new multidimensional model. It brings together a whole particularly broad and varied array of legal principles and practices that are diversely enforceable and arise from a series of initiatives. These initiatives extended from the 1972 Stockholm Declaration on the Human Environment to the 2002 Johannesburg Earth Summit via the June 1992 Rio Declaration on Environment and Development, Agenda 21, and the many conventions adopted in this area including the 1992 Convention on Climate Change to which was appended the Kyoto Protocol that came into force in 2005. The First World Earth Summit, the Rio Conference, provided the decisive impetus. It was organised in Brazil which, in a way, symbolises all the difficulties, expectations and hopes of the South with regard to development. This country has become one of the world's leading agri-food powers, with the much sought-after label of 'emerging country', but at the same time more than 100 million people live in slums while inequalities and pollution are extreme.[43]

The principles adopted at Rio form the foundation for a new law of sustainable development. They primarily bring together development law and environmental law, but more generally include legal rules and practices in the three domains that sustainable development attempts to reconcile (Agenda 21, Preamble 1.1): economic issues (growth and production, social and human issues (human rights, fight against poverty and unemployment) and ecological issues (environmental protection). This multidimensional aspect was subsequently reiterated in all the texts on sustainable development down to the Plan of Action adopted at the 2002 Johannesburg World Earth Summit:

> These efforts will also promote the integration of the three components of sustainable development – economic development, social development and environmental protection – as interdependent and mutually reinforcing pillars. Poverty eradication, changing unsustainable patterns of production and consumption and protecting and managing the natural resource base of economic and social development are overarching objectives of, and essential requirements for, sustainable development.[44]

This explains the inevitable difficulties of application that may occur because of tension and possible contradiction between the principles and rules of the three pillars of development – economic, social and environmental – and which reveal an essential problem as to whether any one of these rationales should prevail over the others. The international financial or commercial institutions tasked with the economic side of development implement legal

[43] Sylvie Brunel, *Le développement durable* (Paris, PUF, Que sais-je?, 2010) 48.

[44] Resolution 2 Annex Plan of Implementation of the World Summit on Sustainable Development of 4 September 2002, A/CONF 199/20, Introduction para 2; daccess-dds-ny.un.org/doc/UNDOC/GEN/N02/636/93/PDF/N0263693.pdf?OpenElement.

rules of an economic order promoting the liberalisation of trade and foreign private investment in poor countries. But this purely economic logic may entail deforestation, desertification, pollution and the exhaustion of renewable energies. The environmental logic may lead to the legal creation of huge nature reserves (more than 15 per cent of land now has protected status) or to the restricted poaching of certain protected species but sometimes to the detriment of the social rights of traditional communities, of indigenous peoples or of rural spheres that may be deprived of their natural, subsistence and social setting.[45] The human and social logic may impose itself to the detriment of ecological considerations whereas it very often accompanies criticism of the liberal financial logic, the disastrous social effects of which are frequently bemoaned. In this respect we see the opposition arise again between North and South since their interests diverge over the different dimensions of sustainable development. Above all, poor countries are eager to maintain their economic growth so as to be able to develop with respect to rich countries for which the environment is becoming a priority. As Sylvie Brunel aptly puts it, the problem is that the rich emphasise the sustainable, while the poor are still thinking development.[46]

These questions of compatibility are still unresolved except on a case by case basis depending on the existing legal systems. But the fact is that, at the present time, the global trend is to put environmental concerns first, and especially concerns about climate, and through them the interplay of economic interests. The combination of the two leaves little room for concern about socio-economic inequalities between states and for the human ends of development. From this point of view, sustainable development, too, is a product of the latest episode of globalisation. Ever since the neoliberal turning point of the 1990s, private firms have become the driving force behind sustainable development, which is no bad thing in itself, of course, since they have boosted sustainable development by contributing to the fight against pollution and by including the concern to improve the social working conditions of their employees. A thousand of the world's largest firms have signed up to the Global Compact initiated by the UN Secretary-General in 1999 at the Davos Forum and therefore agreed to a set of 10 non-binding commitments on the environment, human rights and work. But, overall, the weakness of states which cannot put in place voluntarist policies, the lack of articulation between social and economic legal systems, the lack of control of businesses and of global governance in this area mean that the purely private, commercial and financial logic inevitably wins out over any general and human interest and does nothing to eradicate the poverty in which four billion people still live.

[45] Hervé Kempf, *La baleine qui cache la forêt. Enquête sur les pièges de l'écologie* (Paris, La découverte, 1994) 27 *ff.*

[46] Sylvie Brunel, *A qui profite le développement durable?* (Paris, Larousse, 2008) 9.

It should be emphasised even so that, in its environmental aspects, the law of sustainable development very clearly enshrines the principle of dual legal treatment between industrialised and developing countries and reintroduces a spirit of equity that seemed to have deserted many areas of international law. Some principles of environmental law are designed to commit all states, whichever they may be, such as the principle of participation, the precautionary principle, environmental evaluation and the polluter pays principle. But the specific situation of developing countries is always taken into account to diversify the obligations of each. Enshrinement of this double standard of treatment is perfectly legitimate for developing countries on two grounds: insofar as environmental pollution was caused by the economic activity of industrialised countries, conferring on them specific responsibility in this domain and insofar as developing countries need to further their industrial development which in turn, therefore, contributes to further pollution. Moreover, it is the weak and poor states that are the most affected today by climate change as they have no financial and material means to cope with it.

In this context, the possibility of coming up with equitable legal instruments depends on achieving a balance between the claims of one side to limit environmental pollution and the claims of the other side to be entitled to pollute to ensure their own economic and social development. Now, it will invariably be pointed out that sustainable development law tends to introduce such a balance which reintroduces elements of social justice among states. The 1992 Rio Declaration on environment and development enshrined several principles in favour of developing countries as being essential for achieving sustainable development and most of them are contained in the treaties on the question, thereby becoming mandatory. One example of a treaty-based right that takes up many of these principles is the Convention on Climate Change, also adopted at Rio on 9 May 1992. Its objective is the 'stabilization of greenhouse gas concentrations in the atmosphere' so that they do not cause climate change. Some of the fundamental principles set out in the Declaration are found, particularly the principle of 'common but differentiated responsibilities' which implies that it is the developed countries that bear the main burden for reducing greenhouse gas effects (Article 3(1)); the principle of taking into account 'The specific needs and special circumstances' of developing countries, especially the most vulnerable among them (Article 3(2)); the principle of prohibiting discrimination on the pretext of protecting the environment (Article 3(5)); or the principle of technology transfer (Article 4(1)(c)). Moreover, the Convention draws up a precise list of the different categories of countries by their level of development and vulnerability so as to finely differentiate between the situations of each and their obligations. For example, specific measures must be taken with respect to small island states, countries in arid zones, countries prone to natural disasters or countries whose economic development is highly dependent on the production of fossil fuels (Article 4(8)). Being a framework-convention, the 1992 Convention lays down only very general obligations, but the additional protocol adopted at Kyoto in 1997 and which came into force in 2005 sets far more specific and restrictive obligations for the states parties to the protocol, while reaffirming the principle of 'common but differentiated responsibilities' (Article 10), the need for technology transfers to developing countries (Article 11) and while implementing clean development mechanisms (CDMs) that provide for 'clean' investment by rich countries in developing countries. Moreover, the Conference of the States Parties (194 states) to the Convention that met at Cancun in Mexico in 2010 integrated the Copenhagen Accord into the Convention and adopted a series of measures for developing countries, including the establishment of a Green Climate Fund to aid developing countries financially, a committee for adapting developing countries to climate change, a technology centre on climate to promote climate technologies in developing countries and a mechanism for combatting deforestation.

Alongside the establishment of this differentiated legal regime, several international bodies have been set up to implement the principles contained in the various declarations and resolutions taken by statements within the UN framework, notably the Declarations of Stockholm (1972), Rio (1992), Nairobi (1997) and Malmö (2000). The United Nations Environment Programme (UNEP) created in 1972 is essential in promoting the principles of sustainable development and in organising cooperation among states. The Sustainable Development Commission (SDC) set up in 1992 is tasked with ensuring the implementation of Agenda 21 of 1992 and more generally of controlling and following up on the Earth Summits. The Global Environment Facility (GEF) set up in 1991 manages a financing system for preserving the environment and works mainly with developing and emerging countries. It collaborates with many non-governmental organisations and 10 or so international institutions for development and aims to ensure the financing of several international conventions dealing with sustainable development. This is a crucial aspect because the system's effectiveness depends on there really being financial aid and knowledge transfers to developing countries.[47] Now, it is at this very point that the difficulties accumulate and when doubts arise as to how effective sustainable development law really is. This is particularly so because, since the end of the Cold War, the system has been based entirely on the law of the market, which may well favour the environment market but not really orientate it in favour of the most needy.[48]

Besides, it is particularly striking to see that, while multiplying texts on sustainable, social and human development, the main international actors have

[47] Laurence Boisson de Chazournes, 'The Global Environment Facility (GEF): A Unique and Crucial Institution' (2005) 14(3) *Review of European Community and International Environmental Law* 193 *ff.*

[48] See Alexandre Kiss, 'Emergence de principes généraux du droit international et d'une politique internationale de l'environnement' in Ivo Rens (ed), *Le droit international face à l'éthique et à la politique de l'environnement* (Geneva, SEBES, 1996) 31 *ff.*

for a decade adopted much more specific objectives and much more targeted objectives in terms of health, education, equality between men and women, hunger and poverty. It is as if while multiplying texts on development generally and therefore having a particularly ambitious and wide scope, they were homing in on the objectives to be attained. Among those objectives, reflected in particular under the title of the Millennium Development Goals, one of the main ones is obviously that of the fight against (extreme) poverty. We take this as a particularly significant example of the new humanitarian orientations of the international community.

III The Fight Against Poverty

A The Contemporary Turning Point

It may seem strange to speak of a contemporary turning point and to make the fight against poverty a new focus of the 2000s when it has been one of the major objectives of development law ever since the 1950s. However, it is indeed a decisive contemporary evolution insofar as the fight against poverty is outstripping development everywhere. Even though the eradication of poverty still forms part of development, international texts now invite or compel international institutions, states and all international actors to focus their efforts more effectively on eliminating poverty, on coordinating to achieve this and assigning funds to this goal as a priority. Particularly illustrative of this is the way the UN General Assembly chose not to proclaim a new Development Decade and launched, in 1995, a First UN Decade for the Eradication of Poverty.[49] But above all it is the Millennium Goals proclaimed by the heads of state and government in a solemn resolution of 8 September 2000 that very precisely set out the mission for the international community of halving extreme poverty by 2015.[50] This objective has become one of the priorities of the international community's agenda for the twenty-first century and its acclaim has been as unparalleled as it has been surprising, so swift has it been in securing consensus, in stark contrast with the reluctance and controversy that has constantly dogged development law.

The main international and regional organisations concerned have all fallen into step and redirected their action and aid along these lines. The World Bank Report for 2000 was entitled 'Attacking Poverty', while the 2003

[49] UN General Assembly Resolution 50/107 (26 January 1996) UN Doc A/RES/50/107.

[50] UN General Assembly Resolution 55/L.2 (13 September 2000) UN Doc A/55 L.2. The New Millennium Declaration is a Resolution that was adopted on 8 September 2000, symbolising the international community's new creed. It sets eight development goals (Millennium Development Goals): to cut extreme poverty and hunger; to provide universal primary education; to promote sex equality and women's autonomy; to reduce infant mortality; to improve maternal health care; to combat HIV/AIDS, malaria and other diseases; to protect the environment and set up a global partnership for development.

UNDP Report was 'A Compact among Nations to End Human Poverty'. The World Bank abandoned its first SAPs, adopting Poverty Reduction Strategies (PRSs) instead. From now on all low-income countries must prepare detailed strategies on poverty reduction so as to secure alleviation of their debt and new financing from the World Bank. Hence too the introduction of new classifications like that of 'middle-income country', which are entitled to IMF loans, and others, supported by the IBRD, which are set the priority goal of reducing the indigence and extreme poverty of their populations. Similar moves are made at national level and there are countless declarations by heads of state calling for poverty to be overcome.[51] The G20 meeting at Seoul in November 2010 recalled that the fight against poverty was among the international community's priorities. The year 2010 was also the European Year for Combating Poverty and Social Exclusion. A number of external legal policies were adapted to the new objective. In France, as in many other countries, the fight against poverty was defined in 1999 by the Foreign Affairs Ministry as 'the priority reference for any cooperation policy'.[52]

B Contribution and Limits

The fight against poverty is a fundamental goal of social justice and the measures taken in this area seek to offset the most extreme imbalances the world experiences. The contemporary turning point to promote the fight against poverty is one of the manifestations of a new and much broader ethical impetus from the international community and of new requirements that the post-Cold War world is generating in terms of morals, law and justice. This contemporary shift towards ethics affects other areas of international law like human rights, peace and security or environmental law. It is also reshuffling the cards since it introduces a confusion between law and morals that was thought to have been dismissed, sometimes eliciting a moralisation of law, a legitimacy in terms of value of legal rules and of certain armed humanitarian interventions that implicitly reintroduce the idea of a just war. The current fight against poverty contributes without contest to these new ethical and humanitarian requirements. However, it can also be explained for reasons that are specific to it. It also stems from a twofold feeling of powerlessness in the face of earlier failures of everything relating to specific development

[51] For example, on 2 August 2007 at the UN, British Prime Minister Gordon Brown called for 'a new alliance to defeat poverty'; www.mondialisation.ca/index.php?context=va&aid=6529. See also the address of US President Barack Obama on 22 September 2010; www.radio-canada.ca/nouvelles/internationales/2010/09/22/007-NY-ONU-Obama.shtml and the address by French President Nicolas Sarkozy on 21 September 2010; www.la-croix.com/Actualite/S-informer/Monde/Discours-de-Nicolas-Sarkozy-a-l-ONU-au-sommet-sur-les-objectifs-du-millenaire-_NG_-2010-09-21-579083.

[52] See the Quai d'Orsay website: France diplomatie.

policies[53] and in the face of the current episode of globalisation which, for some, is irresistible and uncontrollable in every way.

But such an evolution is still particularly problematic if accompanied by an associated abandonment of any idea of reform of the existing system or global policy on development.[54] If this is the case, it may be thought that the price to pay to secure material results in the fight against poverty becomes peculiarly high for the poorest states. The humanitarian aspect here imposes itself to the detriment of development law, and like any humanitarian law based on ethics, it takes on the form of an absolute requirement, as a matter of urgency which, accordingly, engenders unanimity. It commands consensus where development failed to do so and leads to political confrontation, for it is far easier to agree on the fight against extreme poverty than on the paths to development and the roads to prosperity.[55] Besides, far from any idea of the NIEO or of discriminatory and compensatory development law, the fight against poverty does not in any way lead to the modification of existing international economic law but, quite the contrary, it seems to be a necessary aspect of it.[56] There is a tradition of thought along these lines and it is not surprising to see its concrete effects today, now that the neoliberal scheme prevails worldwide. A thinker like Friedrich Hayek, for example, who so marked the instigators of the Washington Consensus, is helpful in understanding how international legal practices aimed solely at poverty fit in perfectly with the neoliberal discourse of international institutions. For Hayek, it is the spontaneous interplay of the market that will bring about more equality among individuals, if it is not disturbed by interventionist policies absurdly designed to set up some form of social justice. However, it is quite acceptable even so to act in the case of 'extreme deprivation' so as to ensure a minimum of resources for the least favoured.[57] However, it is more an ethical duty than a real legal obligation. Hayek specifies that this minimum of resources must be supplied 'outside of the market', which suggests it should be above all a matter of coordinating private initiatives, which are directly reminiscent of the moral duty of charity that classical liberal thinking has always entertained.[58] That is why, even if they are as much a fact of international public

[53] On these successive failures and the World Bank's conversion to the fight against poverty, see Jean-Pierre Cling and François Roubaud, *La Banque mondiale* (Paris, La decouverte, 2008) 53 *ff.*

[54] See Dominique Liauzu, *L'enjeu tiers-mondistes. Débats et combats* (Paris, L'Harmattan, 1987) 94 *ff.*

[55] A humanitarian discourse is imposed based on human rights and the protection of individuals, which seeks to stand apart from Third World and neo-Marxist discourse based on inequalities that accompanied development law in the 1970s.

[56] Francine Mestrum, 'De l'utilité de la "lutte contre la pauvreté" pour le nouvel ordre mondial' in Gilbert Rist (ed), *Les mots du pouvoir. Sens et non sens de la rhétorique internationale* (Cahiers de l'IUED, 2002) 67 *ff.*

[57] Friedrich Hayek, *Law, Legislation and Liberty, II* (London, Routledge, 1973).

[58] See Luc Ferry and Alain Renaut, *Philosophie politique, vol 3: Des droits de l'homme à l'idée républicaine* (Paris, PUF, 1985) 149 *ff.*

action as of private (and very dynamic) action, the targeted fight against extreme poverty and the new Millennium Goals are fully consistent with this neoliberal model. And for that matter, confirming this connection, the high profile international action by financial institutions to eradicate poverty seems to have less avowed ends. Such action defuses any crisis of legitimacy of the neoliberal economic model that might arise because of the dismantling of the old social protection that this single development model implies. If the action programmes or adjustment plans are implemented to the detriment of the poorest populations, an excessive social deficit might call them into question. For them to be accepted, aid must be extended by priority to governments that are to set up 'safety nets' for those hardest hit. An example is the new conditions imposed by aid law since aid is now only given to developing countries that adopt policies to fight against poverty and that, at the same time, promote more open markets and foreign investment.[59] The new loans granted by the IMF under its Poverty Reduction and Growth Facility set up in 1999 are another example. As the 2007 report of the Independent Evaluation Office (IEO) states, they are more favourable to public spending (slashed in the early SAPs) and to poverty alleviation programmes. But as the underlying paradigm has not changed in any way, the recommended measures are designed solely to promote growth and the liberalisation of trade at any price.[60] In other words, the economic laws are left to operate, pursuant to the neoliberal creed that continues to prevail, but action is taken to remedy their most patent and most extreme social consequences. The upshot is that the focus on the fight against poverty thus strengthens the existing economic model while leading to a more insidious but real enough negation of any specific law pertaining to development.

By narrowing its purposes, the current fight against poverty or even extreme poverty therefore contributes to consolidating the existing neoliberal situation and the impossibility of finding political and legal solutions for the global development of Third World countries.[61] The narrow focus on the Millennium Goals alone and the fight against extreme poverty becomes an obstacle in itself in the search for solutions, to reflect on international law as it pertains to development and to the idea of a more equitable distribution of

[59] See the Accra Agenda for Action of 4 September 2008, adopted at the Third High Level Forum on Aid Effectiveness; siteresources.worldbank.org/ACCRAEXT/Resources/4700790-1217425866038/FINAL-AAA-4-SEPTEMBER-final-16h00.pdf.

[60] For example, redistributive tax policies could have an obvious effect in reducing poverty, but the World Bank hangs on to its neoliberal policy of out-and-out liberalisation of trade and will not entertain such policies (nor will the states concerned). See Jean-Pierre Cling, Mireille Razafindrakoto and François Roubaud (eds), *Les nouvelles stratégies internationales de lutte contre la pauvreté*, 2nd edn (Paris, Economica/IRD, 2003).

[61] Zaki Laidi, 'Le basculement du « nous » vers le « je ». Réflexions sur le système social mondial' in Yves Daudet (ed), *Les Nations Unies et le développement social international* (Paris, Pedone, 1996) 35 *ff*. The United Nations Conference on Trade and Development (UNCTAD) itself warned about limiting development goals to poverty reduction alone, see UNCTAD *Least-Advanced Countries Report. Escaping the Poverty Trap* (Geneva, United Nations, 2002).

wealth among the world's nations. It is highly significant that there is hardly any talk now of socio-economic inequalities in international texts on poverty since the problem no longer lies there. Developing countries are supposed to have just one central problem, that of poverty and not that of the fight against inequalities. Accordingly, the fight against poverty is seen as the key to everything with the operation of the market. This is particularly misleading. We lose sight of the broader picture and especially of the point that one man's poverty must be viewed against another's wealth. Nor do we try any longer to tackle inequalities by compensatory or redistributive development rules between states. The repercussions of this change are found even in research and teaching. Much of the research in development law has been abandoned, as said, and the subject is no longer taught. It has been replaced by research into policies to eradicate poverty proposed by international organisations.[62]

The overly selective slide in this direction, curbing development law as it has, therefore creates a real predicament and remains problematic insofar as, by the same token, we no longer question the other aspects of existing international legal arrangements or the possibilities of reforming those arrangements to make them more equitable, even if that were to mean rearranging development law and international economic law. It cannot be enough nowadays to refer to goals of humanitarian emergency to solve development questions insofar as it is just as essential to meet the expectations as to social justice in a world that is rife with inequality and tremendous poverty, for the fundamental problem remains and it would be regrettable to see it remain without attempting to provide a solution. In truth, a thorough review of development law is called for, since it may legitimately be thought that it is pointless talking about teaching and enforcing a system of law whose shortcomings the fight against poverty seems to want to palliate.

[62] Highly significant in this respect was the creation of an annual chair in 'Knowledge against Poverty' at the *Collège de France* in 2008; www.college-de-france.fr/default/EN/all/cha_int2008/jpal.htm.

3

An Appraisal

THERE ARE TWO branches of international law which have always been intrinsically related and the achievement of a form of development which is consistent with the joint expectations of equity and effectiveness is probably dependent on their successful articulation and their non-hegemonic use. One of those branches is international economic law. It was built up after the Second World War and is now grounded on a neoliberal model of economics which is inequitable for states and oblivious to the human objectives for which it had been introduced. The other branch is international development law, which groups together a set of specific rules designed to rearrange North–South economic relations more equitably and to confer a special legal regime on developing countries to give them the chance to take on the developing countries on a level playing field. This branch of law dates from the 1960s and 1970s when international society became postcolonial. It was asserted as one of the fundamental demands of the newly decolonised nations, which, through development law, hoped not just to reinforce their economic independence but to establish measures in their favour in order to yield some degree of true equality and not just formal equality among states and so recast the existing international economic order. This impetus was broken with the financial crisis of the 1980s but also with the failure of the collective and planned development models, leaving international economic law in its new neoliberal form to triumph on its own. The New International Economic Order (NIEO) subsequently vanished from the General Assembly resolutions. Even so, international development law did survive to some extent in its classical form and was enhanced by new rules and practices which, while prompting many questions and producing certain debatable effects, do seem to open up fresh prospects for development if the populations concerned make them their own and really do use them for their benefit. Now, what is to be made of this tangle of economic and developmentalist rules and regulations?

It has already been mentioned how contrasting the outcome has been in terms of facts. Many countries have indeed experienced economic development. But that development is unrelated to the principles of development law, and while the spectacular growth of some major emerging states has raised the standard of living for millions of people, this growth exists alongside poverty which subsists in dreadful proportions and alongside inequalities that have arisen in recent years. And so what lies before us is a deeply paradoxical world in that there is 'more poverty in a richer world'.[1] The appraisal of international development law is the subject of this chapter and it can only be recognised that the results as they currently stand are hardly encouraging. It shall be shown how the legal rules and practices of international development law generally work to little effect as they are constantly skewed by the rules of international economic law or by the rationale of overarching economic interests. This results in a persistent gulf between the stated principles and reality and the seeming impossibility of effectively orientating the current legal and economic system through classical and new international development law. This explains the hard fact of the matter that the growth of certain states exists alongside poverty, inequalities and the persistent inequity of the world's legal and economic system.

I The Practices of Classical and New International Development Law

A brief general appraisal shall be given here, which has multiple ramifications that are too voluminous to go into now. Others may care to fill in the outline. What is proposed is an uncompromising critique, but one that should not be misleading. If the results of development law prove so inconclusive, as shall be shown, it is not so much the principle of this law and its foundation stones that need to be challenged as the economic context in which it has been deployed.

A Classical International Development Law

Even apart from the idea of an overall reform of the economic order that was abandoned with the NIEO, classical international development law has not kept its promises. True, the first major legal principles such as the right of peoples to self-determination, the right of permanent sovereignty over natural resources and the right to nationalise assets provided fair compensation is paid or the free choice of economic and political regime have been confirmed by state practice and have incontrovertibly grounded and consolidated the sovereignty of the newly independent nations in such a way that they may really envision their development. But the array of more technical legal norms that were recommended were either not adopted or proved disappointing when applied. The principle of technology and knowledge transfer (Article 13 of the 1974 Charter) worked in part, but ran into many difficulties and fell foul of industrial and intellectual property rights. For more than a decade

[1] See Michel Beaud, *Le basculement du monde. De la terre, des hommes et du capitalisme* (Paris, La découverte, 2000) 23 *ff*.

from 1976 to 1988, developing countries called for a code of conduct in this domain within the United Nations Conference on Trade and Development (UNCTAD) but without any real success. The only partial successes were for technology transfer with respect to the environment (eg Article 11 of the 1997 Kyoto Protocol) and access to medicinal drugs in the event of pandemics, which has probably been the most notable success story. Under the amendment of 6 December 2005 to the Agreement on Trade-Related Aspects of Intellectual Property Rights (TRIPS), the Member States of the World Trade Organization should be able to procure drugs to combat diseases like HIV/AIDS, malaria or tuberculosis through mandatory licences for patented drugs. Moreover, the right of states to group together as commodity producer organisations, like the Organization of the Petroleum Exporting Countries, has not led to a measure of any consequence. Under the influence of UNCTAD, an integrated commodity scheme devised to stabilise prices and incomes for the sake of developing countries was given impetus by the creation of a Common Fund, but it is currently completely ineffective because of the ever-increasing liberalisation of the world market. The right of all developing countries to 'participate fully and effectively' in drawing up and enforcing new international norms (Article 10) has hardly been implemented. As said, the principle of preferential treatment without reciprocity has been included in commercial law, but is limited in its application. The 'common and different' obligations (Articles 29 and 30) are to be introduced above all with regard to the environment, while with regard to the law of the sea, they have been largely relinquished by the change in obligations originally laid down in the 1982 United Nations Convention on the Law of the Sea (UNCLOS) to the benefit of the economic interests of developed countries. Besides, the 1994 Agreement relating to the Implementation of Part XI of UNCLOS is significantly part of the neoliberal turn of the 1990s as it marks the end of a system of redistribution and of technology transfer relating to the sea bed that had been negotiated in the 1980s, putting in its place the open market and joint venture agreements.

It cannot be denied either that none of these principles and rules, when implemented, are truly effective. First of all, it can be pointed out that it is not the legal practices of this classical development law that have brought about the emergence of major nations like China, India, Brazil or the South-East Asian countries. There are many endogenous and exogenous factors that explain this evolution, not just the few legal practices and principles of international law on development.[2] Next, these practices, whether they are in the form of the Generalised Preference System (GPS), Official Development

[2] See Christophe Jaffrelot (ed), *L'enjeu mondial. Les pays émergents* (Paris, Sciences Po les Presses, 2008). On East Asia and more specifically South Korea and the exceptional historical factors for their spectacular growth (and which revise the official version for their success from the financial institutions), see Alice Amsdem, *Asia's Next Giant: South Korea and Late Industrialization* (Oxford, Oxford University Press, 1989).

Assistance (ODA) or Structural Adjustment Plans (SAPs), are always laid down unilaterally either by the country providing the aid or by the institutions. No talk of a partnership or of negotiations can hide the particularly unequal balance of power in this domain where the beneficiary country cannot afford to refuse the conditions imposed on it. Accordingly, these are legal practices that foster the continued dependence of the beneficiary country, not just in the short to medium term because of the unilateral character of the aid, but generally in the long term because the beneficiary countries cannot usually forego the aid although even so they cannot accede to the status of emerging country. Most significantly, the legal principle of the GPS in trade, based on the principle of dual standards and therefore of positive discrimination in favour of developing countries, does not seem to have borne fruit at all, despite it being one of the leading measures of classical international development law. It may save some countries from sinking amid the sea of ever freer trade, and remains essential to that extent. But it does not seem to be a development lever at all. Several recent studies show how ineffective such measures are.[3] By way of example, the European Union's GPS, which is the earliest and most comprehensive, has been criticised in terms of its theory and practice as it excludes certain states (threshold effect) and only really benefits the developing countries with the highest incomes. Because of the constant downward trend of customs tariffs, fresh opposition is now forming between those developing countries that want to maintain their GPS and those which are not GPS beneficiaries and want to secure the freest possible trade, without GPS, with the lowest possible customs tariffs. This is one such aspect of the thriving new South–South struggles. Above all, however, the result of recent years shows that we may be seeing the end of the GPSs because they are economically ineffective but also because of the legal uncertainty they create with the numerous disputes that have formed over them, like the banana case.[4] Besides, under the combined effect of ever more extensive free trade and of the growing power of the emerging countries which represent ever tougher competition, it can be seen that the tendency is clearly to save the GPSs for the least-developed countries while the GPSs attributed to the other developing countries will be replaced by free-trade areas, the philosophy of which is quite the opposite. There is a shift from dual standards and the principle of preferential discrimination to reinforced free trade on the basis of reciprocity and of equal treatment, which is now considered the only effective instrument for the growth of developing countries. The example of the Economic Partnership Agreements (EPAs) the

[3] See, for example, Habib Gherari, 'Tendances récentes des préférences commerciales' in *Mélanges Madjid Benchikh* (Paris, Pedone, 2010) 465 *ff* and Corinne Vidcar, 'Le traitement spécial et différentiel. Plaidoyer contre le système des préférences généralisées' (2005) *Journal du droit international* 319–39. See http://www.wto.org/french/tratop_f/dispu_f/cases_f/ds27_f.htm.

[4] See Gherari, 'Tendances récentes' (n 3) 478 *ff*. On economic controversies on whether special and differential treatment is effective, see Joseph Stiglitz and Andrew Charlton, *Fair Trade for All: How Trade Can Promote Development* (Oxford, Oxford University Press, 2005).

EU is currently forcing African countries to adopt is a direct reflection of this. These agreements are designed to reintroduce the most favoured nation clause and equality of status, to bring about free trade between Europe and Africa. Under pressure from the EU, the African countries in question, which had initially rejected the Agreements, ended up accepting them although they see them as deeply unfair.

The same problems can be found with other weakly binding, but nonetheless binding principles of classical international development law such as the principle of official aid included in several international treaties or the principle of agreements on commodities, cooperation or technology transfers which, to say the least, have not helped poor countries to take off. The inadequacy of these principles, their lack of scope and several local factors specific to developing countries strengthen the impression of the near complete failure of classical international development law. Along these lines, the 2010 UNCTAD report on the least-developed countries tolls the bell for expectations of the development strategies in the world's poorest countries.[5] UNCTAD concludes that the economic development model used for these 49 countries has failed and needs to be completely revised, especially with regard to the dependence of these countries on imported foodstuffs, which has devastating consequences for their populations according to UNCTAD's Secretary-General.[6]

This observation must be taken particularly seriously if we are to change our way of thinking and explore new ways to find suitable legal instruments to help correct the profound inequality between poor and rich countries; but also to correct classical international development law which, by a tragic paradox in its effects, may perhaps only ever have perpetuated the dependence and underdevelopment of the poor nations as it is unable to rectify the deep-rooted unfairness of the global system.[7]

B New International Development Law

It could probably be hoped that the new international development law of the post-Cold War years, which currently applies alongside classical international development law, would be able to impose itself to at least attenuate the economistic version of international economic law. But the fact is that, even if its environmental side has expanded considerably, the new development law runs up in the same way against the rationales of interest or the interplay of other legal rules, in particular of international trade, that constantly

[5] www.unctad.org.

[6] The report says food imports in these countries rose from $9 billion in 2002 to $23 billion in 2008; www.lemonde.fr/international/article/2010/11/26/le-nombre-de-pays-tres-pauvres-a-double-en-quarante-ans_1445160_3210.html.

[7] Madjid Benchik, *Droit international du sous-développement. Nouvel ordre dans la dépendance* (Paris, Berger-Levrault, 1983) 12 and 95 *ff*. He observes that international law cannot be called 'development' law unless it is an effective instrument in the fight against underdevelopment.

prevent it from being fully deployed. It is almost more obvious still that the coexistence of two rationales, one economic and financial, the other social and sustainable, and therefore of several legal systems of unequal scope, works in favour of the former, reproducing the divide between the stated intentions and the actual application and weighing upon what is a decidedly unconvincing outcome.

The differential regime that the environmental aspect of sustainable development commonly introduces between various categories of states is essential to take into account their unequal circumstances. But for so long as the promised financial efforts are not made for developing countries and countries' commitments on the environment are not kept, it is plain that sustainable development is globally ineffective and affects poor countries so much more. This is the case even in a domain where legally compelling treaty-based law holds an important position. At the 2012 Rio + 20 Earth Summit, the overall assessment on sustainable development reported almost complete failure because the world's environment had incurred further damage and the gulf between rich and poor countries had remained or even widened:

> 20. We acknowledge that since 1992 there have been areas of insufficient progress and setbacks in the integration of the three dimensions of sustainable development, aggravated by multiple financial, economic, food and energy crises, which have threatened the ability of all countries, in particular developing countries, to achieve sustainable development. In this regard, it is critical that we do not backtrack from our commitment to the outcome of the United Nations Conference on Environment and Development. We also recognize that one of the current major challenges for all countries, particularly for developing countries, is the impact from the multiple crises affecting the world today.[8]

The Rio Summit also showed that the concerns associated with economic development and with states' economic interests invariably win out over the other human, social and environmental aspects of sustainable development and so much so that they structurally impede their implementation.[9] We observe that unfortunately nothing has changed significantly. True, in the same way as for classical development law, it may be thought that the existing rules avoid the worst and that without them the situation would be catastrophic. But no more than that. By way of example, the general assessment of climate change, which hits poor countries hardest, is particularly worrying. The 2012 UN report on Millennium Development Goals[10] claims

[8] UN General Assembly Resolution 66/288. The Future We Want – Outcome Document. Available at: sustainabledevelopment.un.org/futurewewant.mtml.

[9] See Pierre-Marie Dupuy and Yann Kerbrat, *Droit international public*, 10th edn (Paris, Dalloz, 2010) 870.

[10] 2012 MDG Report; www.un.org/millenniumgoals/pdf/MDG%20Report%202012.pdf. See also Marcello D Varella, *La construction du « développement durable » dans le droit international* (Ed Universitaires européennes, 2010).

that, despite precise commitments by polluter countries, while CO2 emissions declined in 2009, it was essentially due to the economic crisis and once this was over, the increase in world population and economic growth meant that mathematically there would be a near 50 per cent rise in CO2. In other words, if the most powerful states and the greatest polluters of the planet (including the new emerging states) fail to agree on yet more precise and more restrictive objectives in this area, the situation of some countries may become dramatic, especially the situation of small island developing states (SIDS). Some such states like the Cook Islands, Kiribati, the Maldives or Tuvalu, which are particularly vulnerable to sea-level rise brought about by global warming, warned the international community at Cancun in 2010 that for them 'the end of history is in sight' since they are threatened with extinction unless something changes.[11] It remains to be seen whether the Cancun Agreement of the Conference of states parties to the UN Framework Convention on Climate Change will be observed and if it will be enough, for some observers now consider that even if it is complied with, it will not be able to stop global warming. It also remains to be seen whether the WTO will stick to its current position which continues to let the liberalisation of trade prevail over environmental protection despite orientations to the contrary signposted again in the 2001 Doha Declaration in which the Member States reasserted their commitment to sustainable development (point 6).[12] This issue is a decisive one, too, and in itself crystallises all the difficulties of an international legal order that is fragmented into different legal systems in which, for the time being, any new rule devised to curb the rules of international economic law from the outside collides with the autonomous implementation of that system of law. This observation may leave readers unfamiliar with international law disconcerted, and yet the observation is valid because of the specific configuration of international law which is very far removed on this point from domestic legal orders. This does not mean that the rules on sustainable development are without effect, but simply that domestic legal orders are confined to an inevitably limited field of application.

Besides, the same observation holds for social development which involves the same type of problem and loses much of its force in the interplay of rules against it. Globalisation has led to strong economic growth in some countries but has also considerably exacerbated inequalities in income in developed and developing countries alike. The World Bank stated that this was the case for poor countries in its 2006 Report.[13] The Organisation for Economic Co-operation and Development (OECD) also showed this in 2008 in rela-

[11] See ecolonews/blog.fr/2010/12/01/les-etats-insulaires-proches-de-la-noyade-10095905/.

[12] See Raphaël Kempf, *L'OMC face au changement climatique* (Paris, Pedone, 2009) especially 73 *ff*. See the Doha WTO Ministerial Declaration of 14 November 2001; www.wto.org/english/thewto_e/minist_e/min01_e/mindecl_e.htm.

[13] World Development Report 2006, Equity and Development; siteresources.worldbank.org/INTWDR2006/Resources/WDR_on_Equity_FinalOutline_July_public.pdf.

tion to industrialised countries, noting an increase in inequalities in 17 out of the 20 countries studied where growth disproportionately benefitted the highest-income groups.[14] The International Labour Organisation (ILO) recently published a report on social security in which it states that only 28 per cent of the world's population enjoy extended cover while this is particularly important in times of crisis.[15] As is known, the compatibility of ILO norms with those of the WTO remains key to a possible reversal of the trend and the effective promotion of genuine social development. But, for the time being, no progress is being made on the question of the social clause in trade treaties because of North/South opposition on the subject, while the practice of delocalisation allows firms to get around the more protective legislation of their home countries and the question of the responsibility of multinational firms remains patchy. As a former ILO director put it, the provisions of social justice in the WTO declarations seem to be meaningless and the ILO will simply continue to serve as the conscience[16] of the international community if there is no agreement with the WTO and the Bretton Woods institutions about the social dimension of development. It is true that the UN has an Administrative Coordinating Committee on which the WTO, International Monetary Fund and World Bank sit, and which could have facilitated synergy between the economic institutions and the ILO. But the disappointing results accumulate as the countless reports are filed and show just how concerned each institution is about maintaining its own independence above all.

The effective scope of the implementation of legal practices and principles with regard to human development and the good governance and human rights approach is more difficult to assess. The restrictive scope is variable since what is involved is a mixed set of texts ranging from resolutions to the major treaties on human rights and employment norms by way of bilateral agreements and restrictive practices of international economic and financial organisations on the basis of the granting of loans. The indicators of human development and of good governance introduced by international institutions can be used to collect numerous data and to check that the rules imposed or agreed to in this domain are effective.[17] The results collated by the institutions are both unequal and controversial.

The results are unequal. With regard to democracy and human rights, the United Nations Development Programme (UNDP) states that the number

[14] OECD Annual Report 2008; www.oecd.org/dataoecd/39/19/40556222.pdf. See also the UN Economic and Social Division Report on the World Social Situations: The Global Social Crisis, 2010; www.un.org/en/development/desa/news/social/world-social-situation-repor.html.

[15] This is the first such report from the ILO. *World Social Security Report, Providing Coverage in Times of Crisis and Beyond, 2010/2011*; www.ilo.org/wcmsp5/groups/public@dgreports@dcomm/@publ/documents/article/wcms_142224.pdf.

[16] Francis Blanchard, *L'Organisation international du travail. De la guerre froide à un nouvel ordre mondial* (Paris, Seuil, 2004) 225.

[17] Although the results are based on indices that remain controversial. See Carmen Apaza, 'Controverses autour des indicateurs mondiaux de gouvernance' (January 2009) *Problèmes économiques* 36 *ff*.

of countries that have adopted democratic features rose from 60 in 1985 to more than 140 in 2007, which may seem most satisfactory. But it is a figure that, for the time being, hides deep disparities.[18] These figures correspond above all to states that hold elections in their countries but whose populations may at the same time face political and social exclusion, be deprived of public services like clean water and education; states that fail to observe civil and political rights and whose politicians cannot be held accountable for their acts.[19] In other words, they are illiberal democracies that do not yet present the characteristics of pluralistic and social democracies.[20] The World Bank's figures for governance and the fight against corruption reveal more positive results since some countries have made remarkable efforts in these areas. But because, over the same period, the situation has grown worse in other countries, the World Bank in the end observes that the 'overall quality of governance around the world has not improved much over the past decade'.[21] The situation is hardly encouraging, then, as it has changed very little as a whole.

The results are also controversial. Beyond all these figures and results, international law on sustainable and human development raises recurrent questions. First of all, the very idea of connecting the economic development of states and human rights and democracy has been very fiercely criticised by some authoritarian and undemocratic states of the South which have managed to take off economically. They have challenged the effectiveness and the legitimacy of this new approach to development. This is what Singapore's former Prime Minister, Lee Kuan Yew, meant in his celebrated argument about Asian values. He relied on what he thought to be the values of order and authority contained in Confucianism to explain the economic development of his country and to demonstrate that its development owed nothing to Western individual rights that would only have hampered development and could not legitimately apply in Asia. The quarrel it sparked in the 1970s[22] was widely publicised at the time but, in truth, the argument was only made by a few countries that were hardly representative of all of Asia and, while not resolved, it seems outdated nowadays in light of the new empirical conditions in those countries and the advent of new political leaders who have abandoned the argument and renewed the legal discourse on human rights.[23]

[18] The UNDP and Democratic Governance; www.undp.org.

[19] ibid.

[20] See Emmanuelle Jouannet, *The Liberal-Welfarist Law of Nations. A History of International Law* (Cambridge, Cambridge University Press, 2012).

[21] Governance indicators in 2008; web.worldbank.org/WBSITE/EXTERNAL/NEWS/0,,contentMDK:21814712~pagePK:64257043~piPK:437376~theSitePK:4607,00.html.

[22] Lee Kuan Yew, *The Jodidi Lecture: Address by Singapore's Prime Minister Mr Lee Kuan Yee at Lowell Lecture Hall* (Cambridge, Harvard University Press, 1968). See also a reply by Amartya Sen, *The Idea of Justice* (Cambridge, Harvard University Press, 2009).

[23] A Third Way of sorts, in keeping with the aspirations of the populations involved, is being developed around a cultural and therefore Asian approach, but based on human rights and democracy. See Simon Tay, *Asian Values Revisited* (Project Syndicate, 2002); www.project-syndicate.org/commentary/tay1/English. The situation is hard to evaluate from field data. In

And yet, new human and sustainable development law remains controversial in its results, notably because it increases, for the present, the dependency of developing countries, and in particular of the poorest and most vulnerable among them, on the new conditions imposed by international law. Admittedly, current international texts insist on introducing a 'global partnership' (8th Millennium Goal) among equals and not some imposed model and on states making commitments through treaties or unilateral undertakings. This is the case, for example, of the undertaking given in the 2005 Paris Declaration on Aid Effectiveness or the New Partnership for Africa's Development (NEPAD) adopted at Abuja in October 2001, which expresses African states' willingness to move along the road to sustainable development, economic growth and observance of democracy and human rights. The NEPAD reflects Africans' realisation that they themselves must make reforms and support their development by internal transformations of states as much as outside aid. Point 1 makes this plain as it provides that NEPAD 'is anchored on the determination of Africans to *extricate themselves* and the continent from the malaise of underdevelopment and exclusion in a globalising world'.[24] Even so, it is only a 'promise' made by some African heads of state and it is still true that the implementation of many rules and principles on new development law is done by more or less heavily disguised constraint, making the poor states dependent on the state or states which help them to develop.

The dependency of some developing countries increases considerably with new development law. It has been seen that poor countries are increasingly compelled to accept new principles of good governance, democracy and observance of human rights if they are to continue to enjoy development aid and cooperation. The obligations of the beneficiary states have become considerably more onerous, as have the possibilities of restricting and limiting preferences or aid if the conditions laid down are not met. This is attested to by the evolution of international aid law which, from the Monterrey Conference to the 2008 Accra Agenda for Action, has increased the means of political control over developing countries via new obligations to comply with human rights, pluralistic democracy, good governance and the fight against poverty. One might also take the case of the EU's special incentive arrangement for sustainable development and good governance (GSP+). To be entitled to the preference system which is more favourable than its classical version, the beneficiary state must ratify no fewer than 27 conventions: 16 UN/ILO conventions on human and labour rights and 11 conventions on the environment and the principles of good government. The state must then undertake to legislate and introduce measures to enforce these 27

the short term, the introduction of democracy may sometimes destabilise a country and slow its growth. But in the long term economic development and a fortiori human development are fostered. See Daniel Kaufman, *On Democracy and Development: Rejecting the Extremes*; www.america.gov/st/democracyhr-english/2008/June/20080605094537ebyessedo0.3466913.html.

[24] www.afrimap.org/english/images/treaty/file4239af5c8ad12.pdf. Emphasis added.

conventions domestically, and finally it must accept that this implementation is reviewed from time to time. Sanctions are provided should any of the parties be found to have breached their obligations and these include suspension from the preference system.

Clearly, then, these new legal practices related to this new face of development law have become highly politicised and involve greater intervention in poor countries. Conditionality obeys a rationale of selection and effectiveness; but it is a constraint, even when negotiated, and therefore continues to maintain the dependence of the South on the North. Moreover, some populations are punished twice over in that they have predatory and corrupt governments and their countries are then hit by sanctions.[25] More generally, contemporary international law as it relates to development is accordingly the instrument of a very broad social and political control on developing countries designed to ensure the well-being of their populations. Clearly, contemporary international law seems to be more welfarist than before and not liberal and pluralistic like classical development law since it is no longer indifferent to states' internal sovereignty but, on the contrary, tends to impose a model of domestic society in its economic, social and political aspects. It therefore displays the same features and has the same effect as any welfarist form of law. It covers ever more areas of the social life of developing countries, with no limits in sight, since it extends from the basic needs to be met, to the social, political and economic structures to be introduced, and beyond that to the social domains to be transformed. By the same token, alongside contemporary development law a massive international bureaucracy has developed, which deploys a wealth of technology and expertise in its application, creating a highly disturbing situation in which the hoped-for advances cannot hide the many questions, questions which cannot be addressed here, about the scope and workings of this new form of knowledge and power.[26]

II The Fight Against Poverty

The more targeted objectives announced in the fight against poverty and extreme poverty hold out the hope of faster and more satisfactory results, since that was the planned outcome. From this point of view, the 2012 'report card' on the Millennium Development Goals is more satisfactory than the 'mixed' report for 2010.[27] The 2012 Report states that three important goals have been achieved before the 2015 deadline: extreme poverty has been halved, living conditions improved for more than 200 million people, and better access to

[25] See Denis Cogneau and Jean-David Nadet, 'Who Deserves Aid? Equality or Opportunity, International Aid and Poverty Reduction' (2007) 35 (1) *World Development* 104–20.

[26] See Jouannet, *The Liberal-Welfarist Law of Nations* (n 20) 260 *ff*.

[27] Millennium Development Goals Report 2010; www.un.org/millenniumgoals/pdf/MDG%20Report%202010.pdf.

water provided.[28] In addition, the number of people living in poverty has fallen due to the economic development of China and South and South-East Asia, which is an incontrovertible advance for the populations of these parts of Asia. But the Report also states that the situation is worrying in other domains and especially because the gains made in the fight against poverty may be jeopardised by the series of food and climate crises and the world economic and financial crisis of 2007/2008, which weighs heavily on the jobs and incomes of millions of people worldwide. Accordingly, the Millennium Agenda, which had set 2015 as the deadline for achieving the main millennium goals, is unlikely to be achieved and progress may be reversed in some areas.

And that is the most comfortable version of this report card, since things could read very differently if we were to redefine the terms by including the fight against poverty in a more comprehensive appraisal of development covering the systemic relationship between the fight against poverty and other factors related to it.[29] The decline of poverty in Asia is therefore very encouraging if one stops at that. But that would be to forget that the number of poor people has declined because of the uncontrolled economic development of some Asian countries which gives rise to ever more pollution and growing inequalities. It must be accepted, then, that trying to achieve a specific goal like the eradication of poverty might make it impossible to attain another, through ignorance of their interactions. Likewise, if the decline in poverty is unhoped-for progress, it is nevertheless to be related to the globalised economic system, which is thought to have exacerbated poverty in other parts of the world.[30] Obviously that does not invalidate the positive results achieved in some instances, but it does provide an insight into how any evaluation in this domain is particularly difficult to make unless one refrains from connecting together data that would otherwise be dissociated.[31]

[28] Millennium Development Goals Report 2012; www.un.org/millenniumgoals/pdf/MDG%20Report%202012.pdf.

[29] See Pierre-Noël Giraud, *L'inégalité du monde. Economie du monde contemporain* (Paris, Gallimard, 1996) 302 *ff*. Neither the World Bank nor the countries involved wish to take account of inequalities which remain a controversial subject and they refuse tax reforms that might have a redistributive effect. See Jean-Pierre Cling and François Roubaud, *La Banque mondiale* (Paris, La découverte, 2008) 59 *ff*.

[30] World Bank, 'Globalisation, Growth and Poverty' (2002); www-wds.worldbank.org/external/default/main?pagePK=64193027&piPK=64187937&theSitePK=523679&menuPK=64187510&searchMenuPK=64187283&siteName=WDS&entityID=000094946_0202020411335. The fight against poverty has been further exacerbated by the intrusive character of international policies in developing countries.

[31] Paradoxically, the multiplication of data and surveys about poverty do not provide a better understanding of it and so fail to make it easier to combat, for want of suitable indicators. See for Africa, Mireille Razafindrakoto and François Roubaud, 'The existing systems for monitoring poverty: weaknesses of the usual household surveys' in Jean-Pierre Cling, Mireille Razafindrakoto and François Roubaud (eds), *New International Poverty Reduction Strategies* (London and New York, Routledge, 2003) 269 *ff*.

III General Appraisal: International Development Law and International Economic Law

The revelation of these successive results confirms or aggravates an unsurprising diagnosis and requires a more general appraisal to be made of development law. All of this shows the continuation of the destiny of international development law and of all the classical and new principles by which attempts have been made to change the harmful effects of the legal and economic order that prevail in international relations.[32] Those principles do not work or only with tremendous difficulty. They are not usually legally binding and those that are binding are not sufficiently effective.[33] Legal policies are usually ineffective and the most progressive norms are only rarely applied as they are set out in non-mandatory political texts. Some of these rules prevent poor states from sinking; others make the situation worse by imposing sanctions and constraints. None in any event can be cited as having really enabled a state to develop or to achieve the primary objective of development which is to reduce poverty and socio-economic inequalities between states. The fact of the matter is that since 1970, whatever the garb of international development law, it has remained particularly limited in its scope since not only has it not had any real control over the implementation of an inequitable legal and economic system, but it has also often been drafted by the actors of the system to ensure the system is more readily accepted by giving the impression that more equitable rules are being conceded. This may be a complete change of course from what is presupposed to be the initial purpose of development law by which the principles of development and equity are actually used to promote 'forms of voluntary submission' to the existing order which they are supposed rather to inflect and reshape.[34] This finding is not one of radicals or out-and-out ideologists who might be dismissed as dangerous Third World utopians, but it is shared by some of the most prominent personalities in international circles. In 2007, WTO Director, Pascal Lamy, stated:

> [I]nternational relations today are still marked by intolerable injustice [. . .] This is not down to chance. It is a legacy from a politically but not yet economically bygone world: the world of colonialism. Political colonialism ended in the 1960s; economic colonialism has not ended fifty years on and in a new century. It is a fact that must be characterised as such and its features and origins must be studied.[35]

[32] One of the most comprehensive evaluations to date in this area (the result of seven years' work) shows this in detail for Asia, Africa and America. Manuel R Agosin et al, *Solving the Riddle of Globalization and Development* (London and New York, Routledge, 2007).

[33] A situation long denounced as it is an intrinsic problem of development law. See Monique Chemillier-Gendreau, 'Droit du développement et effectivité de la norme' in *La formation des normes en droit international du développement* (Paris, Ed CNRS, 2000) 279 *ff*.

[34] See Axel Honneth, *La société du mépris. Vers une nouvelle théorie critique* (Paris, La découverte, 2006) 245 *ff* and 286 *ff*.

[35] Pascal Lamy, 'Comment sortir de l'injustice des rapports Nord/Sud' in *Qu'est-ce qu'une société juste?* Semaines sociales de France (Paris, Bayard, 2007) 173.

At the Johannesburg Summit in 2002, Kofi Annan stated:

> And let us face an uncomfortable truth: the model of development we are accustomed to has been fruitful for the few, but flawed for the many. A path to prosperity that ravages the environment and leaves a majority of humankind behind in squalor will soon prove to be a dead-end road for everyone.[36]

The ILO World Commission's 2004 Report, based on a study of 73 countries also found:

> [W]e have reached a crisis stage in the legitimacy of our political institutions, whether national or international. There is an urgent need to rethink current institutions of global economic governance, whose rules and policies it [the report] says are largely shaped by powerful countries and powerful players. The unfairness of key rules of trade and finance reflect a serious 'democratic deficit' at the heart of the system.[37]

All told, along with Joseph Stiglitz and on the basis of the ILO World Commission's 2004 Report, five problems with globalisation and the current legal and economic system can be identified.[38] Globalisation is believed to have 'vast potential'[39] but it must be observed that:

(1) The rules governing globalisation are unfair as they are designed once again primarily with the interests of the advanced industrial nations in mind. Certainly, some emerging countries have benefited from them, but the rules are not equitable.
(2) Globalisation gives precedence to a model of materialistic consumption which prevails over other values such as the environment or human objectives.
(3) Economic and financial international law of globalisation constrains the sovereignty of developing countries, and even deprives those countries of part of their sovereignty and their freedom to decide in areas that are essential to the well-being of their citizens.
(4) Contrary to the idea that globalisation benefits everyone, there are losers on both sides, North and South.
(5) The political, economic and legal system that globalisation has imposed on developing countries is unsuitable and leads to the Westernisation and, more specifically, the Americanisation of their economies and cultures.

To be brief, and so as an example only, one might cite the trade agreements which are commonly acknowledged to be neither free nor fair. Masses of obstacles to trade have remained in place in rich countries and, at the same

[36] Johannesburg World Summit on Sustainable Development Report 2002; www.johannesburgsummit.org/.

[37] ILO Report 2004: 'Fair Globalization: Creating Opportunities for All'; www.ilo.org/fairglobalization/report/lang--en/index.htm.

[38] Joseph E Stiglitz, *Making Globalization Work* (New York and London, Norton, 2006).

[39] ILO Report 2004: 'Fair Globalization: Creating Opportunities for All' (n 38).

time, masses of subsidies remain as developing countries are compelled to open up their markets. The scandal of the agricultural market is familiar enough and yet, for the time being, no real breakthrough has been made towards changing it. Subsidies from industrialised countries in this domain are thought to top $1 billion per day, while 70 per cent of the populations in poor countries live from farming and survive on less than a dollar a day. The world cotton scandal is regularly denounced. Annual subsidies of some $3 billion to $4 billion, which make the United States one of the biggest exporters of the commodity, have ruined farmers in several of the world's poorest countries. In addition, the provisional agreement of 2004 between the US and Brazil alone did not put an end to what was a particularly unjust situation for all the other producers. The distortions arising from subsidies create a state of glaring injustice which, despite the few safety barriers set up, is lawful under existing international trade law. Likewise, the 2005 Hong Kong agreement for the least-developed countries has been presented as 'one of the high points of hypocrisy and cynicism'.[40] The United States has opened its market to a whole range of products that have been carefully selected to exclude those that are really important for the country. So, for instance, a country like Bangladesh is now free to export aircraft engines, which it is incapable of manufacturing, but not fabric and clothing, which are its main output. This unfairness, in the interplay of existing rules is found everywhere, whether in finance with regard to investments, in basic commodities or in technology and knowledge transfers.

[40] Stiglitz, *Making Globalization Work* (n 39) 83.

4
Prospects and Alternatives

THE APPRAISAL WHICH has just been made is obviously open to refinement or criticism on any particular point, in respect of any particular rule, and it would be either naive or pretentious to claim to have exhausted the issue since our discussion has been confined to general results and to pointing out a few specific difficulties. However, it seems hard to dismiss the overall tendency since the succession of reports, figures and results consulted converge to underscore a joint powerlessness of law and politics in this domain that makes development law illusory and even reveals a dark side to this law if it, in fact, merely contributes to concealing the unbounded market-oriented and financial rationale of international economic law. The value of the attempts to temper the neoliberal economic model of development lies, however, in the difficulties encountered by those attempts. For they show that enquiry into classical and new international development law is inseparable from enquiry into international economic law. In line with the purpose of this book, which is to look primarily at the legal remedies to the socio-economic inequalities among states (that being the prime objective of development law), we shall examine the current options available in this field on the basis of a reflection on the existing legal and economic order.[1] In other words, other aspects of the matter, especially the aspect of human rights or certain hegemonic features of the new development law, shall be left aside and what shall be highlighted is three possible legal solutions that are

[1] In concentrating on the aspects relating to international economic law alone, other aspects of this multidimensional problem are omitted. For example, the equitable character of the rules of the economic system would not change other basic issues like the fact that some countries have structural growth handicaps and institutional weaknesses that exclude them from gaining equal access to the market and the world development process. See Denis Cogneau and Jean-David Naudet, 'Who Deserves Aid? Equality of Opportunity, Interanational Aid, and Poverty Reduction' (2007) 35 *World Development* 104–20. Or again it would be necessary to highlight objective internal factors specific to postcolonial states (especially demography) and their personal subjective responsibility in the improper development of their populations, as evoked above, which means that one can no longer attribute, as with the Millennium Development Goals (MDGs), all the economic and social evils attendant on those states to the existing legal and economic system. The ruling elites very often use the inequalities and injustices of the international system or of international institutions as scapegoats to elude their own obligations. See Ebrehim Beigzadeh and Ali-Hossein Nadjafi, 'Malentendu Nord-Sud autour du droit international: réalité ou mythe' in Ruiz-Fabri, Jouannet and Tomkiewicz (eds), *Select Proceedings of the European Society of International Law* (Oxford, Hart Publishing, 2008) 224 *ff*.

underpinned by economic and political theories that contrast in the way they combine social justice and economic efficiency on a worldwide level.

I Solutions Relating to the Existing Legal and Economic Order

A Solution One

The first solution is to wager everything on present-day economic international law alone and maintain the existing system considering that its inequitable character is part of a natural process that will eventually bring about greater equality among states. This first type of solution to Third World problems imposed itself fully with the fall of the Berlin Wall which signalled the failure of alternatives to capitalist development. It means that one must continue to open markets as widely as possible and to deregulate for the benefit of private actors, to maintain the World Trade Organisation's (WTO) existing rules and regulations, modifying them only marginally in line with the existing balance of power and maintain the lead set by the international financial institutions. According to this perspective, precedence is given to private law or to mere regulatory public law. It is not a system of law that would claim to determine or to introduce equity into the material circumstances of peoples or states or to purposefully plan sets of rules to promote sustainable development. What counts above all is that private property rights are upheld, contracts are protected, trade is made secure and loans are repaid so as to give people incentives to work and invest.[2] That also means that any market shortcomings can be attributed to failure to comply with neoliberal principles and that the responsibility for 'backwardness' in development is down to the developing countries themselves, to their poor governance, their instability, their corruption and the absence of the rule of law; but never to the system itself.

The strength of this current perspective should not be underestimated. It is not a movement that results solely from the greed and grasping of the groups that direct the economy, even if this is incontrovertible,[3] but it is also the product of a coherent ideology that hypostases belief in the market, individual freedom and deregulation. The existing system relies on a particular neoliberal ideology which, contrary to what might have been suggested, does not renounce justice of society (both domestic and international) or the idea of protecting the environment, but considers simply that these phenomena arise from the spontaneous interplay of the market. The inequality of mate-

[2] See Jacques Brasseul, *Introduction à l'économie du développement*, 3rd edn (Paris, A Colin, 2010) 80 *ff*.

[3] Joseph Stiglitz, *Freefall: America, Free Markets, and the Sinking of the World Economy* (New York, Norton, 2010).

rial conditions among states is thus part of the market order, which must not be disturbed because the interplay of the market must favour everyone's chances and lead in itself to better overall circumstances for each of us. A utilitarian vision of world society results from this, in which it is considered that the overall increase in wealth, property and advantage will have positive 'fallout' for the greatest number and therefore that this society will be fairer as it amasses more resources and achieves economic growth. By the same token, the need for a New International Economic Order (NIEO), for a fair and equitable economic system based on interventionist development law and on discriminatory practices, is thought of as wholly nonsensical and mistaken because not only does it upset the order of the world market, which spontaneously creates wealth, but it runs counter to the equality of opportunity of all to benefit from the market by favouring one specific group of states.

The current situation shows nonetheless that while this solution is economically effective in part, it remains socially inequitable. While the existing legal and economic order has shown that it can promote development for some states and counter poverty, it is therefore a part of the solution. But it is also a large part of the problem, for it helps to maintain and engender fresh instances of poverty and inequality in unacceptable proportions and in what is this time a movement affecting North and South alike, even if it is the much more vulnerable South that suffers most. In other words, the facts themselves prove that the utilitarian vision of world society is an illusion, for even if global wealth increases there is no positive 'fallout' for the greatest number, no spontaneous justice that emerges from the world market and no equitable distribution of the wealth produced. The latest phase of economic globalisation which the existing system has favoured has thus brought about unprecedented growth in world trade, output and investment, which has benefitted a number of countries, but it has also led to new imbalances: the sidelining of the poorest states, the increasingly unequal distribution of wealth and the constant destabilisation of markets and economies because of repeated major crises which have had devastating human and social repercussions.[4] The result of this is that present-day international economic law makes lawful an order that is intrinsically inequitable. The fact that the world's wealth is increasing and that a greater number of states are developing economically does not ensure that the overall distribution of wealth will be fair.[5] Some even speak of a 'return to Marie Antoinette' to describe the record peaks in the unequal distribution

[4] See the dossiers 'Crise: la faute à la . . . finance?' (January 2009) 2963 *Problèmes économiques* and 'La mondialisation sous le choc de la crise' (July 2009) 2976 *Problèmes économiques*.

[5] Nor is it ultimately economically efficient for the world as a whole since it engenders as much in the way of crises and instability as it does wealth. Hence the need to reintroduce human and sustainable purposes in economics and the return to the Keynesian school of thought after the high point of neoliberalism. See Bernard Gazier, *John Maynard Keynes* (Paris, PUF, 2009) 104 *ff*. The Neoliberals are not self-critical and think that if the system is not economically efficient it is because it has been thwarted by interventionist political measures. They advocate leaving the markets to operate. See Pascal Salin, *Revenir au capitalism pour éviter les crises* (Paris, O Jacob, 2010).

of current wealth.[6] As the World Bank itself observed in 2005, we now live in a world which has never been so rich and yet which exhibits 'extraordinary deprivation' and 'staggering inequalities'.[7] The question as to whether some have gained is less important than whether the distribution of gains has been fair. 'As long as the sharing of potential gains from globalization is viewed as unfair by many, the inequalities [. . .] will be deemed unacceptable.'[8]

B Solution Two

The second solution stands at the opposite pole to the first, even if they share the common feature of condemning any and all international development law. The second solution is proposed by post-developmentalists and consists in arguing for the abandonment of any idea of development but also of the world economic system and therefore of both international economic law and international development law. Post-developmentalists denounce the poor countries' hot pursuit of development in the celebrated collective task of 'catching up' that mobilises substantial financial resources while often being thwarted as it helps to maintain the exclusion and exacerbates the poverty it purports to eradicate. The result of this is that all the legal and economic practices that support it are constantly widening the gulf they are supposed to be filling in.[9] Accordingly, international development law is seen as a machine for producing exclusion and indigence together with development and wealth, precisely because of the liberal economic, free-trade and capitalist postulates on which it is still ultimately based. By a cynical trick of history it has even contributed to perpetuating the world economic system and therefore a certain balance of power in favour of those who truly benefit; namely the strong and the rich.

Post-developmentalist criticism is particularly convincing in denouncing this pursuit by states of ever greater growth which cannot end and which eventually means the exhaustion of the planet's resources and therefore its own extinction. But the question is what alternative can be proposed to remedy this situation and also the socio-economic inequalities between states. It

[6] Jean-Paul Fitoussi, *La démocratie et le marché* (Paris, Grasset, 2004) 8. On rich and emerging countries see the dossier 'Les inégalités responsables de la crise?' (July 2011) 3023 *Problèmes économiques*.

[7] World Development Report, Equity and Development, 55; siteresources.worldbank.org/INTWDR2006/Resources/477383-1127230817535/082136412X.pdf

[8] ibid. Africa has experienced very positive growth since it has been more liberal, especially with the marked increase in foreign direct investment (FDI). But not all African economies have benefitted in the same way and the poor states have been completely left out. See 'L'Afrique à la recherche de financements' (January 2009) *Problèmes économiques* 32 *ff*. The inequalities that are exploding because of the system contribute to the return to crises, revealing a vicious circle. See 'Les inégalités responsables de la crise? (July 2011) 3023 *Problèmes économiques*.

[9] See Serge Latouche, *Le pari de la décroissance* (Paris, Fayard, 2006) and Gilbert Rist, *The History of Development: From Western Origins to Global Faith* (London and New York, Zed Books, 2002), 1 *ff*.

has to be admitted that the solutions advanced here are far less convincing, at least for the time being. They generally recommend an anti-modernist and parochial or even cultural vision of economics, of law and society, an economics of downscaling too, the effects of which seem particularly costly with regard to the populations of a world that is as interdependent, acculturated and interbred as ours is. The problem is that at the present time, when all societies are interdependent, it is hard to imagine the return to a traditional and near-autarchic communitarisation of societies, with a minimal international law that might be not just viable but might also correspond to the actual aspirations and life experiences of populations. To leave the countries of the South in a state of poverty or frugality far from Western industrial indigence might be a naturalistic myth that recalls vice versa the evolutionist myth based on economic growth at any cost. It is also to consider that the advances already acquired in Europe, North America and now Asia are to be reserved to those who already enjoy them and to keep the rest of the world as a sort of reserve of fauna, flora and traditional human communities to be sure that no further harm is done to them. And so it is hardly surprising to see that this post-developmentalist position enchants some in the North but none in the South as the former Third World continues to fervently desire the same industrial development which occurred in the West. That is why the positions of those who wish to escape development seem to lead to such a radical solution with respect to the current context that despite their salutary denunciations, this solution seems for now at least to be neither economically efficient nor even socially equitable. And yet the discussion obviously remains open, as the need for a change of economic model is being increasingly felt because of the major social and ecological changes it prompts and it cannot be ruled out that future reflection in this domain will be totally convincing and will impose its solution.[10]

C Solution Three

Meanwhile, it is the third solution that is opted for here. However critical it may be of past mistakes and of the illusions elicited by international development law and international economic law, the third solution remains on the terrain of the principle of development and of a market economy. It consists in making a fresh commitment to the reform of existing international economic law with a view to introducing a new NIEO, a legal and economic order that is compatible with the establishment of international social justice. It consists in establishing an international order that is both economically efficient and

[10] There is not yet sufficiently broad and coherent economic and political thought to provide a satisfactory alternative along these lines, but the increase in recent work in the field suggests it may be in the making. See Philippe Fremeaux, 'Faut-il encore chercher la croissance (verte)?' (April 2011) 301 *Altérnatives économiques* 61–62.

socially equitable. If the various norms of international development law and the more targeted attacks on poverty are mere stop-gap measures that do nothing to change the socio-economic inequalities and the economistic paradigm currently in place, then any new resolution or convention, any new legal commitment that fails to address the inequitable character of the system and its lack of regulation will invariably be biased and inevitably of limited effect. Thus, world poverty decades and world development days shall follow one after another, along with incantatory legal discourse that tells a consensus-based and reassuring tale but which in reality will merely repeat the mistakes of the past. The third solution therefore looks to change the rules of the world economic system, to recast the financial institutions of Bretton Woods and to modify the General Agreement on Tariffs and Trade (GATT) rules to make them more equitable so that the relations between the various Norths and Souths will be rebalanced at last. It is not a matter of re-doing the facade of the building for the umpteenth time by adding exceptions, provisional discriminatory measures or parallel regimes to the existing system, as they have proved ineffective or limited in their scope. An attempt must be made to change the economic system in its normative and institutional aspect by placing the principle of equity at the very heart of things.

In point of fact, the idea of *equitable* globalisation has become the byword of these last 10 years and a direct reminder of the general call for equity that underlay the NIEO in the 1970s. A new discourse, first identified in economics, seems to have made its mark in the 2000s. In 1992, Agenda 21 spoke of the need 'to achieve a more efficient and equitable world economy' and in 1995, at the ceremonies in San Francisco for the Fiftieth Anniversary of the United Nations, the organisation's Secretary-General, Boutros Boutros-Ghali, called for a 'new social contract' between North and South so that the world's wealth could be better shared out.[11] In 2000, the New Millennium Declaration, which rounds up the international community's commitments for the new century, mentions 'equity' in its second paragraph as a principle to be defended worldwide, along with human dignity and equality. It further asserts that the 'central challenge' for the new millennium is to make globalisation 'equitable' for all, and especially for the developing countries and countries in transition. In 2001, the WTO launched a new round of talks at Doha, Qatar, on the liberalisation of trade but this time in terms of 'development'. The programme recognises the connections between trade and development and places the needs and interests of developing countries at the heart of future negotiations. In 2002, at the World Summit on Sustainable Development in Johannesburg, the delegates adopted a resolution giving a commitment to 'building a humane, equitable and caring global society cognizant of the need for human dignity for all'. In that same year the Monterrey Consensus reaf-

[11] www.liberation.fr/monde/0101145567-boutros-ghali-veut-ranimer-la-flamme-onusienne-pour-le-cinquentenaire.

firmed the objective of equitable globalisation (Point I, 7). In June 2004, the United Nations Conference on Trade and Development (UNCTAD) once again redirected its objectives via the Sao Paolo Consensus that set itself up as a reaction to the Washington Consensus. To do this, it showed that globalisation caused 'special difficulties' for developing countries and notably called 'to strike a balance between the objectives of efficiency and equity'.[12] In 2006 the new Nobel Peace Prize Winner, the economist and founder of the first micro-credit institution, Bangladeshi Muhammad Yunus, was rewarded for his efforts to 'create economic and social development from below' and he called for the creation of a High Committee for Equitable Globalisation. In that same year the World Bank published its report entitled 'Equity and Development'. In 2007, at the International Labour Organisation (ILO) forum, the EU undertook to promote measures for 'fair globalisation'.[13] On 10 June 2008, the ILO voted unanimously for the Declaration on Social Justice for Fair Globalisation which was inspired by the Philadelphia Declaration and defended the need for 'a strong social dimension to globalization in achieving improved and fair outcomes for all'.[14] In short, the debate about globalisation became a debate about social justice in a globalised economy.

Yet, it must be determined whether these declarations about the fairness of globalisation and the economic system are to remain part of the 'enchanted' discourse of the actors of international society and simply put up a smoke-screen leaving the system to continue in operation unchanged. This would be the inconsequential swing of the pendulum where, after a very liberal phase, there is a return to a more social phase while basically nothing has actually changed in terms of the dominant legal and economic practice. Worse still, the idea of fairness may be used by the main decision makers and international institutions solely to ensure acceptance of the painful social consequences of the same ultraliberal policy by instrumentalising the use of fairness in the same way as the fight against poverty. And there is ground for caution in view of the many declarations made by the main international players that have not been acted upon. The fact that the Doha Round has proved a failure to date is not reassuring.[15]

To go beyond the stage of discourse, the nature and legal scope of fairness in such a context needs to be specified. What exactly is fair globalisation or a fair economic order in international law? How can it be transposed into law? The inclusion of these expressions in resolutions or non-binding undertakings seems to point to a very broad new direction for which it is hard to discern any

[12] www.unctad.org/en/docs/td410_en.pdf.

[13] 2007 ILO Forum, 3658; www.politiquessociales.net/Mondialisation.

[14] Report of the World Commission on the Social Dimension of Globalization, February 2004, Point 9; www.ilo.org/public/english/wcsdg/index1.htm.

[15] This reflects the ambiguities of the declaration. See Laurence Boisson de Chazournes and Makane M Mbengue, 'La déclaration de Doha de la Conférence ministérielle de l'OMC et sa portée dans les relations commerciales/environnement' (2002) 4 *Revue Generale de Droit International Public* 855–92.

concrete applications, not just in economics but also in the form of legal rules, since fairness is frequently contrasted with law. It seems to me entirely possible to think of the principle of fairness as a legal principle on which to base any discussion of substantial and formal norms of the international economic system. The thing here is not to take fairness as equity in its technical or legal sense and use it at the stage of application of the law, but to use it as a general principle for creating or revising the legal norm and, in so doing, return it to its original meaning as a rule of justice related to equality and applied to a specific situation: by equity, equal things are treated equally and unequal things are treated unequally.[16] If we use this original meaning of the principle and apply it to our subject matter, fairness as an objective and as a basis will have, as a logical consequence, to go beyond the simple formal equality between states so that it can move towards a truly equal situation among them. But unlike the rules of classical international development law that planned for that in a limited way, this new outlook looks to equalise situations in favour of developing countries and the least developed countries can no longer remain simple exceptions to a system that renders them ineffective.[17] Consideration of fairness should be at the core of any revision of existing agreements, the core of the current legal and economic system. It must become a fundamental legal rule of the international order, in institutional and normative terms and therefore in the dual form of *a guiding principle* for the WTO, the International Monetary Fund (IMF) and World Bank and as *a general principle of international economic law*.[18] From then on, through its generality and its flexibility, the principle of fairness may lead to a whole battery of legal solutions to the problems raised. It may guide the negotiation of substantive rules and formal procedures in force so that the actual economic capacities of states to develop in accordance with their social and political projects are made fair, whereas unfavourable conditions make it impossible for some states to accomplish those projects.

With regard to the basic rules, resorting to equitable principles should logically lead to a re-discussion of the term of free trade in favour of fair trade, to the wiping-out or at least further alleviation of the unbearable weight of debt, to the creation of a food fund for basic food resources[19] and to the negotiation

[16] On this point see Michel Virally, 'L'équité dans le droit' in *Le droit international en devenir* (Paris, PUF, 1990) 407 *ff*.

[17] Some argue for the extension of special and differential treatment for the sake of fairness. This is recommended in the 2002 High-Level Group Report on Financing for Development at the Monterrey Conference, once again evoking the need for 'fair trade'. Report of the Conference on Financing for Development (March 2002) A/CONF.198/11, p 8; www.un.org/Docs/journal/asp/ws.asp?m=A/CONF.198/11.

[18] Some even propose making it a public world good. See Lisa Martin, 'L'économie politique de la coopération internationale' in Inge Kaul, Isabelle Grunberg and Marc Stern (eds), *Les biens publics mondiaux. La coopération internationale du XXIème siècle* (Paris, Economica, 2002) 55 *ff*.

[19] A proposal argued for by Mohammed Bedjaoui, 'Faim et pauvreté' in *Mélanges Benchickh*, 201 *ff*. See also the five proposals to combat food crises by Olivier de Schutter, UN Special Rapporteur on the Right to Food; www.srfood.org/index.php/en/component/content/article/1394-g20-agriculture-5-priorities-to-%20end-food-crises.

of an international tax system as a corrective and redistributive instrument designed to restore a certain economic and social equality among states.[20] But the re-founding of rules for a new NIEO also means modifying formal rules since that is probably the most realistic way to obtain basic rules that are themselves equitable. The mere existence of an inequitable procedural system in terms of representation and negotiation produces inequitable basic rules that are characteristics of the current system. It is invariably the rich countries that draft the texts that serve as a basis for negotiation and that decide the essential economic questions, including those on development. The way to achieve a truly fair situation between poor and rich countries therefore involves reinstating an old and essential Third World demand: the desire to be better represented in the international organisations and to carry equal weight in negotiations on norms and their implementation. This means nothing more nor less than the right for developing countries and the least advanced countries to be truly treated as equals with the same interest as all other countries and the same respect due to any state.[21]

But the extreme complexity nowadays of the technical briefs means that even if they were properly represented by fair rules, the least advanced countries would be greatly disadvantaged in international negotiations on international rules which means that not only does their representation need to be strengthened but their capacity to negotiate on a level playing field does too. This implies, as a prior condition, being able to maintain permanent representations at the WTO while some countries are still unable to do so. This also means having fair access to information so as to have the means to make well-informed choices. There are numerous examples of situations where developing countries are kept out of the main talks and can do nothing to change an unequal situation with regard to trade and finance as they do not have the power to be kept informed, to make themselves heard and to be able to influence negotiations in any way. For example, while global warming is threatening to radically change the living conditions of inhabitants of low-lying coastal areas, small islands and semi-arid zones, the states that are the potential victims are unable to carry any weight in global talks on climate.

[20] For example, for a legal analysis of investments and 'fair and equitable treatment' that appears increasingly fundamental in case law, see Pierre-Marie Dupuy and Yann Kerbrat, *Droit international public* (Paris, Dalloz-Sirey, 2010) 795 *ff*. For a philosophical analysis of international taxation and the principle of a worldwide redistributive system, see Thomas Pogge, *World Poverty and Human Rights* (Cambridge, Polity Press, 2002) 202 *ff* and Jean-Marc Ferry, *L'Europe, l'Amérique et le monde* (Paris, Ed Pleins feux, 2004) 46 *ff*.

[21] The confiscation of power by the former great powers is rightly contested by the new emerging countries that are spearheading changes along these lines. Singapore's former Ambassador to the Security Council, Kishore Mahbubani, pointed out this contradiction: 'The twenty-first century is living a serious paradox: it is the world's most democratic nations, the Western nations, that are doing their utmost to maintain this anti-democratic world order. In those countries, a minority could never impose decisions on the majority: but this is precisely what the West is doing on the world scale' (our translation). Cited by Philippe Marchesin, 'La revanche pour le Sud' *Le monde* 30 October 2010, 19.

Moreover, the poor countries are at an even greater disadvantage when they engage in bilateral agreements, with some rich countries preferring this option for this very reason. However unfair the Trade-Related Aspects of Intellectual Property Rights (TRIPS) Agreement might seem, having been drafted mainly by a dozen lawyers from the industry,[22] it is a multilateral international norm, that is the subject of in-depth studies and tests, whereas many of the recent bilateral agreements between the United States and developing countries (Chile, Jordan, Vietnam, Morocco, etc) contain rules for the protection of intellectual property that are more restrictive for small countries. The TRIPS Amendment, adopted by the WTO in 2005, shows that the WTO process of multilateral discussions and negotiations can mobilise public opinion and secure advances that would be impossible bilaterally. For the first time ever an official WTO text clearly affirms that the protection of public health takes precedence over intellectual property and that text must serve in interpreting TRIPS in this specific domain.

All these proposed reforms briefly evoked have already been detailed in many ways and are familiar enough now. Moreover, under the influence of the financial crisis, progress has been made in recent years on the formal representation rules as shown by the new structure of the Financial Stability Board, the Basel Committee on Banking Supervision and the IMF reform. This is a slow start, however.[23]

The growing importance of the principle of equity is at the heart of the endeavour to reconstruct a new economic order for postcolonial society as a whole. Fairness may become the fundamental principle, both the means and the end, for orientating the provisions of international economic law and international development law. The third solution therefore advocates changing the current legal and economic order into an equitable order corresponding to nothing more nor less than a liberal-social order. It is a social order as it sets up mechanisms geared to solidarity, the redistribution of funds and positive discrimination for less favoured states. But it remains liberal as the principle of the market and of free trade, even remodelled as fair trade, is maintained. As such it is hoped that it will be both economically effective and socially equitable. This third liberal-social option also highlights the need to differentiate in people's minds and in actual fact a form of economic and political liberalism that is part of the solution on a world scale, not the deregulated, unbridled and destabilising ultra-liberalism the world is experiencing now. This is far from certain, for the contemporary neoliberal model tends to generate, in a symmetrically opposite way, a fiercely anti-liberal consensus which seems just as excessive in its conclusions in that, by condemning any

[22] Susan Sell, *Private Power, Public Law: The Globalization of Intellectual Property Rights* (Cambridge, Cambridge University Press, 2003). Historically, no international agreement has ever been so favourable to multinationals, which is why it was challenged in 2001.

[23] On the IMF see, for example, Christian Chavagneux, 'Le FMI a-t-il vraiment changé?' (April 2011) 301 *Alternatives économiques* 30 *ff*.

model of a liberal economic system of law, it is attacking the wrong enemy and precluding itself from coming up with an alternative on the basis of the liberalism of international law in a social and equitable version capable of providing chances of sustainable development for all.

Although these aspects cannot be expounded here, it should be pointed out that the introduction of equity into international economic law involves twofold action: action in favour of sustainable development that enshrines a principle of inter-generational equity and entirely re-orders the economy in terms of moderate, social and environmentally friendly development; and a specific international action in favour of the least favoured nations, which is what the Millennium Development Goals (MDGs) are about. On the first point, the re-orientation of international law in terms of inter-generational equity and sustainable development (including human and social ends), which is included in the Preamble to the GATT II, is considered as the ultimate purpose of this reconstruction. Assuming that the existing legal and economic order is made socially equitable for all states, what might such a reform mean if it is still an order that continues to propagate a model of unlimited growth and of out-and-out consumption to which states frantically commit themselves? On the second point, the reforms recommended with regard to the equitable equalisation of states' circumstances are not aimed at completely equal outcomes, but plainly the reforms are insufficient in situations of serious human distress over major diseases, hunger, extreme poverty or illiteracy, for it is essential to achieve certain outcomes in such cases. This point is essential and maintains the MDGs as an absolute priority in a fairer international society reconfigured by equity in which the least favoured must be able to benefit from specific, targeted international action. The effort to make fundamental rights to water, health and food mandatory, as mentioned above, is also decisive. But this time round, the enshrinement in law of those fundamental rights and the action in favour of targeted objectives to combat the most serious humanitarian situations would be part of a global reform of the economic order and would therefore not systematically be limited in their effect by an order that constantly produces as much indigence and inequality as it does wealth.

II The Possible Implementation of a New Economic Order?

The forceful criticism of the neoliberal model voiced in recent years, the deconstruction of the legal practices that accompany the model and the proliferation of international legal texts advocating 'fair' globalisation might, however, be a turning point which does not materialise in anything but words and so fails to lead to a realistic and binding legal (and economic) alternative. It is not by chance, for example, that the GATT round on development, the Doha Round, which aims not just at opening up more markets but at correcting certain imbalances in the world, is on hold for the time being. Unsurprisingly, it reflects an extreme reluctance to go down this road, with great tension underlying the talks. Given the scale of the changes evoked here with the introduction of the principle of equity, the question arises as to why this recasting of the rules of the existing legal and economic system via the principle of equity, this new NIEO, might be thought any more realistic than in 1974 when the first NIEO was proclaimed? This is a crucial question in light of history and of the aborted attempts to impose the first NIEO and it constitutes, it seems to us, a real test on the basis of which to weigh up the empirical conditions for bringing about the third solution. It is from this perspective that three arguments can be made, suggesting there is a more realistic context today for inflecting the legal and economic order towards greater equity.

First, the challenge for this new NIEO is to tie in with the presuppositions about a critique of the dominant legal and economic system but allowing for the lessons of the past. The international context has completely changed anyway. What is needed is an overhaul of the existing economic rules, not based on the repetition of soft law, on resolutions, which ultimately produce bitterness and disillusion on what has become a highly contestable ideological base, but an overhaul of the rules based legally on the principle of equity and based pragmatically on targeted legal combats and on the negotiation of the revision of existing agreements and statutes of international economic institutions in all of the major sectors involved: trade, investment, finance and in the new sector of international taxation. What was impossible in the 1970s because of major ideological divides and an impassioned climate, which was understandable in view of events, is probably more achievable in the pragmatic context of the 2010s.

Secondly, we need, I feel, to free ourselves of the common terms in international texts on 'fair globalisation' insofar as globalisation per se is no fairer than it is unfair. It is a complex process of interdependency, thought of here in economic terms, which has nothing to do with justice, which does not aim to produce either justice or injustice, fairness or unfairness. To argue otherwise would be to unwittingly repeat the confusion of orders astutely denounced by André Comte-Sponville about capitalism.[24] There is no internal regulatory mechanism for the process of globalisation that can act with respect to ethical challenges, with the result that seeking to make the process of economic globalisation intrinsically equitable is utopian. However, it is possible to impose on it legal limits from the outside based on the principle of equity. Such a viewpoint leads to two subsidiary considerations. It implies that globalisation is not an inevitable or irreversible economic process to which we can ascribe political and economic failings or successive world or national crises that shake the planet, exonerating political leaders in North

[24] André Comte-Sponville, *Le capitalisme est-il moral?* (Paris, Albin Michel, 2004) 92 *ff*.

and South alike and the world's economic and financial operators from their responsibility in maintaining an inequitable and unstable system. It presupposes, too, that we address the 'crisis in law' that has hit international society in this domain since the end of the Cold War, so that the law of the market ceases to be almost systematically the law of the jungle.[25] We return here to the idea that economics must be subordinate to politics and to the legal limits that it may introduce so as to avoid the ultimate de-politicisation of all international relations sought by neoliberals. In point of fact, this outlook also requires an in-depth investigation, that cannot be carried out here, of the role of the state and of official and unofficial centres of power and decision making, which have reformed differently under the effect of globalisation, for the re-enhancement of law and politics first supposes that those liable to act on norms or to impede them can be identified. Thus, for example, many private actors such as multinationals, Anglo-Saxon audit firms, business associations or international cartels directly influence the formulation of the rules of globalisation so as to promote their own interests. Accordingly, it is essential to come up with reforms that take due account of the weight and influence of these new sources of power if they are to be effective.[26]

Thirdly, it may be thought that the recourse to equity coincides with the interests of states and even of private operators so that it is genuinely fostered. No change to the existing legal and economic system seems feasible unless three assumptions are met: if it corresponds to the interest of states, to a fundamental motivation of their public opinion, or if all are aware of the global catastrophes that threaten them.[27] But even if catastrophism and the reaction of public opinion are beginning to mobilise people over the environment (but not poverty), it has to be observed that for the time being only the driving force of self-interest still dominates, with the result that it alone seems able to set things moving. In other words, no equitable reform of the existing system can be contemplated unless this reform serves not only the poor states but also the economic interests of the most powerful private and public players. Now, interestingly, this is perhaps just where things might change compared

[25] Supiot, *L'Esprit de Philadelphie: la justice sociale face au marché total* (Paris, Seuil/La République des Idées, 2010) 91 *ff*. As an economist and specialist of development, Joseph Stiglitz also lambasts the fact that international institutions present ultraliberal globalisation as inevitable when economic alternatives are possible. See Joseph E Stiglitz, *Making Globalization Work* (New York and London, Norton, 2006) 3 *ff*.

[26] Christian Chavagneux, 'Les multinationales définissent-elles les règles de la mondialisation? Les multinationales de la mondialisation' (March 2011) 3014 *Problèmes économiques* 20–25 and Susan Strange, *The Retreat of the State: The Diffusion of Power in the World Economy* (Cambridge, Cambridge University Press, 1996) 16 *ff*. And in any event, it is necessary to think about 're-founding power' in international terms as is convincingly demonstrated in Mireille Delmas-Marty, *Les forces imaginantes du droit (III). La refondation des pouvoirs* (Paris, Seuil, 2007).

[27] For the two driving forces of interest and public opinion see Jürgen Habermas, *Après l'Etat-nation. Une nouvelle constellation politique* (Paris, Fayard, 1988) 121 *ff*, *The Postnational Constellation* (Cambridge, MA, MIT Press, 2001). For catastrophism, see Jean-Pierre Dupuy, *Pour un catastrophisme éclairé. Quand l'impossible est certain* (Paris, Seuil, 2002).

with earlier years. It turns out that the latest economic theories now seem to support the introduction of equity into economics. Updating an old debate over the equity–efficiency pairing, these theories show that a more equitable situation is favourable to the economic efficiency of markets and therefore profitable to all.[28] If the world became more equitable, it would provide greater opportunities for all, rich and poor states alike, since 'Good economic institutions are equitable in a fundamental way: to prosper, a society must create incentives for the vast majority of the population to invest and innovate'.[29] Excessive inequalities lead to conflict, frustration, skewed competition for states themselves, the impossibility for some to have access to the market, lack of innovation and creativity and total economic non-productivity. It is also common knowledge that the recommended economic and social policies do not really work unless developing countries and their populations make them their own and become genuinely involved. This ownership process cannot work unless states and populations feel that the dominant model contains principles of social justice both within states (democracy and human rights) and between states.[30] This is particularly important as until now many of the measures imposed by the system and the conditionality of aid nurture a tremendous feeling of powerlessness, frustration and resentment. In short, these new analyses tend to show that only a socially equitable model can be truly economically efficient since equity is a factor of greater efficiency. Accordingly, even the dominant states and the major private operators of the day might see their interest in its application and so make the prospect of this new NIEO less unrealistic as the essential pathway to resolving the problems of inequality and poverty in the world.

In actual fact, I remain very pessimistic while describing this possibility for there is a fundamental ambivalence in this use of equity which may reproduce the eternal problems with which we are confronted today in this domain because of the intrinsic and original ambivalence of legal practices related to development. The new economic and legal discourse of 'fair globalisation' may be mere rhetoric taken up by public and private actors of globalisation and diverted from its initial objective, that is, far from re-directing the neo-liberal model of development, it can, on the contrary, secure its acceptance by attenuating its most painful human and social consequences.[31] That being

[28] See the World Bank, *World Development Report 2006: Equity and Development*.

[29] ibid p 9.

[30] The concept of 'taking ownership' has become a new leitmotiv of donors and of the major development agencies while it is open to much manipulation. However, despite harsh criticism of the existing system, some of the South's most radical actors insist on this re-appropriation of economic development by their populations and the reform of the system. These issues must be conceptually redesigned from the South primarily. See Yash Tandon, *En finir avec la dépendance à l'aide* (Geneva, CETIM, 2009) 204 *ff*.

[31] See Branislav Gosovic, 'Global Intellectual Hegemony and the International Development Agenda' (December 2000) 166 *Revue internationale des sciences sociales*, UNESCO 507 *ff*; Olivier Favreau, 'Conventions et régulations' in Robert Boyer and Yves Saillard (eds), *Théories de la régulation: l'état des savoirs* (Paris, La découverte, 1995) 65 *ff*; Robert Boyer, 'Justice sociale et

the case, as some commentators suggest, there might only remain social resistance from 'below' based on a counter-hegemonic use of international development law to truly bring about a reform of economic international law and development law. But in truth even those who advocate this seem to doubt their ability to really change things.[32]

III The Principle of Equality in Question: From Formal Equality to Equity

At the very least it still remains for us to size up the rearrangements that are occurring within international law by showing how the principle of equality is profoundly problematised with respect to these legal changes. A new logic of equality has been implemented with international development law, which seeks to restore a degree of material and economic equality among states without restricting itself to the former international law based entirely on the principle of an abstract conception of equal sovereignty. It is no longer a question of just the absence of formal discrimination between states but of positive action to purposefully benefit the poorest states which, because of their economic and social circumstances, are discriminated against de facto. This is why it is no longer equality but equity that is invoked to change international law. Now, while there is nothing surprising about the introduction of equity with respect to the requirements of economic and social justice for poor states, it does illustrate a complex evolution of the principle of equality in international law which deserves to be examined to complete this first part in order to better understand current attempts to reformulate it by taking account of the specific circumstances of our postcolonial international society.

The colonial and imperial society of the last two centuries was not a society of equal states but a hierarchical and unequal society based on the distinction between civilised states, which were subjects of international law, and semi-civilised states, which enjoyed certain specific norms of international law, and uncivilised peoples, who did not benefit from international law.[33] The uncivilised or barbarian peoples and the insufficiently civilised states were perceived essentially by the civilised states in ethno-cultural terms. The civilised states were convinced of the need to dominate them and guide them towards civilisation, and therefore towards the club of equal and sovereign states that were wholly subjects of international law. Against a background

performances économiques: de la synergie au conflit?' in Jérome Affichard and Jean-Baptiste Foucauld (eds), *Justice sociale et inégalités* (Paris, Esprit, 1992) 33 *ff.*

[32] Balkrishnan Rajagopal, *International Law from Below: Development, Social Movements and Third World Resistance* (Cambridge, Cambridge University Press, 2003).

[33] See Emmanuelle Jouannet, *The Liberal-Welfarist Law of Nations. A History of International Law* (Cambridge, Cambridge University Press, 2012) 135 *ff.*

of racism and prejudice, their inferiority was judged as being quite natural and justified by their different, inferior nature. As it was thought to be related intrinsically to their ethno-cultural characteristics, their weak technological and economic development was also invoked to justify their legally inferior status. The non-civilised peoples were reduced to the legal status of objects of international law, while the semi-civilised states did not enjoy full legal personality and capacities in international law. Therefore, neither group could enjoy equal status and rights to the civilised states and all relations codified by classical international law between civilised and non civilised states shared the common features of dependence and inequality. This was captured by the international lawyer Antoine Pillet in 1894:

> There are no equal rights between civilised states and non-civilised or less civilised states [. . .] Between the condition of the ones and the condition of the others there is a flagrant inequality and that inequality is, in this matter, the true basis of their relations.[34]

In short, by a complete reversal of its principles, classical international law reinforced and justified a superiority of law, power and organisation for the benefit of civilised nations that ran directly counter to the liberal principles of equality and sovereign freedom that applied among civilised states. Decolonisation put an end to this discriminatory legal system and was to extend legal equality of the classical law of nations to all states or political entities formed into sovereign states in the eyes of international law. When they gain their independence, these peoples formed into states become full subjects of international law and therefore states that are formally equal to the long-standing subjects of international law, although their material circumstances are plainly less favourable and unequal to those of other states. Being legal equals, they are subject to the same rights and duties of international law.

However, the principle of formal equality that applies to them because of decolonisation has contrasting effects. It has positive effects. Unlike the former colonial and imperial society which was inegalitarian and hierarchical and which compartmentalised each state in its own place, the new postcolonial society is founded on the equal standing of all states, old and new, and appears a more open society. Admittedly, the postcolonial world is not without its real inequalities and everyone is fully aware of the enormous differences in circumstances between states in the aftermath of independence, but these differences no longer tie people or certain states down to a different and inferior legal status. A fundamental gain has therefore been secured: the removal of a radical heterogeneity between states justifying that it is impossible to have equal international standing and rights. Postcolonial international law no longer considers them legally incapable or semi-incapable

[34] Antoine Pillet, 'Le droit international public. Ses éléments constitutifs, son domaine, son objet' (1894) *Revue Generale de Droit International Public* 24–25. Emphasis added.

because of some supposed uncivilised or semi-civilised ethno-cultural nature and a deficient economic condition that allegedly keeps them in an inferior position to other states. The decolonised states have made no mistake about the importance of this recognition. Once decolonised, they demand before anything else the application of this equal status and equal rights as attested by one of the major resolutions of the time, Resolution 2625 of 24 October 1970 (Declaration on Principles of International Law concerning Friendly Relations and Co-operation among States), since it sets out sovereign equality between states as a fundamental principle of postcolonial international law: 'All States enjoy sovereign equality. They have equal rights and duties and are equal members of the international community, notwithstanding differences of an economic, social, political or other nature.'[35]

However, this new, purely formal, legal equality among sovereign states has not erased the differences and the socio-economic inequalities even less; and it is at this stage that difficulties arise for, by the same token, it is not sufficient to given chances of equal economic development for all, and especially not for developing countries fresh from colonisation. The principle of formal equality between states therefore also has negative aspects on which the NIEO (and classical development law) sought to act but which complicate the scope of its principles and of those principles that now relate to 'fair globalisation'. There is a shift from the fight for equal standing and therefore of equal rights among states to the call for a right to different treatment. Formal equality is maintained but after having been perceived as a powerful instrument for the liberation of decolonised states, it is progressively perceived as also being a potential instrument of oppression for the benefit of rich and dominant states, as it masks the flagrant imbalance in the economic and social circumstances of states. In other words, there is a glaring contrast between the equal *attribution* of rights and the unequal *distribution* of goods.[36] It therefore produces disenchantment and leads to states wanting to extend the equality of rights by an equalisation in circumstances and therefore to finding rules for sharing fairly in a deeply unequal society which seems condemned to pay for development in terms of wealth by new inequalities forever. Now, allowing for this means bringing back distinctions in status that formal equality sought to overcome. And so after securing the removal of differences in circumstances that previously justified negative discrimination, decolonised states now want to rely on socio-economic differences to establish positive discrimination; having suffered from an unequal legal status they call for a legal status that is both equal and unequal. This plainly complicates the question of equality since the new legal call for different treatment does not replace formal equality between states but exists alongside it. Hence, for example, the call for compensatory inequality for the benefit of the less

[35] www.un.org/documents/ga/res/25/ares25.htm.
[36] Paul Ricoeur, *Parcours de la reconnaissance* (Paris, Gallimard, 2004) 312.

favoured countries, which exists alongside the principle of formal equality of all states. Some commentators have seen an inconsistency in international texts between provisions that affirm equality among states 'without discrimination' and the provisions that seek to take account of differences so as to establish a preferential system. It is a contradictory form of logic that is operating here; but, at the same time, the wager of introducing the principle of equity into the international legal and economic order is about deepening the principle of legal equality among states along these lines, that is, equitably, by taking account of the actual inequalities that set them apart: redesigning the rules of international law in economic matters so as to protect the freedom and sovereignty of states, their legal equality and to introduce greater equality concerning states' development.

This new aspect of the principle of equality envisaged in terms of equity replies therefore to the question of inequalities between states and of the economic and social organisation of international society. It corresponds to the concern to end discrimination in the circumstances of states, arising from the colonial period, in order to restore, along with the legal equality in rights, true equality of opportunity for states in their economic development and equal results for the most serious humanitarian situations (MDGs).[37] But it is not a matter of envisaging complete equality in material conditions, which no state or commentator would venture to advocate today. The objective is obviously not to claim to achieve perfect equality, which is unachievable, but to right the situation of deep inequality in circumstances with respect to the market, to technologies and to medicinal drugs and therefore to the real possibility of developing. The result is that there will always remain inequalities that are considered acceptable and it is not a matter of the right of each state to have exactly the same resources and to enjoy the same income.[38] Such a point of view relates to strict egalitarianism, which has already been the subject of many deconstructions and on which there is no need to insist for not only is it completely unrealistic but, moreover, it is totalising in its effects since it corresponds to a new form of domination based on the most complete equalisation possible of the circumstances of each and on the elimination of any form of difference.[39]

[37] See Geneviève Koubi and Gilles J Guglielmi (eds), *L'égalité des chances. Analyse, évolutions, perspectives* (Paris, La découverte, 2000).

[38] Not every inequality is considered unfair, but with respect to the circumstances and requirements related to the principle of equity, what are unfair are the inequalities that can be remedied which arise from the unfair economic and social system. The same can be said of unjust situations, other than inequality, that can also be remedied. On the idea of reparable injustice see, for example, Amartya Sen, *The Idea of Justice* (Cambridge, Harvard University Press, 2009).

[39] Pierre Rosanvallon, *Le capitalism utopique. Historie de l'idée de marché* (Paris, Seuil, 1999) 232. He also shows that this implies getting rid of the representation of a single, open and homogeneous, world economic area.

IV Conclusion

The current situation shows that the question of development remains one of the most fundamental problems for international society, a problem that is at least as essential as the questions of international peace and security, and which is even inseparable from them. This is what the drafters of the United Nations Charter had suspected in adding the objective of development to that of international peace (Article 1), and therefore the promise of achieving them both together, for peace was newly thought of in 1945 as being dependent in the long term on the economic and social development of states, and vice versa. The history of the former Third World provides a better understanding of the evolution that ensued and the legal rationale at work since the 1950s through development law, with a view to ending the glaring socio-economic inequalities among states in the aftermath of decolonisation. That history also shows the dark side of this body of law which has always been instrumentalised in part, to be turned against those who were supposed to benefit from it and to form a sound foundation for Western hegemonic power by subordinating it to an inequitable legal and economic order and maintaining economic, then political and social dependence on liberal standards that have not yet been fully appropriated or formulated internally by the populations in question. Unless it is itself seriously re-thought, especially in conjunction with the reform of economic international law, international development law will be unable to reflect the hope for social justice that it has held within itself since the Third World first called for legal reform in the 1970s.[40]

For, in spite of its ambivalent effects, classical and new international development law – as it has been defined here as separate from international economic law – also reflects the aspiration to an equitable and humane international society, and therefore a fundamental requirement of social justice at world level related to the emergence of postcolonial society. In this respect, it must also be pointed out that the goal of a more equitable legal and economic order, in the service of genuine human and sustainable development, potentially concerns all the world's states for since the end of the Cold War we have been immersed in a globalised economic system which, with its growth spurts and multiple crises, will not cease to create new winners and new losers. It may well be that the former dominated nations will shortly be fighting hardest to maintain unfair rules that henceforth they may use to their own

[40] Balkrishnan Rajagopal, 'Droit international contre-hégémonique, repenser les droits humains et le développement comme stratégie pour le Tiers Monde' in Emmanuelle Jouannet, Hélène Ruiz-Fabri and Mark Toufayan (eds), *Droit international et nouvelles approches sur le Tiers monde* (Paris, Société de Législation comparée, 2012). The article summarises the arguments in Rajagopal, *International Law from Below. Development, Social Movements and Third World Resistance* (n 32).

benefit. The major new emerging states which previously criticised the existing legal and economic order no longer reason themselves other than in terms of catching up along the lines of the model of accumulation of wealth production, and one cannot fail to notice that these states, which fully accepted the neoliberal rules of international economic law, are paradoxically feared more today by the North than those states which, in the 1970s, violently decried the injustice of the rules of the world economic order. This does not mean that all the socio-economic injustices and inequalities of the past have been settled and are over and done with. Far from it. They are simply to be compounded by new inequalities in the North related to the advent of an ultra-liberalised global society.

This point deserves attention for the situation seems therefore more complex than it might appear from certain discourses. One particular type of discourse on globalisation has had a marked tendency to consider the post-colonial divisions that underpin our world history as obsolete, considering them as hidden away for good behind the representation of a united and borderless world, which no longer has any major structural fracture, is subject to global governance characterised by free trade, democracy and human rights, and has supposedly become one again after the previous bi-polarisation of the world.[41] Now, although the world has indeed changed in many ways and although inequalities affect both North and South, as has been emphasised here, I cannot agree with such a representation. Not only does it seem wrong in the consensus-based image of the present it tends to portray, but it very opportunely glosses over the economic and social inequalities inherited from the past. The point is not to get pointlessly hung up on the past but to make allowances for it and its effects which persist over time. Besides, any plan to completely eliminate this past from the current economic and social problems would be especially unwelcome since the end of the Cold War ushered in another type of claim based on identity and memory. It is hard to see how these issues can be eluded by sweeping history under the carpet; on the contrary this would only make matters worse.

[41] Emblematically see Francis Fukuyama, *The End of History and the Last Man* (New York, The Free Press, 1992).

Part II

International Law and Recognition: A Decent International Society?

Today, there is an international demand for recognition that is so intense that it has taken on the appearance of an international social phenomenon of the same kind as is generated by expectations of development. For convincing evidence of this, one need look no further than the many demands that have emerged within this domain in the last two decades from all sides. Various social groups such as minorities, indigenous peoples, women, homosexuals and again, and this is probably the most disconcerting aspect, certain states themselves, have expressed a desire for full international recognition of their equal dignity and specific identity and have called for an end to the intolerable stigmatisation and marginalisation from which they suffer. Although it may be connected with them, this need for recognition lies on a separate plane to expectations about development, since demands for recognition relate to the respect of the identity and culture of each group. In other words, the issue is no longer about how to correct socio-economic differences among states, but about the cultural and symbolical representations of them and about the means to restore the value of scorned identities or subservient cultures.

This intrusion of recognition from all directions creates a new problem for international law insofar as, to date, recognition has only been dealt with very secondarily and without any great interest being attributed to it. This is evident in the fact that none of the major international texts after 1945 speak of recognition and the principle of recognition is never directly mentioned in the UN Charter. The very idea of the need for recognition and its legal treatment did not occur to the decision makers after the Second World War, even though demands were already being made by formerly dominated states that felt stigmatised or by the minorities that had so troubled Europe since the nineteenth century, and even though, for that matter, certain post-war texts, without saying as much, made a first fundamental move towards the legal recognition of states and then of individuals as subjects of law. There is nothing surprising in the fact that the need for recognition and its legal treatment did not really emerge until the 1990s, because it was the specific circumstances of the post-Cold War context that elicited the intrusion of issues of recognition on the international scene and the onset of a new era that was increasingly dominated by these questions. And yet, it is not clear whether the emergence of this phenomenon of international recognition has been accorded all the importance it deserves, although a whole series of new legal instruments attests to the interest that political decision makers have taken in it. There are several reasons for this, two of which stand out. First, while presented as incontrovertible today, identities, which lie at the heart of recognition, are considered by some observers as very dangerous and therefore as things to be blocked out rather than enhanced by law.[1] Second, in line with standard international practice, the legal instruments adopted with respect to recognition have been adopted in a disorderly way, in response to needs being expressed in a piecemeal fashion. They therefore remain in disarray, without any connection necessarily being made between them and without it being realised that recognition is the guiding principle. However, attention must be paid to them if we are to grasp the most essential changes in international law, for what is at play is another decisive evolution of the principle of formal equality of the old classical liberal law but also of international social justice as it began to emerge with the legal instruments based on development. As Nancy Fraser highlighted for internal societies, since the end of the Cold War, the new struggles for recognition have shifted the nature and criteria of social justice in part, but this time on a worldwide scale. For they are superimposed upon and overlap with the earlier economic demands, giving rise to the idea of an international society that, it is hoped, will become not just *equitable*, through development law which is, at last, efficient, but also *decent*, that is, based on respect for others by means of the international law of recognition.[2]

Even so, the legal transposition needs to be reviewed and understood, as do the implications of this second very general evolution insofar as it has still not been presented in this way in terms of research, at least not to my knowledge, and as it raises a substantial web of difficulties. And so it needs to be supported and questioned in depth, argued out and resituated within a historical perspective so that we may better understand its emergence and importance. Because of the new context arising from the fall of the Berlin Wall, recognition has become a new paradigm of international society, which may be presented as the counterpart to the development paradigm that arose after the Second World War, which has accordingly given rise to an international law of recognition as a remedy to the many infringements of identity and culture (chapter five). It is possible to identify a whole set of rules and legal practices that can be grouped together so that they have the same objective of responding to new expectations in this domain. Without prejudging more global and technical research that should subsequently be made into these subject areas, we shall examine those which seem the most significant because they particularly reflect the challenges associated with preserving

[1] See the arguments in Michel Wieviorka, *La différence. Identités culturelles:enjeux, débats et politiques* (Paris, L'aube, 2005) especially 40 *ff*.

[2] Avishai Margalit, *The Decent Society* (Cambridge, Harvard University Press, 1996). However, the issue is considered a moral one, not in terms of law and justice as is done here.

cultures and identities and the legal logic that distinguishes them. The preservation and promotion of the diversity of cultural expression is made through the 2005 United Nations Educational, Scientific and Cultural Organization Convention (chapter six); the existence of rights relating to identities, including human rights (chapter seven); and the reparation of historical prejudice associated with racism and colonialism (chapter eight). While taken for granted but also held to be problematic, all these rules and legal practices require some general reflection on the overall architecture that is sketched out progressively with this second evolution, in particular the way the rules and practices are superimposed on or articulate with the other two branches of international law that have been drawn on as part of this study – international development law and international economic law (chapter nine).

5

The Evolution of Recognition Internationally

THE CURRENT PHENOMENON of recognition is rooted in an international world that has always been heterogeneous and multicultural, but which has only lately come to fully accept the reality of this. Recognition encompasses all forms of demand pertaining to sex, nation, language, history, culture and religion and covers the entire globe from east to west and north to south. And yet, the more specific existence of an international law relating to recognition is not self-evident and results from a stepwise evolution that invites us to understand that this body of law, like the recognition on which it is based, has several meanings. This evolution follows a complex and unusual pathway, related in part to the uneasy legacy of colonisation, where the expectation of recognition internationally was reflected before the Cold War by a call for equal standing and equal rights while, in the new post-Cold War context, expectations of recognition selectively take the form of specific and inverted demands for a right to be different. This dissociation of expectations and of the legal responses that were to be successively given through international law should not be surprising since it merely reflects the different possible modalities of recognition. Far from being a homogenous process, recognition is a phenomenon that may vary depending on the state of international society, the expectations of those who make up that society at any given time, and the nature of their refusals of recognition.

I From the International Law of Civilised Nations to Postcolonial International Law

Up until decolonisation, international law was a stigmatising body of law that merely reflected the distortion in power among states, the feeling of superiority of a whole political class and the latent racism of an entire age. It was itself an instrument of refusal of recognition and of domination since it was based entirely on the fundamental discrimination between civilised and uncivilised nations. Accordingly, after decolonisation, the recognition of equal status for all was to be the clearest manifestation of the recognition of the identity of new states. This recognition of their status, which put an end to the discrimination of the colonial period, did not lie in the affirmation of a right to be different but in the affirmation of a right to be equal, which ignored differences; indeed it was indifferent to differences.

A The International Law of Civilised Nations

As seen above, classical international law introduced the distinction between civilised states, which were subjects of international law, and uncivilised or semi-civilised countries or peoples, which were not. The distinction was drawn on the basis of a criterion of culture and civilisation, or more specifically an ethno-cultural criterion since ethnic and racial considerations underpinned the cultural and civilisational criteria.[1] It is true that the difference in economic and social standing and the absence of technological and industrial development of non-European states and peoples were also factors that meant Europeans held them to be 'backward' or 'immobile' peoples who could not claim the status of fully civilised states and therefore of subjects of law. But it is true nonetheless that the basis for the difference in status introduced by classical international law was, above all, of a cultural order. More specifically, classical international law posited the existence of a 'standard of civilisation' to which any people wishing to become a subject of international law must measure up and which was nothing other than the standard of Euro-American civilisation. In 1884, James Lorimer said: 'Despite this tendency to generalise, a common, tacit and permanent international law will only ever exist between nations whose moral standards and intellectual culture are identical'.[2]

Unsurprisingly, Euro-American civilisation and culture were held to be incontrovertibly superior by the vast majority of jurists of the time, who were mostly white and Western. Despite their efforts to try to demonstrate some interest for other cultures, they could barely conceal their contempt and distrust of them and often their racism. This civilisation and culture had underpinned Euro-American international law in its entirety since the Enlightenment. It was the celebrated threesome of rationalism, humanism and liberalism that was thought to have given rise to technological and industrial progress, the practice of contracts, the existence of independent courts, the abolition of slavery and the observance of civil and political freedoms. The states or peoples that had not yet integrated its values were perceived as deprived of this degree of reason, of willpower and of maturity that would have enabled them to be considered as legal persons and therefore as subjects of law, capable of creating and using the rules of international law. The international lawyer Raymond Piédelièvre captured the general opinion of

[1] See Joseph Hornung, 'Civilisés et barbares' (1885) XVII *Revue de droit international et de législation comparée* 456 *ff.*

[2] James Lorimer, 'La doctrine de la reconnaissance, fondement du droit international' (1884) XVI *Revue de droit international et de législation comparée* 335.

his contemporaries in asserting that '[I]nternational law essentially presupposes reciprocity, that is, a sufficiently well-developed conscience among the nations whose foreign relations it governs, and their deliberate and persistent will to apply the precepts of law and justice in their mutual relations'.[3]

Hence, one of the best known justifications for the colonisation process which is fully integrated in international law, the 'sacred mission of civilisation', justified colonisation and was recognised as entirely lawful by international law, for it was to enable the uncivilised nations to accede to Euro-American civilisation by gradually modifying their identity from an uncivilised to a civilised people. As Nathaniel Berman shows, the aim was not to completely eliminate what composed the identity, albeit uncivilised, of the dominated peoples but, in a more subtle and more ambivalent way, to metamorphose that identity so that it fitted in with Western civilisation which was considered the high point of all civilisation, the goal which any human being should naturally aim for.[4] Berman cites the case made by the French Government in *Nationality Decrees Issued in Tunis and Morocco* (PCIJ, 1923) in which it is explained that the civilising mission of France in North Africa was to 'liberate' the true identity of the Arabs, which was not French, but which 'evolves within the broader framework of Western conceptions'.[5] The French Government thus intended, through the effect of colonisation, to act on the pre-colonial identity of the dominated peoples to give birth to a new and fuller identity which ultimately would 'reveal to the Arabs their true identity'.[6]

Besides this, it is particularly interesting to observe that the possible inclusion of some states within the sphere of subjects of the Euro-American law of nations was then based on the legal technique of recognition. Recognition was defined as the unilateral, individual or collective legal act by which the civilised states attested to the sufficiently advanced degree of civilisation and therefore of the maturity of a political entity to be part of the 'community of civilised states'. Thus, its new status as a state that was fully civilised, fully sovereign and a full subject of international law was made binding.[7] In other words, this act of recognition put an end to a political entity's exclusion and disqualification, an entity which had previously been discriminated against for being insufficiently civilised.[8] Recognition was therefore an essential act

[3] Raymond Piédelièvre, *Précis de droit international public ou Droit des gens* (Paris, Cotillon, 1894) vol 1, 19.

[4] See Nathaniel Berman, *Passions et ambivalences. Le colonialisme, le nationalisme et le droit international* (Paris, Pedone, 2008) 277 *ff*. See also Nathaniel Berman, 'Les ambivalences impériales' in Emmanuelle Jouannet and Hélène Ruiz-Fabri (eds), *Impérialisme et droit international en Europe et aux Etats-Unis* (Paris, Société de législation comparée, 2007) 150 *ff*.

[5] Case presented in the name of the Government of the French Republic: *Nationality Decrees in Tunis and Morocco* PCIJ, 1923, Series C No 2, p 3 (our translation).

[6] ibid (our translation).

[7] See *Annuaire de l'Institut de droit international*, Ed nouvelle abrégée (1928) (Paris, Pedone, Session de La Haye, 1875) vol I, 70 *ff*.

[8] See especially the three types of recognition invented by James Lorimer, *The Institutes of the Law of Nations* (London, Blackwood and Sons, 1883–84) 91 *ff*.

in classical international law, the 'password' for joining the club of civilised states, subjects of international law. But it was restrictive and discriminatory. The act of recognition of the time did not work towards recognition of the differences that constituted others and their identities. On the contrary, it was an act of recognition of the similarity of values and of the degree of civilisation attained by a state or people that had previously been thought of as ethno-culturally different. Since it was based on similarity, recognition did not aim to grant an equal legal status to new subjects despite their differences, but an equal legal status based on the similarities in culture and civilisation. Integration into the 'community of civilised nations' and the attribution of equal standing and rights was achieved by forced assimilation and uniformisation, that is, when the newly recognised state had erased, at least superficially, the differences of culture or civilisation that opposed it to the Euro-American states and it displayed an acceptable degree of 'civilised conscience'. For Paul Fauchille, in 1921, 'States' participation in positive international law presupposes a certain identity or similarity in mores, customs, social or legal institutions, a common practice of the same processes, a reciprocity in the forms of relations'.[9]

In actual fact, evaluation of the criterion of civilisation gave rise to all manner of political manipulation and the certificate of 'civilised nation' was awarded depending on the changes in international diplomacy. Recognition depended pre-eminently on political and pragmatic considerations. Countries that were included as and when international relations evolved were Turkey, China, Japan and the countries of South America, while all of Africa was excluded, with the exception of Ethiopia, which even so finished by being invaded by Italy – as were many Asian countries. However, apart from political and economic considerations that guided the act of recognition, it was no less true that dominated peoples wanting to be recognised as civilised were forced to adopt certain institutions, certain private and public rights and certain of the most fundamental practices of Euro-American states, starting with the principle of the modern state and the Western concept of law. Evidence of this is the way Turkey forced itself to revise its judicial, commercial, civil and criminal law by imitating the French model and therefore by conveying values that were not always readily compatible with its Islamic tradition. The example of Japan is also a striking example of the mimicry non Euro-American states were forced to engage in in order to play a part on the international stage. The transformation of Japan's education policy in the 1870s was a major turning point towards the European Enlightenment and the country's complete and deliberate re-casting in the mould of the state and the modern West.[10] Gradually, the governments of Oriental states all ended up adopting institutions of Western inspiration. This imitation spread all the

[9] Paul Fauchille, *Traité de droit international public* (Paris, Rousseau, 1922) 30–31.
[10] See Carol Gluck, *Japan's Modern Myths* (Princeton, Princeton University Press, 1985).

more at the time as the belief in the superiority of Euro-American civilisation was largely shared by many of the elite non-Western nations. What Jalal-Al-e-Ahmad termed 'occidentosis' for Iran, for example, refers to a period when there was no end to the copying of Western customs and ways of life.[11] Euro-American civilisation generally, like international law which was a pure product of it, reflected something that was morally good and desirable that decked out Europeans of the time in an eminent form of prestige and naturally destined them, even in the eyes of the elite of many dominated peoples, to propagate it among those who had no experience of it.

Besides, one cannot fail to notice that the need to comply with the Euro-American code of culture and civilisation obeyed a logic of domination that was found worldwide. Up until the twentieth century, the foreign relation systems of other regions of the world were cosmogonies subject to the hold of a dominant state and culture that decreed that the others were inferior, including Europeans. In this way the Sublime Porte saw itself as the hub of an Islamocentric system until the eighteenth century.[12] And if it conceded a system of capitulations, removing foreigners from the ambit of Turkish law, it was also because there was no question of infidels being subject to the same law as true believers. With its civilisation that went back more than four thousand years, China called itself the 'Middle Empire', submitting its neighbours to its cultural code and viewing Euro-Americans as barbarians. It was hardly surprising, then, that the conflicts relating to British imperialism in China were crystallised by denials of recognition and by humiliating situations that were experienced on both sides.[13]

After the First World War, the League of Nations maintained the colonisation of the world through a system of mandates and the principle of a civilised law of nations based on the distinction between civilised and uncivilised peoples. At the same time, certain thinkers in the colonised world, including the great minds of the Indian Renaissance, Sri Aurobindo and Rabindranath Tagore, were already warning the West about the idea of setting up a free and universal world order that failed to recognise the rights of peoples to self-determination and failed to abandon its vision of child peoples under the guardianship of adult nations.[14] Moreover, it is anecdotal but highly significant that the drafters of the Covenant of the League of Nations declined to include in the Covenant the principle of the equality of peoples and races proposed by the Japanese, which the Japanese took as an affront. After many discussions contesting this proposal, it was decided instead to include equal

[11] Jalal Al-I Ahmad, *Occidentosis. A Plague from the West* (Berkeley, Mizan Press, 1984). See also Albert Memmi *The Colonizer and the Colonized* (Boston, Beacon Press, 1965).

[12] Yasuaki Onuma, 'When was the Law of International Society Born? An Inquiry into the History of International Law' (2000) 2 *Journal of the History of International Law* 33.

[13] Notably, the British Ambassador Lord Macartney's refusal in 1793 to kowtow which, for Alain Peyrefittte, is the origin of the permanent cultural conflict between China and Westerners. See Alain Peyrefitte, *L'empire immobile, le choc des mondes* (Paris, Fayard, 1989) IX.

[14] Armand Mattelart, *Diversité culturelle et mondialisation* (Paris, Poche, 2006) 19.

treatment of nationalities in all countries, which was far removed from the Japanese proposal. Admittedly at the time, Japan refrained from speaking of its own discriminatory policy towards other Asian peoples, but the fact is that rejecting the principle of equality among the races meant implicitly recognising their inequality, inevitably causing a terrible sense of stigma and discrimination.

Things only began to change after 1945, the Second World War having shuffled the pack of cards somewhat, and the UN Charter recorded certain fundamental principles on this point. It must be seen, however, that despite its apparent openness, the Charter is still based on the most discriminatory principles of the colonial system, which limits the scope of the stated principles from the outset. The UN Charter enshrines internationally a whole set of principles that could have worked towards a greater movement of recognition like the right to self-determination, human rights, the principle of non-discrimination on the grounds of race and the principle of equality between men and women and of 'nations large and small' (Preamble, (2)). Taking up Japan's fight in the League of Nations, China asked that the racial question be re-examined by the representatives in San Francisco. By simple but incontrovertible reasoning, given the state of mind at the time, China argued that its citizens were treated as subhuman in the United States because China itself had been considered a racially inferior sub-state. Like all the states emancipated in 1945 but still feeling the stigma of past discrimination, China asked that racial equality be recognised together with China's identity as a state and people as being of equal dignity with others so that its citizens could enjoy truly equal treatment abroad and not some inferior status.[15] Indeed, it obtained satisfaction with the solemn proclamation of the principle of equality and the prohibition of discrimination on the basis of race among peoples, states and individuals.

But even though the drafters of the Charter incorporated these new principles, contradiction was already at the heart of the UN text since it also set up the regime for non-self-governing territories (Chapter XI) and the trusteeship system (Chapter XII) which took over from the mandate system of the League of Nations and so perpetuated the colonial domination of the victorious powers.[16] The right of peoples to self-determination as a goal of the United Nations (Article 1(2)) was of very limited scope and liable to elicit the same misunderstanding as that caused by some of Woodrow Wilson's speeches in 1917 and 1918. It was not intended for colonised peoples but was applicable to peoples that were already free and that ought to be able to decide on their form of government independently of any foreign influence. So the Charter and international law after 1945 continued to draw a legal

[15] See Olivier de Frouville, 'Une conception démocratique du droit international' (2001) 39 *Revue européenne de sciences sociales* §108; ress.revues.org/659#bodyftn189.

[16] See generally Mark Mazower, *No Enchanted Palace. The End of Empire and the Ideological Origins of the United Nations* (Princeton, Princeton University Press, 2009).

difference between peoples depending on their level of development and their capacity to govern themselves (Articles 73 and 76), as well as their degree of civilisation. Non-self-governing territories were even expressly defined ethno-culturally as shown by the works of the Special Committee of the time. For the Committee, a territory was presumed to be 'non-self-governing' if it were 'geographically separate or ethnically or culturally distinct from the country administering it'.[17] All the new and potentially emancipating principles were therefore dominated by a conception of international political relations inherited from colonialism, for even when scope was given to these principles in the Charter, the Charter continued to share with the old colonial system the same stigmatising political, social and cultural structure that was its trademark.

B Postcolonial International Law

A genuine process of recognition, putting an end to the cultural and social representations of the past, therefore presupposed far greater transformations than those in the 1945 text and it was not until the decolonisation movement of the 1950s and 1960s that any ethno-cultural distinction between peoples was finally abandoned as the pre-condition for attributing international legal personality and the status of sovereign state. The independence movement brought about the virtually general inclusion of former dominated and colonised peoples within the community of subjects of international law, based on the lawfulness of the right to self-determination (Resolution 1514 of 14 December 1960) and not on the criterion of civilisation and the old legal technique of recognition. Decolonised peoples automatically enjoyed legal personality and legal capacity as new states, and a legal status equal to that of their former colonising states. In this way the stigmatising effects of classical international law, induced by the concepts of semi-civilised states or uncivilised and non-self-governing peoples, disappeared at last along with the difference in status that derived from it. At the same time the idea of a 'community of civilised states' was abandoned and superseded by the idea of an 'international society'. The idea of society meant unity in the observance of the multiplicity of cultural and civilisational values of each state, whereas the idea of community reflected the necessary sharing of the same values.[18]

And so it was within this period and not in 1945 that an initial and spectacular phenomenon of recognition of the Other really occurred internationally, with international law putting an end, in law if not in fact, to centuries of devaluation and stigmatisation of colonised peoples through their automatic

[17] Cited by Michel Virally, 'Droit international et décolonisation devant les Nations Unies', *Le droit international en devenir. Essais écrits au fil des ans* (Paris, PUF, 1990) 334 *ff.* The Committee was tasked with giving its opinion on the principles that should inspire members when interpreting the provisions of Chapter XI by Resolution 147 (XIV) of 12 December 1959.

[18] See Emmanuelle Jouannet, *The Liberal-Welfarist Law of Nations. A History of International Law* (Cambridge, Cambridge University Press, 2012) 148 *ff.*

and generalised accession to the status of state and full subjects of international law. The very fact that former colonised peoples were being considered subjects of international law and equal subjects of law to others, in particular to their former colonisers, with the same rights and obligations, is a fundamental form of recognition of their identity in that they are at last considered and treated legally as having equal dignity to others.[19] That apart, this legal evolution did not give rise to any far-reaching internal upheavals in international law since it actually applied to all the states of the globe, without bringing in any discriminatory criterion, the liberal pluralistic principles of sovereign freedom and formal equality on which international law had been based since the old seventeenth-century law of nations. What it represented for the Euro-American states until the time of decolonisation was simply extended to all: a formal body of law which, from the wars of religion in Europe, had been built on neutrality and tolerance with respect to states' choices of culture, political system and religion, and which therefore was used only to justify the exclusion of non-European states by a diversion of its founding precepts. Being now extended to all, it showed itself for what it was originally, a legal instrument of emancipation proclaiming formal equality of all and its indifference to differences, enshrining the observance of de jure cultural pluralism where, contrary to its original principles, it had previously imposed uniformity in accordance with a single model of civilisation.

C The Limits of the Process of Recognition

In truth, this 'neutrality' of international law and the observance of cultural pluralism cannot conceal the fact that they were all easier to proclaim as, in the 1960s, all the human societies of the world were being reshaped along the lines of the Western states and of their underlying values. European colonisation and domination, the yardstick of civilisation, had already begun to produce their effects by redefining the identity of non-European peoples through the prism of European legal and political culture and in doing so constantly eroded the traditional form and content of their ways of thinking about law and politics. Short of having penetrated the deep-seated cultural and social structures of these societies, colonisation and even simple domination were often reflected by the imposition of all the main components of Western legal systems.[20] The fact is that during the years following independence, the movement of legal Westernisation continued and even swelled. No

[19] On this fundamental process of legal recognition of the Other as being equal to oneself, see Axel Honneth, *The Struggle for Recognition. The Moral Grammar of Social Conflicts* (Cambridge, Polity Press, 1995) and Charles Taylor, *Multiculturalism and the Politics of Recognition* (Princeton, Princeton University Press, 1992).

[20] Mikhaïl Xifaras, 'Les ambivalences impériales – commentaire' in Jouannet and Ruiz-Fabri (eds), *Impérialisme et droit international en Europe et aux Etats-Unis* (Paris, Société de Législation comparée, 2007) 185 *ff*.

sooner did they gain independence than the new governments set up modern states based on the former values of the colonising powers, for they saw in this form of state a guarantee of modernity and development. The mimetic impetus was in fact in full flow in an attempt to 'modernise' the country. In other words, decolonisation paradoxically completed the process of 'civilisation' because of the willing submission of newly independent nations to Western legal practices and to existing international law. Not without cruel irony, decolonisation continued to reshape the identities of those nations as non-Western peoples in the legal categories of existing international law and therefore to bring about the Westernisation of the world.

Even if it counted as recognition for the new states of their identity as free and sovereign peoples, access to the status of subject of law, equal to others, did not end the feelings of denial of recognition of their cultures and their identities overnight. This was because the legal and social changes brought about did not eradicate the stigmatising cultural and symbolic representations underlying all international relations, as inherited from such a long history of domination. For one thing the era of development law had begun in the 1950s with the same implicit logic of discrimination between developed and underdeveloped countries and the same inevitably stigmatising effects.[21] It was not by chance, as said, that the newly independent nations preferred to call themselves the 'Third World' or teamed up as the 'Non-Aligned Movement', for they were asserting their re-found pride and indirectly combatting what remained a dark side of development law. Léopold Sédar Senghor expressed this best when speaking at the 1955 Bandung Conference which, he claimed, reflected worldwide 'awareness of their eminent dignity by coloured peoples' and 'the death of the inferiority complex'.[22] However, this situation of new states at the bottom of the development ladder continued to belittle them, and the repeated failures of development policies merely increased the new feeling of stigmatisation. It is only with the current success of the major emerging states that the feeling of pride and self-esteem seems to have become a reality for some of them. Not because that success breaks the belittling symbolic structure of the development ladder and what it presupposes, but because those states at least are now at the top of the ladder and no longer at the bottom.

For another thing, being culturally dominated has remained an ongoing point of confrontation with the North. The tragic ambivalence of the de-colonised states, always subject to Western economic hegemony, torn between their desire to modernise and their desire to re-discover their identity, was to remain a constant feature of the contemporary postcolonial world.

[21] Firouzeh Nahavandi, *Du développement à la globalisation. Histoire d'une stigmatisation* (Brussels, Bruylant, 2009) 30 *ff*.

[22] Cited by Yadh Ben Achour, *Le rôle des civilisations dans le système international. Droit et relations internationales* (Brussels, Bruylant, 2003) 155 (our translation).

It is one of the reasons why their call for recognition was to evolve over time to take the form today of a right to legally protect their cultures and for some a call for reparation for the historic wrongs inflicted on the identities that were battered and bruised by colonisation. By the same token, their new demands are part of a much more global movement that was to affect all of post-Cold War international society and that is crystallised in the demand for a right to be different.

II Cultures and Identities During and After the Cold War

This renewed figure of recognition as the right to preserve one's ethnic, cultural or civilisational difference is rooted in the concern of newly decolonised states to re-enhance their forgotten cultural and historical heritage and involves rehabilitating the highly disconcerting idea of cultural identity. But it was not until the end of the Cold War that it really became a fundamental claim for many social groups, including former decolonised states, since from then onwards, the need for recognition itself became a total social phenomenon that ran through all societies.[23]

A During the Cold War

The question of cultural identity is not a new one and is part of the rationale of the independence movement and of an ambition of emancipated states to return to their roots so as not only to assert their independence but also to fully reconstruct their specific character.[24] From the time of decolonisation, the new or formerly dominated states constantly called for their cultural independence and, to achieve this, for an identity based on the existence of their own cultures, meaning cultures through which they could be distinguished from their former colonisers and which revealed the value of their pre-colonial heritage.[25] In 1956 a founding congress was organised in Paris at which great writers of Third World Africa, including Léopold Sédar Senghor, Aimé Césaire, Richard Wright and Frantz Fanon gathered around Alioune Diop, the editor of *Présence africaine*. Alioune Diop welcomed the participants:

[23] Alain Caille (ed), *La quête de la reconnaissance. Nouveau phénomène social total* (Paris, La découverte, 2007).

[24] Internally, this type of claim goes back further, to 'subaltern anticolonialism' and then to the anticolonialism of elites before independence. See Tamara Sivanadan, 'Anticolonialism, National Liberation and Postcolonial Nation Formation' in Neil Lazarus (ed), *The Cambridge Companion to Postcolonial Literary Studies* (Cambridge, Cambridge University Press, 2004) 41 *ff*.

[25] See Oruno-Denis Lara, L'histoire et l'élaboration d'une identité culturelle' in *Histoire et diversité des cultures* (Paris, United Nations Educational, Scientific and Cultural Organisation, 1984) 309 *ff*.

> If the Bandung meeting is for non-European minds the most important event since the end of the war, I think I can say that this First World Congress of Black Culture will be the second event of this decade for our peoples.[26]

Denunciation of the ravages of colonialism on native cultures and their impoverishment for the benefit of European domination were at the heart of these presentations. There were reports of cultures that were invaded, destroyed and humiliated; structuralist anthropology meant it could be posited that cultures were equivalent and entailed the recognition of the specificity of each culture as a source of identity of peoples and individuals, of their dignity, their flourishing and their creativity. Pre-colonial historical memories that had been buried were rediscovered and contributed to the formation of this identity. Nonetheless, beyond this common diagnosis, the contributions were split into two camps, constantly oscillating between those who radically preached a complete split between the cultures of the colonisers and the colonised and those who advocated a dialectical approach between the two. This was the case of Aimé Césaire with the concept of creolisation and Léopold Senghor with the concept of negritude.[27] Similarly, the relationship to cultures divided intellectuals over the importance they were to be given within the new national liberation states. For some, the new nationalist culture should not turn its back on Europe and the world but understand other cultures and grow richer through contact with them. Others were far more radical in their opposition to the West and in their defence of national cultures which were turned in on themselves; this they saw as a necessary attitude if they were to restore their identities.

The fact of the matter is that beyond the stances of the great Third World thinkers, the protection and the flourishing of their culture became a common objective for all new states fighting for the 'decolonisation of their identities'[28] and struggling to re-appropriate their cultures that had been destroyed or marginalised by colonial domination. In 1966, in the impassioned and revolutionary context of the Tri-continental Conference of Havana, which convened 82 non-aligned countries of Africa, Asia and Latin America, the delegates proclaimed in the Final Declaration the right of peoples to conserve and develop their cultural heritage and undertook to fight against Western 'cultural imperialism' so as to foster their 'true' arts and cultures. In 1976 at Port-Louis, the Organisation of African Unity Member States adopted the Cultural Charter for Africa. In the Preamble, the text recalls that '[C]ultural domination led to the depersonalization of part of the African peoples,

[26] Alioune Diop, Opening Address, *Présence africaine*, June–November 1956, 9 (our translation).

[27] Aimé Césaire, *Discours sur le colonialisme suivi de Discours sur la négritude* (Paris, Présence africaine, 2000) and Léopold Sédar Sengor, *Ce que je crois: Négritude, francité et civilisation* (Paris, Grasset, 1988).

[28] A term borrowed from Alain Renaut, *Un humanisme de la diversité. Essai sur la décolonisation des identités* (Paris, Flammarion, 2009).

falsified their history, systematically disparaged and combatted African values, and tried to replace progressively and officially, their languages by that of the colonizer'.[29]

The African states asserted their commitment to cultural diversity, the return to African values and languages, the conservation of the cultural heritage and many other measures to promote this return to their origins. At Bogota in January 1978, the states of Latin America and the Caribbean even more clearly made 'cultural identity' the basis of peoples' lives which sprang from the past and extended into the future so that it never stood still but was both historical and prospective, constantly moving, improving and developing.[30] In Mexico City in 1982, the United Nations Educational, Scientific and Cultural Organisation (UNESCO) adopted a Declaration on Cultural Policies promoting this idea and calling to fight against all forms of cultural domination. In particular, the Declaration affirmed that 'The assertion of cultural identity therefore contributes to the liberation of peoples. Conversely, any form of domination constitutes a denial or an impairment of that identity'.[31] The connection with development is also asserted, that is, the necessity to adopt an economic and social development that can preserve cultural identities but that is also cultural in itself because 'Culture constitutes a fundamental dimension of the development process' contributing to 'the satisfaction of man's spiritual and cultural aspirations'.[32] People began to think that the development of poor countries failed because the cultural factor was overlooked and that economic development must be reconciled with the different socio-cultural environments. All earlier theories of development were alike in terms of putting economics before cultural factors. Accordingly, the different actors involved considered an alternative development process based more on the resources offered by the populations in question and which was more mindful of their cultural specificities.

The claim as to identity and culture was to be reflected in various ways in the different states. Sophie Bessis clearly shows the paradoxical management of this question in many postcolonial nations that wavered between imitating the West and returning to tradition.[33] The ruling elites played constantly on the two levels. Some tended to promote a strictly nationalist and egalitarian culture, others to open up to a mix of cultures or even to copy Western culture while attempting to preserve their own traditions. This was case of countries like Iran. Yet others were to be much more radical about a return to their roots, their origins or their religions, as in the case of Zaire or of some

[29] www.au.int/en/treaties.

[30] portal.unesco.org/culture/en/ev.php-URL_ID=35221&URL_DO=DO_TOPIC&URL_SECTION=201.html.

[31] Point 2; portal.unesco.org/culture/en/files/35197/11919410061mexico_en.pdf/mexico_en.pdf.

[32] ibid point 10.

[33] Sophie Bessis, *L'Occident et les autres: Histoire d'une suprématie* (Paris, La découverte, 2001) 314 *ff*.

Arab countries. At Mecca in 1962, the Muslim World League (Rabita al-Alam al-Islami) was formed, which in its final Declaration stated that 'Those who disavow Islam and distort its call under the guise of nationalism are actually the most bitter enemies of the Arabs'.[34] Again in the 1960s, tribalism was reinvented with Joseph Désiré Mobutu who undertook the Zairianisation of the Congo and therefore what he thought of as the cultural heritage of Zaire in its purest form. The aim was to develop forms of identity (tribalism, religionism, culturalism), that were sometimes re-invented, on which to base legitimacy. These forms of identity are plainly different from Third World nationalism characterised by secularity and egalitarian socialism (nationalist identity) and from the calls for hybrid cultures (cultural mixing or multiple identities).[35]

The question of culture or identity was therefore certainly not ignored by the Third World during the Cold War. Nonetheless, the forms of domination and stigmatisation, related to colour, culture and the history of colonised peoples were still minor and secondary matters in international (and domestic) terms compared with economic and social issues that implicitly blotted out their significance. The newly decolonised countries did not make a fundamental issue of it, for not only were they concerned primarily with their economic development but, in addition, many thought it would suffice to ensure their material prosperity to secure a postcolonial society that was liberated and at peace, in which identities and cultures would have the scope to thrive. Their priorities lay elsewhere, which was no surprise in view of the conditions of deprivation of some countries and the constant preoccupation with development. But as it so happened, apart from the fact that the economic and social solutions failed, many identity claims that had been thought secondary were in truth just as decisive and were crying out to be heard. The end of the Cold War saw them surge back as absolutely crucial issues and showed that the different manifestations of the desire for identity, which had been voiced before, were indeed a sign that they were a fundamental and unavoidable requirement. The phenomenon was to take on such scope that it would very soon turn, in part, and rightly so, back against the decolonised states. For while denouncing the fact that other states failed to recognise them, the decolonised nations did little themselves to apply the techniques of recognition within their own societies, on the contrary, they bolstered, engendered or allowed many situations to arise where certain social groups, religions, cultures or ethnic groups were stigmatised or marginalised.

[34] Cited by Abdulladh M Sindi, 'King Faisal and Pan-Islamism' in Willard Beling (ed), *King Faisal and the Modernization of Saudi Arabia* (London, Groom Helm, 1980) 186.

[35] They often reflected reversed racism to that of the former coloniser. See Marielle Villasante Cervello, 'La négritude: une forme de racisme héritée de la colonisation française? Réflexions sur l'idéologie négro-africaine en Mauritanie' in Marc Ferro (ed), *Le livre noir du colonialisme* (Paris, Lafont, 2003) 971 *ff*.

B After the Cold War

From 1989 onwards, the question has therefore surfaced again and spread as it has gone beyond the context of decolonisation alone. Everywhere and on all continents claims have arisen relating to identity and culture, a sign that, far from being settled, the problem runs very deep, to the extent that it is now becoming one of the most characteristic and most worrying features of the new globalised society. The new calls take on many forms depending on each particular context, but they are particularly striking when they are the source of a number of very deadly conflicts, as in Rwanda or in the Balkans.[36] This sometimes very violent incursion of the identity issue has upset and surprised a post-Cold War world that thought it had at long last been re-unified around common values. In truth, however, it can be explained by two closely related events: the end of the Cold War and the new episode of globalisation.

Although questions relating to identity and culture have long been discussed by national liberation movements and decolonised states, the Cold War had contributed to stifling most calls from groups and minorities because of the strategic rivalry between the two blocs and the dead weight of the East/West ideological rift that led to two supposedly universal social models being imposed. Cultural (religious, linguistic, national and ethnic) identities were even perceived by several governments as dangerous for the cohesion of the state and their claims were duly put down.[37] And so, when the Cold War ended, a new world of diversity unsurprisingly emerged, there was an awakening of the aspirations of peoples, of minorities and of individuals who were able to speak for themselves, to find their identities that had been trampled on by the East/West stand-off and by nationalist policies and, to do this, to revive their culture, their religion or their nationality even, and so endeavour to find their identity by asserting themselves, if need be, against others, which is a familiar phenomenon in social science.[38] In this new international society that is no longer carried along by the great socially transforming ideologies of the Cold War, suffering and injustice began to express themselves in a different, more personal register that affected the personality of individuals and of groups.

This is to be compounded with the impact of the new episode of globalisation. This is not just economic; it also refers to greater interdependence between peoples, ideas, cultures and knowledge. Now, in terms of culture, globalisation has had paradoxical results.[39] It has been hailed as engendering true

[36] Kalevi J Holsti, *The State War and the State of War* (Cambridge, Cambridge University Press, 1996) and François Thual, *Les conflits identitaires* (Paris, Ellipses, 1995).

[37] United Nations Development Programme 2004 Report, 'Cultural Liberty in Today's Diverse World'; hdr.undp.org/en/reports/global/hdr2004/.

[38] See Denys Cuche, *La notion de culture dans les sciences sociales* (Paris, La découverte, 2010).

[39] See especially Jean-Pierre Warnier, *La mondialisation de la culture* (Paris, La découverte, 2008).

cultural hybrids through the proximity and reduction in distance that it implies. It has also diminished the sense of isolation that reigned in so many poor countries and has provided access to knowledge that did not exist. But it has also been perceived as promoting the hegemony of a single Western (mainly American) cultural model around the world. This hegemony is considered as resting on the new means of communication but also on the legal rules of ultra-liberalised international trade which allow US or Western cultural products to dominate domestic markets.[40] In this, globalisation still raises collective fears as to a possible homogenisation of ways of living and thinking. So it is no mean paradox to see that globalisation has thus contributed to producing cultural and identity-related reactions whereas it was thought it would spell the end of them.

It is in line with the logic of this paradoxical process that globalisation should have particular repercussions on North–South relations, since it has aggravated the old feeling of cultural domination at the same time as it has made for closer ties among populations. While still wanting what globalisation brings, many countries and populations of the South still fear that their cultural identities will continue to be denied overall by a North that continues to maintain its cultural hold via liberal economic globalisation and the outpouring of Western cultural products, for such products break with the traditions of the former colonised or dominated peoples and kill off their cultural specificities. This perception reinforces the feeling that was born at the time of independence, that Third World memory, history and culture would come to be marginalised or destroyed because of the imperialism of the North. Moreover, the communications revolution related to globalisation means that everyone has become increasingly aware of these disparities, which, much more rapidly and massively, bring about collective frustration, feelings of injustice and sporadic revolts against what are perceived as unacceptable effects. In truth, states have themselves been outpaced by identity phenomena; because states have been weakened post-Cold War but also because, in some cases, they have paid for the exacerbation – which they had once played on – of a feeling of national and cultural identity that was defined in the systematic opposition to the West. Proof of this is the situation which countries such as Algeria or Tunisia find themselves in, which, having finally chosen 'openness' with the West, have had to cope with strong religious and identity reactions, especially Islamic reactions, that is, from those whose radical religious and identity ideology they had at one stage fostered.

However, one must not overstate the tropism of North/South relations in appraising a phenomenon that, in truth, involves the entire globe and that therefore extends well beyond the postcolonial divide. Cultural reactions

[40] Undoubtedly promoting the emergence of the 'culture-world' within the meaning of the opinion put forward by Lipovetsky and Serroy, that is, the end of traditional heterogeneity in the sphere of culture and the universalisation of market culture. A 'culture-world' that here becomes worldwide. See Gilles Lipovetsky and Jean Serroy, *La culture-monde. Réponse à une société désorientée* (Paris, O Jacob, 2008) 9.

affect just as much South–South as North–North relations, although the ramifications cannot be developed here: in the North between the East and West or between Europe and the US; in the South between the countries of Africa and Asia. Moreover, these reactions are as much internal as they are external to the countries of the South and North, East and West, which have all experienced the horrors of the awakening of religious, cultural or ethnical identities and which oppose majorities to minorities. This turmoil has broken out notably in the North, in the English-speaking world, where former settlement colonies must face the new demands of the native peoples that they have ignored for so long, or in Europe after the collapse of the Eastern regimes, where populations and minorities have sought to reconstruct their identities that were broken by the ideological straitjacket of communism. But this same turmoil also affects all these countries because of the vast migratory movements that have led to, prior to now, unknown multicultural societies which are putting an end to a certain idea of national homogeneity. Such movements may be sources of social and cultural mixing but they may also be perceived as a threat to the social cohesion of the old national states. In addition, several governments have irresponsibly manipulated the fears these movements raise in order to win back a majority or consolidate power via 'cultural nationalism' or the principle of a purportedly threatened 'national identity'.[41] There is little need to labour this point but at least it can be seen how much the phenomenon becomes 'total' and sometimes fuels irrational fears in return. The problem will not be solved by ignoring it, and the fact is that far more innovative and audacious mechanisms have been set up internationally than in much domestic legislation. To properly appraise these new legal practices requires an awareness that it is a paradigm of recognition that has overtaken the world in the space of two decades.

III International Law and Recognition

A A New Paradigm

The awakening of identities and the multiple contemporary aspirations to recognition have taken on such momentum that we can speak of the emergence of a true paradigm of recognition, that is, a new system of representation that influences and conditions the way in which domestic and international actors act and react in this domain. The fact that the phenomenon has acquired this status should come as no surprise for, however it manifests itself, it also reflects the fundamental need for recognition that is now generally thought to be one of the most essential truths about individuals and groups and of which there is greater awareness with the ending of the Cold War and the advent of

[41] Samuel Huntington, *Who Are We: The Challenges to America's National Identity* (New York, Simon and Schuster, 2004).

the new episode of globalisation.[42] The need for recognition was first investigated in the 1990s by several contemporary authors in light of the situation in democratic societies, along two main lines: that of a policy that respected cultural differences within what had become multicultural societies and that of the denials of recognition within any current democratic society. On the first point, Charles Taylor, for example, has shown that the issue of identities and of cultural differences was at the heart of the fight for recognition in the most varied societies in ethno-cultural terms, that those differences drove countless political and social conflicts and made necessary a general policy of recognition that was 'hospitable to difference'.[43] On the second point, Axel Honneth's work has prompted general thinking based on scorn and lack of respect.[44] Based on a particular re-reading of Hegel, Honneth shows that we all want to escape from scorn and to gain genuine recognition for what we are in three separate spheres: in the private and family sphere where we seek the love of our relatives; in the sphere of cooperation and work where we aspire to the social esteem owed to us as a function of our productivity; and in the public sphere of law and politics where we expect legal respect, that is, equal legal recognition of our standing and our rights.[45]

Other commentators have taken up these ideas, reintroducing or deepening the concept of identity or by relating them to the demand for justice. It can be considered that the need for recognition appears to be based more generally on the idea that individuals or groups aim in the same way for the recognition of their individual and collective identity[46] and that this identity is determined in part by their relationship to others. The concept of identity refers to a system of mental representation of the self and others that is deep-seated in each individual (and each group) and that helps to define them. Individually, it implies that people are defined not just in some abstract way by a common identity, having equal dignity with others, but also by a specific identity that is determined by their belonging to cultures and by their specific values. People's identities are therefore intimately linked to the cultural systems in which individuals and groups live, to their changes and their transmission from one generation to the next.[47] If the need for recognition of this

[42] See Tzvetan Todorov, *La peur des barbares. Au-delà du choc des civilisations* (Paris, R Laffont, 2008) 129 *ff*. On the sociological causes and manifestations of this phenomenon, see Alain Caille (ed), *La quête de la reconnaissance. Nouveau phénomène social total* (n 23).

[43] Taylor, *Multiculturalism. Examining the Politics of Recognition* (n 19). See also Patrick Savidan, *Le multiculturalisme* (Paris, PUF, Que sais-je?, 2009).

[44] Honneth, *The Struggle for Recognition* (n 19).

[45] ibid 92 *ff*. See also the interpretation by Paul Ricoeur, *Parcours de la reconnaissance* (Paris, Gallimard, 2004) 293–340. Analyses based on these foundational works have been made in moral, political and social philosophy but also in anthropological and psychoanalytical sociology.

[46] Bruno Ollier, 'Les identités collectives: comment comprendre une question politique brûlante?' in *Les identités collectives à l'heure de la mondialisation* (Paris, Les Essentiels d'Hermès, CNRS Editions, 2009) 8 *ff*.

[47] Stuart Hall, *Identités et cultures. Politique des Cultural Studies* (Paris, Ed Amsterdam, 2008). This work is a collection of some of Hall's essays in French.

identity is analysed sociologically as a fundamental requirement of human beings, which can no longer be defined just by seeking self-interest and can no longer be reduced to the *homo oeconomicus* of the Utilitarians, but by the fact that people aspire just as much, if not more, to be recognised by others for what they are.[48]

Hence for some there are specific injustices that are cultural and not socio-economic.[49] Injustice results more specifically from what I shall call here 'denials of recognition' in the broad sense, which arise from disregard for that common or specific identity, from the disregard for the value of a culture, a way of life, of the dignity of an individual as a person and from the infringement of their physical integrity.[50] Such denials of recognition may be acts designed to marginalise or stigmatise or to culturally dominate others which mean that individuals, peoples, minorities, groups or even certain states, not only cannot be full members of a society (domestic or international) but cannot be respected for what they are and cannot live and act in accordance with their cultural preferences. These denials then cause feelings of indignation, lack of self-esteem, humiliation and finally of injustice, that give rise to unbearable suffering and can be radicalised by engendering extremely violent conflicts. To avoid conflict and to satisfy the fundamental need for recognition of identity that is in everyone, one must be able to ensure respect for that identity by others and by society as a whole, which, given that we are dealing with cultural infringements, implies altering the cultural or symbolic representations of society. This gives rise to a whole series of measures that are liable to be adopted politically and legally and that range from granting equal status to the re-evaluation of disregarded identities, via changes in means of communication and representation to be more favourable to identities and to the protection or promotion of the cultural products of the groups or individuals that are the subject of discrimination.

[48] Alain Caillé, *Théorie anti-utilitariste de l'action. Fragments d'une sociologie générale* (Paris, La découverte, 2009) 5.

[49] Fraser, *Qu'est-ce que la justice sociale? Reconnaissance et redistribution* (Paris, La découverte, 2011) 13 *ff*. To stay within my remit, I am summarising here a much debated and more complex subject. For example, transposing the issue of recognition to the domain of justice is a question that divides. See the exchange between Honneth and Fraser in *Redistribution or Recognition? A Political Philosophical Exchange* (London, Verso, 2003). Besides, Fraser relies principally on 'social identity' and not individual identity and remains very reticent about what she calls 'identity politics', which she interprets very restrictively. See especially Patchen Markell, *Bound by Recognition* (Princeton, Princeton University Press, 2003) 19 *ff*. This is why, while using the double formulation of justice she introduces and setting myself in the field of justice, I am far closer to the views of Charles Taylor on identity, which are more relevant when seeking to conceptualise existing international legal practice.

[50] The use of recognition has become so commonplace today that it refers to a whole range of experience, injustice and suffering that may seem different in kind. Many of these experiences are deliberately lumped together here which are sometimes considered differently by authors and not necessarily from the standpoint of injustice. For different views see, for example, Honneth, *The Struggle for Recognition* (n 19) 130 *ff* or Fraser, *Qu'est-ce que la justice sociale?* (n 49) 83 *ff*.

In this it is easier to understand the gesture which involved internationally adopting several legal instruments on identity and culture and so responding to several different types of denials of recognition, with the more or less clearly expressed wish to take charge of them, which testifies to a rather remarkable development of international law in this direction.

B A New Body of Law

It is in this way that in an ever more complex, ever less stable, post-Cold War, international society that is beset by multiple calls for recognition of identities and cultures, a new branch of international law has emerged which is that of recognition. It is not formulated as such internationally but it is no less clearly pregnant, to my mind, both in the multiple demands about identity and culture made in the language of law and in the different legal solutions proposed by international law and that all clearly converge in this direction. Accordingly, it ought to be identified for what it is and we should allow ourselves to speak of the international law of recognition to describe a set of legal institutions, discourses, practices and principles that had not heretofore been sufficiently theorised and grouped together, although they have the same subject matter that sets them apart from others in that it relates specifically to the need for recognition. As a consequence, then, this international law of recognition appears as the exact counterpart of the international law of development and as forming an essential component of what might be a fair international society.

It must be made clearer, however, what this need for recognition is that present-day international law attempts to answer, because it differs from the first process of the recognition of others that decolonisation led to and that was based on a policy of 'equal dignity'. Henceforth, to take up a very suggestive formulation by Alain Touraine, peoples but also states, groups and minorities want to be recognised by international law as 'equal but different'.[51] They clamour not just, as decolonised states did, for legal equality that grants the same legal status to all despite their differences, but for the legal recognition of certain differences that protect their difference. In other words, they no longer settle for being recognised by international law as simply equal, which implies having equal rights, but they want to be respected as different, as belonging to cultures or to groups which themselves are recognised as particular and that found their identity, which may imply rights that can differ.[52] The provisions adopted are not temporary rules as in development law, based on the difference in circumstances between states and designed to ensure a degree of equalisation of conditions, which, if it were achieved, would cause

[51] Alain Touraine, *Pourrons-nous vivre ensemble? Egaux et différents* (Paris, Fayard, 1997).
[52] On this distinction between the two processes of recognition, see Taylor, *Multiculturalism* (n 19).

those rules to disappear; no, the provisions adopted aim to enshrine existing differences permanently. In light of these distinctions, it is at last realised that this new form of recognition involves a completely different representation of identity, for it is no longer a shared identity through equal status that is claimed, but a specific identity, meaning that states, peoples, groups or individuals consider themselves as authentically unique.[53] Where the post-colonial international law of the Cold War was once based exclusively on the abstract liberal principles of formal equality and equal rights, post-Cold War international law is less abstract and progressively approves an international policy of recognition based on the right to be different and the right to preserve one's cultural identity.

It remains then to make a closer study of existing legal practice to show in what way and why law has been mobilised internationally in some specific instances to meet the problems of identity and culture and the aspirations to recognition. It is proposed that this investigation be conducted by concentrating on three areas that make up this new international law on recognition, since they bear on three elements that are essential in preserving identities and cultures. The first area is that of recognition of the diversity of cultures which aims to combat the phenomena of cultural domination related to globalisation in particular; the second is the granting of particular rights that preserve the identity of a group or an individual; the third is that of recognition of the wrongs inflicted in the past and the reparation of historical crimes, an area that relates to the construction of identities over time and no longer in space and by which it can be seen how states, peoples or individuals try to reconstruct their 'narrative identity'. From this study it very clearly appears that a legal status of difference is gradually being established in international law that stands alongside the legal status of equality and that this change truly does meet a very deep-seated need of our present time. But it is also confirmed that this evolution remains oddly fragile in some respects and raises many questions that are not necessarily resolved and several dark sides to which we shall return. How can the contemporary need for recognition be satisfied internationally? How can one ascertain which identities are to be recognised and protected? Whose identities? Because everyone wants to be recognised, should all cultures and identities be legally enshrined? How does the legal preservation of certain cultures and identities sit with other branches of law, including human rights and economic international law? The fact is, for example, that the 'general thirst for recognition' that characterises our age has ambivalent effects. It reflects aspirations to recognition that are legitimate coming from groups, peoples, states or individuals that have long been stigmatised and it sees a possible path towards a solution in law. But how can one fail to see that this thirst for recognition sometimes also expresses the need for

[53] These developments are inspired by Sylvie Mesure and Alain Renaut, *Alter ego. Les paradoxes de l'identité démocratique* (Paris, Flammarion, 1999) 9 *ff*.

social certainty, at any price, in a globalised world that deprives individuals, groups or peoples of their bearings, even within more community-based societies. This, it can be readily seen, might lead them to manipulate certain rules of the law of recognition by way of reassurance in proclaiming radical and fundamentalist identities that directly infringe people's fundamental rights.[54]

[54] See especially Amin Maalouf, *In the Name of Identity: Violence and the Need to Belong* (New York, Arcade, 2000); Amartya Sen, *Identity and Violence: The Illusion of Destiny* (New York, WW Norton, 2006) and Arjun Appadurai, *Fear of Small Numbers. An Essay on the Geography of Anger* (Durham and London, Duke University Press, 2006).

6

Law and Cultural Diversity

ETHNO-CULTURAL PLURALISM IS a very ancient phenomenon in human history inasmuch as human societies have always been the vectors of thousands of different cultures because of the movement and mixing of populations, trade and also because of the countless conflicts that have set them against each other. It is this diversity which is intrinsic to human life, that has finally been taken on board by post-Cold War international law because of a consensus that has suddenly formed with the new conviction that there is a 'heritage of humanity' to be protected. The main explanation for this very broad agreement lies in the hitherto unknown force of attraction of the paradigm of recognition and the requirement to protect cultures as a necessity, and through them identities, some of which seem to be under threat of extinction.[1]

One could probably delve deeper into the sociological phenomena at issue here, but it can be taken as established at least that cultures reflect what it is that makes human groups distinctive and so reflect their collective identity within which individual cultural identities are constructed.[2] It can therefore readily be understood that whatever upholds and fosters the diversity of cultures can play a fundamental part in the flourishing of cultural identities and this is what is attested to by the 2005 United Nations Educational, Scientific and Cultural Organisation (UNESCO) Convention on the Protection and Promotion of the Diversity of Cultural Expressions. It should not be forgotten that the Convention does not merely reflect the concern to safeguard economic interests in the cultural domain, although they do of course have their place, but it also reflects the necessity to adapt to a world which, since the end of the Cold War, has experienced a slide away from 'politics' towards 'culture', a world which sees issues of identity, culture and economics intertwine and which makes respect for cultural identities a new requirement.

[1] With respect to the internal affairs of democratic states, see Patrick Savidan, *Le multiculturalisme* (Paris, PUF, Que sais-je?, 2009) 34 *ff*.

[2] Discussion about the definition of culture and cultures is recurrent. That proposed by UNESCO has the merit of being internal to international law practice, which is our subject here. UNESCO's Universal Declaration on Cultural Diversity reaffirms that 'culture should be regarded as the set of distinctive spiritual, material, intellectual and emotional features of society or a social group and that it encompasses, in addition to art and literature, lifestyles, ways of living together, value systems, traditions and beliefs'. Preamble, Declaration of 2 November 2001; unesdoc.unesco.org/images/0012/001271/127160m.pdf.

In this respect, the impact of globalisation evoked earlier was decisive to the framing of the 2005 Convention. As has been seen, globalisation fosters closer relations and exchanges but it also fosters conflicts between diverse and plural cultures that are no longer stifled by the two-way ideological split of the Cold War. These conflicts may also be driven by states fearing they will be dominated by a particular culture whose expansion may be favoured by the generalisation of free trade and the current deregulation for the benefit of the more powerful. Admittedly, and it is hardly surprising, the cultural hegemony of American culture is feared more than any other. It will be recalled that the 1980s, when the ultraliberal economic Washington consensus was elaborated, was the time when the United States under Ronald Reagan and the United Kingdom under Margaret Thatcher slammed the door on UNESCO. The aim of the two political leaders was clearly to set up a thoroughgoing Western neoliberal order in this domain for the benefit of English-speaking cultural industries and to put an end to what they considered the anti-Western waywardness of the UN system. Moreover, 20 years later, the attacks of 11 September 2001 and the ensuing fight against Islamic terrorism have raised new points of contention, which are more cultural than economic, between Western and non-Western cultures and have convinced some Westerners of the need to see their own culture prevail, under threat from other civilisations or the new 'barbarians'.[3] But these sticking points and Western cultural predominance have also been compounded by South–South regional hegemonies that should not be underestimated as they reproduce, albeit on a smaller scale, the same logic of domination as that of the United States on a global scale, notably with the cultural hegemony of Egypt in the Arab world, Brazil and Mexico in the Latin American world, and India and China in much of Asia.

The phenomenon of domination is so powerful that it will eventually deprive those who are subject to it the opportunity of developing their own cultures and therefore of protecting their identities. Bearing this in mind, therefore, it was essential that states should enshrine the legal principle of the 'diversity of cultural expressions', as they did in 2005.

I From Cultural Exception to the Diversity of Cultural Expressions

A Cultural Exception

The principle of 'cultural exception' is that which was first invoked most frequently in international law and which, in the post-war years, served as a defence for European states against the hegemony of American culture. At

[3] See Pierre Hassner, *La violence et la paix. Tome 2: La terreur et l'empire* (Paris, Seuil, 2006).

that time, it was not a matter that involved the South. From the post-war period onwards, the principle of cultural exception was at the heart of a bitter legal and political controversy that opposed Europeans and Americans over the very substantial commercial gains the US wished to derive with the Marshall Plan, but also over a different conception of culture between them. Without going back over the many aspects of the discussion on the subject, it can be recalled that two conceptions were and still are at loggerheads. The European conception is that cultural goods and services are not goods but creations that enhance the cultural life of each people and its identity, with the result that they cannot be subjected to the same legal rules as other wares. They should benefit from a special regime that takes the name of 'cultural exception'. The US conception views cultural goods and services as wares like any others and therefore liable to the same common rules of free trade.

The principle of cultural exception then resurfaced at the time of the 1994 talks among General Agreement on Tariffs and Trade (GATT) Member States (Uruguay Round) over the General Agreement on Trade in Services (GATS). It was integrated in a very limited way in the form of an absence of supply in the audio-visual sectors and through a series of exemptions to the most favoured nation clause, making it possible to remove, to some degree, some cultural productions from the laws of the market.[4] However, there were many who felt it was a failure in view of what was at stake and so wished not to confine themselves to the World Trade Organisation (WTO) and to the commercial aspects in discussing the legal status of culture and cultural exchange. UNESCO seemed like the natural forum for reinvigorating legal reflection in this area. Now that these questions had been brought back before it, this was the turning point for UNESCO and it consequently revived the old idea of 'diversity of cultures' by proclaiming a Universal Declaration on the subject, working to draw up a binding legal instrument that might truly protect and promote that diversity.

Now, this orientation, which was to be enshrined in the adoption of the Convention in 2005, was not self-evident in view of the history of UNESCO, as surprising as that may seem, for the principle of protection of cultural diversity was only considered later on as something that ought to be an objective of the international community. This can be seen if this development is put into historical perspective.

B The Diversity of Cultural Expressions: The 2005 UNESCO Convention

Culture truly became a worldwide concern after the Second World War with the creation of UNESCO on 16 November 1945. But the new organisation arose entirely from concerns about war, which was perceived at the time as a wholesale defeat of the mind, and not strictly from any desire to open up to

[4] See Serge Regourd, *L'exception culturelle*, 2nd edn (Paris, PUF, 2004) 11 *ff*.

the world and for the cultural de-centring of Western positions. The establishment of UNESCO responded foremost to a desire for peace on the part of a Euro-American world that had been traumatised by war, while cultural diversity did not feature among the organisation's original objectives.

First of all, it should be recalled that it was primarily over questions of information and communication that states were to square up to one another within UNESCO during the Cold War. From 1973 onwards, the Third World states, led by the Non-Aligned Movement, attempted to impose on UNESCO a New World Information and Communication Order (NWICO) that might be the counterpart of the NIEO (passed by the General Assembly in 1974). They decried the imbalance in information exchanges and the infringement of their political and economic independence which that implied. They also called for the legal preservation of a wealth of information sources and channels that might ensure their independence. However, NWICO largely lost all credibility because the states that clamoured for it engaged in national policies of repression of the freedom of information and authoritarian control over all media. The historical context of the time meant that many states, including the USSR, were demanding the establishment of NWICO internationally while violating the most elementary rights to information at home. Very soon the NWICO became a political issue that crystallised the ideological opposition in the two camps and caused the most serious crisis UNESCO had ever experienced with the withdrawal of the United States and the United Kingdom in the 1980s.

Then, in terms of culture proper and no longer of information, it can be observed that cultural diversity was not originally one of UNESCO's objectives. It is true that Article 1(3) of the Constitution speaks of 'preserving the independence, integrity and fruitful diversity of the cultures and educational systems of the States Members'.[5] However, that Article is at best quite a conventional national competence clause, the goal of which is not to preserve diversity but simply to prevent any intervention by the Organisation in states' internal cultural affairs. Given the historical post-war context, it was world peace that was the primary objective of UNESCO and culture appeared as one of the best instruments to secure that peace. It was a means to an end. The process to be implemented was quite straightforward: through the spread of culture it was hoped to construct the 'defences of peace' 'in the minds of men' and secure the 'support of the peoples of the world' in the fight against racism and intolerance (Preamble), and it was yet more profoundly assumed that the development of the arts, of ideas and knowledge, might ultimately bring mankind to share the same values and culture. Even the original philosophy of UNESCO appears to be a world away from the promotion of cultural diversity since, in the words of its then director, Julian Huxley, the

[5] UNESCO Constitution of 16 November 1945; portal.unesco.org/en/ev.php-URL_ID=15244&URL_DO=DO_TOPIC&URL_SECTION=201.html.

organisation's task was 'to help the emergence of a single world culture' that would make the world one.[6] And unsurprisingly in the aftermath of the war, the cultural unity in question was a 'new humanism' of a Western type, based on science and education, that could go beyond the differences between cultures and ideological divides and also transcend its Euro-American intellectual roots to found a universal culture.

Even so, UNESCO always considered that the plurality of cultures was an inescapable fact underpinning its action and the most notable development in this domain reflects the way in which it was to gradually transform this plurality into a legal principle of diversity. It so happened that the 1972 UN Conference on the Human Environment in Stockholm associated the theme of natural biodiversity with that of cultural biodiversity, considering these were two realities that were equally threatened by the Western model of growth. In the same year, UNESCO adopted the World Heritage Convention linking the conservation of nature and culture that inaugurated the Organisation's very active policy to protect cultural property and peoples. Twenty years later, at the Rio Earth Summit, came the introduction of the odd but highly suggestive idea of preserving the equilibrium of 'cultural ecosystems'. In Rio, the Convention on Biological Diversity was adopted and the Convention on the Diversity of Cultural Expressions of 2005 echoed it. In 1995, UNESCO launched the idea of 'creative diversity'. This was aimed at 'the flourishing of human existence in its several forms and as a whole'.[7] But above all it was to lead to clarification and consolidation of the idea of 'cultural diversity' which, because of fears prompted by the growing strength of globalisation in the 2000s, was eventually to be solemnly declared 'common heritage of humanity' (Article 1) in the Universal Declaration on Cultural Diversity unanimously adopted by the UNESCO Conference in 2001, an essential guiding text that marked a turning point in this field.[8] The analogy with nature and the living world was taken up again as the Declaration considers 'cultural diversity is as necessary for humankind as biodiversity is for nature'. Even if it is dubious in its principles,[9] the comparison between the diversity of cultures and the diversity of living organisms has a strategic purpose above all: it is a reminder that we get upset over the threat to certain life forms but not about threats to arts and minority languages that affect the cultural heritage of mankind. That same year the UN declared the 21 May as World Cultural Diversity Day for Dialogue and Development. In 2004 the United Nations Development

[6] Julian Huxley, *Unesco. Its Purpose and its Philosophy*, Preparatory Commission of UNESCO (London, 1946) 61; unesdoc.unesco.org/images/0006/000681/068197eo.pdf.

[7] Report of the World Commission on Culture and Development. *Our Creative Diversity* (Paris, UNESCO, 1996); unesdoc.unesco.org/images/0010/001055/105586e.pdf.

[8] portal.unesco.org/en/ev.php-URL_ID=13179&URL_DO=DO_TOPIC&URL_SECTION=201.html.

[9] Jürgen Habermas, *L'intégration républicaine* (Paris, Fayard, 1996) 226 *ff.* It is particularly problematic as it suggests an evolution of cultures similar to a biological evolution of species: Claude Lévi-Strauss, *Anthropologie structurale II*, 2nd edn (Paris, Plon, 1996) 385 *ff.*

Programme (UNDP) gave over its annual report to 'Cultural Liberty in Today's Diverse World' and announced that 'cultural diversity is one of the central challenges of our time'.[10] This entire development culminated on 20 October 2005 with UNESCO adopting the Convention on the Protection and Promotion of the Diversity of Cultural Expressions (which came into force on 18 March 2007).[11]

Of the 154 countries present, only the United States and Israel voted against it and only four countries (Australia, Honduras, Liberia and Nicaragua) abstained. This shows the extent of international consensus about an instrument which, once it came into force, became legally binding on all those who ratified it. And yet it is not that the United States did not pull out all the stops to try to oppose it during negotiations. The United States re-joined UNESCO in 2003 in order to undermine talks on cultural diversity. For the US, cultural diversity is just the cultural face of a new NWICO that must be countered; these are two sides of the same coin designed to impede the free movement of information and cultural products and the freedom of any individual to be able to choose the culture and cultural products they wish. But where NWICO had the Cold War as its backdrop, cultural diversity has globalisation. So things had changed entirely and the United States was to find itself progressively isolated. Its patent bad faith in negotiating the Convention – when it claimed to be combatting cultural diversity in the name of 'freedom', whereas it made most of the world's profits because of that 'freedom' – saw almost all the other participants rally against it, especially the developing countries 'in what took on the appearance of a fight against hegemony'.[12] Even apart from the fact that the figures show how cynical this line of argument is in respect of the profits the United States makes – in the context of total disequilibrium of the economic balance of power, freedom here benefits might alone – it does not want to see or understand what was becoming evident in the course of negotiations, namely the fundamental connection between culture and identity and the need to respect the identity of peoples through their cultures. The refusal to shift its point of view from the centre and to base it on something other than its own experience prevented

[10] UNDP Report, *Cultural Liberty in Today's Diverse World*, 2004.

[11] The question of information has not been abandoned but has evolved to be considered less in state to state relations than contemplated in terms of access to information for civil society and the creation of independent media. UNESCO's New Communication Strategy, adopted in 1989, marked the end of NWICO and reflected this turnaround, indicative of the post-Cold War world, away from states and towards individuals and civil society. For many, the lesson to be learnt from NWICO is to continue to protect cultures and information flows while moving towards more democratic media, greater freedom of expression and even recognition of a right to communicate.

[12] Hélène Ruiz-Fabri, 'Introduction' in Hélène Ruiz-Fabri (ed), *La convention de l'UNESCO sur la promotion et la protection de la diversité des expressions culturelles. Premier bilan et défis juridiques* (Paris, Société de législation comparée, 2010) 40. On the economic issues, see especially Yves Theoret (ed), *David contre Goliath. La convention sur la protection et la promotion de la diversité des expressions culturelles de l'UNESCO* (Montréal, Hurubise, HMH, 2008) especially 62 *ff*.

the United States from understanding this issue in a very different context to the Cold War, based on the paradigm of recognition and from seeing to what extent European and Third World countries, and pretty much most of the planet, might feel culturally dominated and not just in terms of their financial interests and sovereign independence but more deeply still in what it is that constitutes their identity.

The fact is that the Convention is far from negligible in its scope. The diversity of cultural expressions became a standard to adhere to in itself. Ethno-cultural plurality was an accepted fact; but this is a transition to a norm, to a legal principle of 'diversity' designed to preserve and promote this 'plurality', which engenders new rights and obligations that extend much further than 'cultural exception'. With the principle of the 'diversity of cultural expressions',[13] the principle of 'cultural diversity' is made relative, even if it continues to produce these effects within the WTO framework. In fact, there is continuity between the two principles but they have not been introduced at the same level and one is more restrictive than the other. The principle of cultural diversity or of diversity of cultural expressions aims primarily to safeguard cultures and the cultural policies of each country against possible domination by a single cultural model because of the ever greater economic liberalisation of trade. It too, like the principle of cultural exception, is part of the logic of the need for states to fight against the excessively liberal importing of dominant cultural products, for the hegemony of the industrialised or emerging states on the markets of poor countries is still just as much of a threat to the diversity of their cultural expressions. It relies in the same way on the idea that cultural products and property are not wares like others and that they must be removed from the common regime of trade.

Their common points apart, the principle of cultural diversity is nonetheless profoundly different from the principle of cultural exception, in many ways relating particularly to its nature and its scope, and in such a way that it invites us to take a whole new look at the issues involved. The most significant thing in this respect is to observe from the outset, taking up the philosophy of the Universal Declaration of 2001 (Article 1), that the text of the Convention roots the principle of the diversity of cultural expressions in a conception of culture that very clearly associates culture in the broad sense with the identity of individuals and groups (Preamble, 2005 Convention).[14] And so this conception invites us to unequivocally understand that any domination of one culture by another seriously jeopardises individuals and groups in what gives them their precious and unique character and individuality. The concept of 'cultural property' defined shortly after confirms, if there were need, this fundamental connection between culture and identity since it is defined as

[13] I shall not explore the distinction between 'cultural diversity' and 'diversity of cultural expressions', both concepts being defined in the 2005 Convention but only the latter being the subject matter of the Convention directly. For convenience, they are used interchangeably here.

[14] unesdoc.unesco.org/images/0014/001429/142919e.pdf.

a symbolic good that is a vector of 'identity, value and meaning' (Preamble and Article 1(g)), in the same way as the concept of cultural content that is defined relative to identities (Article 4.2). The vast scope of application of the principle (Article 3) suggests, in another way, its broader and virtually infinite perspectives, if it is considered that there is culture in everything, since far from being limited to audio-visual domains and cinema, it encompasses all 'cultural expressions', a particularly vague term that refers to an inevitably subjective and potentially very broad interpretation of the object of the Convention. As for the legal regime provided for by the Convention, it will be observed that unlike the cultural exception, the principle of diversity of cultural expressions is not an exception within a system of commercial liberalisation but has the status of a general rule. In this, whereas the cultural exception is a struggle for targeted protectionism, cultural diversity is generally applicable. Besides, this general legal regime contains three elements that seem highly significant.

First is the fundamental principle around which all the rights and obligations of the Convention revolve, namely, that it is recognised that each culture has equal dignity and therefore deserves equal respect (Article 2.3). Then, as the Convention itself states, the objective is a double one: the aim is not just to preserve the diversity of cultural expressions but also to promote that diversity. The faculty of preserving different cultural expressions legitimates the national measures taken by states to protect their cultural creations, property and products, which runs counter to the principle of liberalisation of trade. But the objective of promoting diversity goes even further as it means that diversity is considered as intrinsically beneficial and compels states to encourage ever more cultural diversity, heterogeneity and multiplicity. As a third point, it should be emphasised that states are under an obligation to apply in their own territory the principle of diversity they wish to see applied in international relations (Article 5.2).[15] Externally, the principle of diversity commands equal treatment of the cultures of each state and the right to respect of each in its singularity, the right also, sought primarily by states, to freely establish their own cultural policies and to be in a position to preserve them. That is to say that a state has the legal opportunity, insofar as it observes fundamental human rights, to limit its citizens' access to foreign cultures so as to protect their own. Internally, however, states also have legal obligations inasmuch as they must protect and promote diversity in their own territories and therefore respect sub-state or indigenous cultures and promote individual creative freedom and freedom of expression. Besides, it is significant that the 2005 Convention is presented by UNESCO as an agreement 'that ensures artists, cultural professionals, practitioners and citizens worldwide can create, produce, disseminate and enjoy a broad range of cul-

[15] See also Articles 6, 7, 8, 10 and 11 in particular. Article 5(2) stipulates an obligation of 'consistency' and not 'conformity' with the Convention.

tural goods, services and activities, including their own'.[16] Whereby we find again the tipping point of international law that we have already seen several times towards the rights of individuals and more generally a conception of the human being understood in terms of freedom, that is, someone who must be given the opportunity to make 'choices' (Article 2.1). This is a humanistic conception whose constant repetition through the many instruments studied shows the extent to which it is at work deep down in all classical liberal international law to the point of it becoming, unnoticed, the centre of the entire edifice of international law. This is a trend that is so powerful that we shall have the opportunity to observe its effects later on.

In any event, the principle of cultural diversity (and of the diversity of cultural expressions) here without contest takes on the nature of a fundamental principle of international law and it is an essential reflection of the new paradigm of recognition. Against the exponential character of homogenising globalisation, this principle alone enshrines diversity and singularity to stave off the identical repetition of the same model. That the principle of diversity should also be at the heart of states' defence of their economic interests and their cultural industries is an obvious fact that does not in any way remove this strong and essential dimension, the effects of which can be measured with respect to the colonial and postcolonial history of international law. The enshrinement of the principle of cultural diversity tends to end centuries of denial of recognition of customs, cultures and traditions of certain peoples who have been dominated and marginalised for so long. And it emerges from this that the 2005 Convention appears as a decisive legal instrument that, provided it is properly applied, can contribute to significantly altering the forms of self-representation and the structures of cultural and symbolic evaluation that still dominate on a world scale through the legally recognised position and the dignity at last rendered to the culture or civilisation of each. It is no longer a matter of passively accepting the domination of a cultural model; nor is it a matter of leaning towards the formation of a universal culture as in 1946, since, on the contrary, the very principle of 'diversity' consecrates the plurality of all existing cultures. In addition, by the same token, the affirmation of identity by any human being or people within their culture becomes meaningful. Assuming that, by virtue of specific rights conferred on members of minorities or specific cultural rights, each human being could affirm their cultural identity, what would this be worth if it were expressed in a framework that itself were culturally dominated? Lastly, this is a decisive inflection, at least in law, that is beginning to operate here and that involves the right of recognition as a remedy to a specific type of injustice, for it amounts to affirming that earlier classical international law, which was liberal, pluralistic and formal, was unable to satisfactorily meet the need

[16] www.unesco.org/new/en/culture/themes/cultural-diversity/diversity-of-cultural-expressions/the-convention/what-is-the-convention/.

for respect of different cultures and that its would-be 'neutrality' in cultural matters, based on the respect of equal sovereign freedom of states in cultural and economic matters, did not work and amounts to imposing de facto one or more dominant cultures (and therefore one or more dominant cultural identities). As a consequence, in a true reversal of perspective, it is the legal recognition of cultural diversity that was to enable the consolidation of states' sovereign equality in cultural terms, while this was strained by the formalism of classical liberal international law. In other words, the enshrinement in law of the principle of cultural diversity becomes the instrument for greater equality among states.[17]

II Difficulties and Questions

For as powerful and interesting as it is, the principle of cultural diversity still raises a number of questions. Apart from the strictly legal problems related to the 2005 Convention that will not fail to arise, two difficulties of a more general nature need to be raised here. They are familiar enough now and have been widely discussed in the social sciences, but it seems important to resituate them in terms of international law.

The first difficulty stems from the fear that the principle of diversity, as it is enshrined in several international legal instruments, might be construed and applied for traditionalist or regressive ends to compartmentalise cultures and therefore people within those cultures. The principle of diversity enshrines for good in law the fact that there is no longer just one single model of civilisation and culture, but a multiplicity of cultures and civilisations that have equal dignity which are to be promoted. Now, some commentators see in this not a remedy for cultural injustice but a far greater evil. The risk is that groups or members of those groups might no longer be defined by multiple membership, by the possibility of a hybrid or cross-bred cultural identity, but that they might be characterised and recognised as such on a solely ethno-cultural and even sometimes ethno-racial basis, which would be that of a single group and would pin them down to a particular status for good. Moreover, one might, in addition, by the same token rekindle conflicts between groups, minorities or states that would perceive their culture in a wholly irreducible way and in which each would tend to want to make their own cultural system of values prevail over others. The principle of diversity would then have a double and paradoxically regressive consequence for a principle that purports to be emancipatory: collectively, it would reactivate ethno-cultural or civilisational conflict among groups, regions or states, and on an individual level, it might mean individuals being locked up in 'identity dictatorships' or

[17] See Savidan, *Le multiculturalisme* (n 1) 80 *ff* for considerations on domestic law that shape these views.

conversely being arbitrarily excluded from their cultural communities. This would cause new denials of recognition of the culture of groups and of the plural identity of individuals.

As seen, such an interpretation relies on a narrowly differentialist and relativist understanding of the principle of diversity that leads to identifying any culture with a sort of entity that retreats into itself where any external influence is perceived as an infringement of its identity. What for some is necessary, as it is a matter of maintaining authenticity as a criterion of cultural identity and what for others is just an irreversible effect of the contemporary development of cultures; that development supposedly leads to inevitable conflict between the world's major cultures which would naturally tend to reject any outside interference and would seek, at the same time, to impose their model of values on others. This was Samuel Huntington's argument about the 'clash of civilisations', which was very fashionable in the 1990s and 2000s, as it included within a coherent argument a whole complex of fears of the United States over the way the post-Cold War world was changing.[18] In what was a very interesting attempt to achieve a fresh understanding of the changes in international relations and future conflicts, Huntington begins with one of the fundamental postulates on which the paradigm of recognition stands: cultural predominance. This explains, he claims, why cultures, and even more so the great cultural complexes that form civilisations, have become the driving forces of international society, in place and instead of the role played previously, during the Cold War, by ideologies, nationalist ideas or socio-economic inequalities. It is cultures that are to become the new catalyst for antagonism in international society, for the great civilisations, that are growing in power with the new context of the end of the Cold War, notably the Confucian and Islamic civilisation, inevitably lean towards universality just like Western civilisation and will therefore threaten the West itself in its own values.[19] In which case, the West would have no alternative but to react and defend itself to ensure the survival of its own culture and civilisation.[20] Hence Huntington's view that future conflicts will be mostly cultural and the new blocs that will wage war will no longer be ideological but civilisational. In truth, it will be agreed that, without necessarily possessing the countless failings it has been caught up in, such a study raises far more problems than it solves and the simplicity of some of its analyses has persuaded some but put off the great majority of readers. Several observers have subsequently extended and radicalised Huntington's view by considering that the attacks of 11 September confirmed, in a particularly tragic manner, the truth of his analyses, while others, who were more numerous, excoriated his Manichean arguments that completely ignore the plural, complex, fluid and interactive phenomenon of civilisations, that ignore

[18] Samuel Huntington, *The Clash of Civilisations and the Remaking of World Order* (New York, Simon and Schuster, 1996).

[19] ibid 183 *ff*.

[20] ibid 301 *ff*.

the complex sedimentation that makes a culture, mixing, the multiple hybridisation among cultures, especially at the time of globalisation, to the benefit of membership of cultures or civilisations that are considered to be fixed and very often mutually exclusive.[21]

Beyond these often relevant criticisms, it cannot be denied, however, that Huntington testified to an acute awareness of the decisive importance of cultural factors in the post-Cold War world and that, at least apart from certain obvious aporias in his thought, he sparked a genuine debate about these essential questions to which there is no doubt cultural diversity must be connected.[22] Although it must be realised that the effect achieved was not consistent with what Huntington recommended, for, paradoxically, if one thinks of the conflict-torn society that inevitably arose in the months following the attacks of 11 September, faced with the risk of a cultural clash that was suddenly felt right at the heart of numerous societies, a genuine internationalist impetus occurred in favour of a dialogue between civilisations and of whatever might secure exchanges between cultures and the understanding of the Other, with the renewed conviction that such a dialogue was becoming a decisive feature for maintaining peace. A whole series of actions and texts adopted internationally bore testimony to this, which aimed to reinstate that old principle of dialogue to give it renewed importance and vigour. This was the case with regard to the uninterrupted succession of resolutions adopted by the UN General Assembly to this end, the constant association made by UNESCO between respect for diversity and dialogue, or the creation under the aegis of the UN in 2005, further to the Islamist attacks in Madrid in 2004, of an Organisation of the Alliance of Civilisations (OAC).[23]

Now, if the 2005 Convention is replaced in such a context as being an additional instrument to this end, adopted just four years after the events of 11 September, it is not hard to understand that the legal principle of cultural diversity that it enshrines seeks to cater for importance taken on by the phenomenon of plurality of civilisations and of cultures while being resolutely part of the optic of dialogue.[24] Thus, bringing about an imperceptible shift in concerns about cultures and identities, the Convention very clearly enshrines a legal objective of communication among cultures so as to avoid any self-segregation by each culture. This objective is set out in three forms, including that of an 'intercultural dialogue' that becomes the necessary corollary of the

[21] See for example Seyla Benhabib, *The Claims of Culture. Equality and Diversity in the Global Era* (Princeton, Princeton University Press, 2002) 187 *ff.*

[22] The idea of a war of civilisations is far from new and countless authors have written on the subject with the same underlying assumption that one civilisation is superior to others. See Yadh Ben Achour, *Le rôle des civilisations dans le système international. Droit et relations internationales* (Brussels, Bruylant, 2003) 51 *ff.*

[23] It so happened that the UN had declared 2001 the International Year of Dialogue among Civilisations (A/RES/55/23, 11 January 2001).

[24] The same is true of the Universal Declaration of November 2001 that calls for a dialogue among cultures (Article 7).

principle of diversity (Article 1.c). If the state has the opportunity to preserve its cultural expressions via several protective measures, it must therefore also promote interaction between cultures and individuals. The requirements about the freedom of movement, of information, of communication and of access to all cultures also point in this direction. Diversity is not thought of, in law, as the simple juxtaposition of different cultures with no connection among them, but as the search for dialogue and exchange, both to identify shared values but also to avoid conflict in connection with identity-related or ethnic entrenchment in the face of cultural globalisation that remains hegemonic. The upshot is that a differentialist and strictly culturalist interpretation of the principle of diversity cannot be considered compatible with the purpose and the object of the 2005 Convention and of all the current international texts on cultural diversity.[25]

Having been re-introduced amid a media circus, the principle of dialogue is itself open to multiple criticism because of its fuzzy character, its lack of binding power, because it may conceal the hegemony of a single culture, or because of the way it may be readily instrumentalised to ease the conscience of an international community that fails to address the economic and social problems of poor countries that provide a base for radical traditionalist beliefs. These are all ambivalent effects and potential dark sides that are not to be underestimated. But the principle of dialogue does have the advantage of helping to guide the interpretation of international texts on cultural diversity in a not strictly culture-related direction. Thus, the international law on cultural diversity does appear, at least in its original aims, to be an attempt to transpose the complex act that characterises the paradigm of recognition within globalisation:[26] on the one hand, it must avoid identically reproducing the same cultural or civilisational model, but on the other, the preservation of cultures it introduces must not restore the radical otherness found in the international law of the colonial world. The positive dynamics of cultural diversity must provide a way past the ethno-cultural barriers that earlier colonial society had erected as impassable. From the existing cultural, civilisational and ethnic differences, international law had induced legal inequalities among states and peoples from which very few managed to escape. The present-day legal recognition of diversity has not been made fundamental in terms of accepting other peoples, states and groups notwithstanding their singularity and their cultural difference just so that they can be ring-fenced in their cultural difference and otherness as they had been under colonialism.

The second difficulty lies in the principle of equal dignity of cultures which is the basis of the principle of diversity stated in the 2005 Convention and

[25] Including domestically where the principle of diversity must apply in compliance with human rights and fundamental freedoms.

[26] On this development see Alain Renaut, *Un humanisme de la diversité. Essai sur la décolonisation des identités* (Paris, Flammarion, 2009) but also for internal democracy see Sylvie Mesure and Alain Renaut, *Alter ego. Les paradoxes de l'identité démocratique* (Paris, Flammarion, 1999).

other international texts and which raises an equally important general problem. This principle establishes a strict equivalence among cultures internationally, which is problematic in that it is far from being an established fact that all cultural practices can be considered as equivalent and of equal dignity. To take up familiar examples that particularly illuminate the issues involved here, can it be considered that a cultural practice like the excision of young girls has equal dignity with others? As Charles Taylor points out, to answer yes on this point is to fall again into a strict culturalist perspective that is overstated and particularly contentious.[27] There is therefore a limit to safeguarding the integrity of each cultural practice which lies in the observance of the fundamental rights of individuals, that is, in the observance not of equal dignity of cultures but of the equal dignity of human beings, which is ultimately the foundation of the entire edifice. It is what is reflected by, among other things, and particularly forcefully in the light of the example chosen, the Additional Protocol of the African Charter of Human and Peoples' Rights on Women's Rights in Africa, adopted in 2003. Under the Protocol 'harmful' traditional practices are now prohibited, particularly genital mutilations, as being contrary to the human rights of women (Article 5(b)).[28] In other words, what we shall call 'strong' culturalist arguments; strictly differentialist arguments, are clearly disavowed here by the very existence of a regional instrument of the sort. Likewise, this is precisely what the Universal Declaration of 2001 (Article 4) and the 2005 Convention (Article 4) indicate as they stipulate very plainly that one cannot invoke cultural diversity to vindicate the infringement of human rights.

That said, the question may recur because of the cultural interpretation of human rights themselves following 'weak' culturalist arguments that remain relevant.[29] This leads us ultimately to the need to understand the precise role that human rights play internationally and to what extent they in turn reflect a form of cultural imperialism. This is a point we shall return to later. At any rate, it can be pointed out here, that the question of the equal dignity of cultures seems to stand apart from the more specific question of the equal dignity of cultural practices or expressions insofar as a culture is more than just one or two cultural practices developed in its midst. It would be particularly simplistic and contrary to the spirit of the new texts of international law to discredit an entire culture by denouncing one of its practices or expressions. This is a point that is seldom emphasised, whereas it seems crucial to me if we are to safeguard what constitutes the singular and new force of the legal principle of equal dignity of cultures in our post-Cold War and postcolonial worlds based on recognition, without jeopardising the principle of the equal

[27] Charles Taylor, *Multiculturalism. Examining the Politics of Recognition* (Princeton, Princeton University Press, 1994).

[28] The Protocol came into force in 2005; www.achpr.org/english/women/protocolwomen.pdf.

[29] See the development on human rights below.

dignity of individuals, but without abandoning, either, the idea that a culture can no longer, in law, decree itself superior to others and returning to a hegemonic policy against which the principle of diversity has been erected. The denunciation of the degrading character of a few cultural practices or expressions, in the North as in the South, is used strategically by some commentators to discredit certain cultures as a whole and to challenge the principle of the equal dignity of cultures and the perfectly legitimate need to adapt human rights to those cultures.[30]

[30] See Celestine Nyamu, 'How Should Human Rights and Development Respond to Cultural Hierarcy in Developing Countries?' (2000) 41 (2) *Harvard International Law Journal* 381–419.

7

Recognition through Rights

IN POSTCOLONIAL AND post-Cold War international society, the international law of recognition is not limited to the legal enshrinement of the objective principle of cultural diversity. It also takes the form of individual or collective subjective rights that must be guaranteed within states themselves and which protect and promote the identities of individuals and groups and put an end to stigmatisation and marginalisation.[1] These rights are the essential complement to the right of cultural diversity, just as cultural diversity is essential to any effective exercise of them.[2] The legal guarantee of cultural diversity is in itself not enough to recognise what constitutes the dignity of each individual, nor their specificity, if this is to be more specifically protected. That guarantee must be accompanied by the granting of subjective rights that endow each individual with specific rights that are binding on their states but that also confer on the most vulnerable groups – minorities, indigenous peoples – the legal means to preserve their identity against the majority groups within states.[3]

The whole dynamic of subjective rights is therefore at work here and opens up both new perspectives and new difficulties. These are to be examined by distinguishing several categories of rights and I shall try to show how these may be situated within the issue of recognition which casts light on certain less familiar essential questions. First, we can group together the rights bestowed on specific groups or individuals because of their membership of those groups: these are the rights of minorities and of native peoples. We can

[1] The recognition of rights has been examined by Honneth and Ricœur, but they emphasised the rights common to all (eg civil, political, economic and social) and not specific rights. See Axel Honneth, *The Struggle for Recognition* (New York, Polity Press, 1996) 92 *ff* and Paul Ricoeur, *Parcours de la reconnaissance* (Paris, Gallimard, 2004) 311 *ff*.

[2] Conditional upon the interpretation given above to the principle of cultural diversity, which cannot be invoked in violating fundamental human freedoms and rights, which would again entail the downward spiral of cultural entrapment. See Amartya Sen, *Identity and Violence. The Illusion of Destiny* (New York, Norton, 2006) 103 *ff*.

[3] The underlying objective is also to confer more autonomy on them in the pursuit of their personal or group projects. See Axel Honneth, *La société du mépris. Vers une nouvelle théorie critique* (Paris, La découverte, 2006) 254 and Alain Caillé, *Théorie anti-utilitariste de l'action. Fragments d'une sociologie générale* (Paris, La découverte, 2009) 167–68. This shows that internationally, the issue of the right to be different does not necessarily run counter to human rights but may supplement their objective of autonomy of the individual and therefore of the 'capabilities' of human beings.

then identify the rights conferred on individuals regardless of their membership of a group but working on very different assumptions, and we shall thus look at cultural rights, human rights and women's rights. All these categories of rights provide a striking picture of the diversity of practices of recognition and of the way in which legal instruments respond to aspirations that are both similar and unlike by swinging constantly between the concern to see the differences of individuals and groups respected and the concern for protecting their equal dignity.

I Rights of Minorities and Indigenous Peoples

The domination and stigmatisation of certain minority groups is as old as the history of human societies. For sure, not all minorities and peoples have been stigmatised but even so very many groups have been and still are for multiple reasons, be it migration, conflict, colonisation for exploitation or settlement, domination, slavery or forced movement of populations. It is obvious, too, that colonisation, where it occurred, made this phenomenon worse. Settlement colonies led to a complete denial of the identity of native peoples, while exploitation colonies often generated ambivalent attitudes, marked by a fascination for the Other and a rejection, but which ultimately led, all the same, to the marginalisation of colonised peoples and, within those peoples, to discrimination among ethnic groups (majority or minority groups) to the detriment of others. Precolonial, colonial and postcolonial situations are inseparable here, for the current claims are the outcome of all this history in which past and present are inextricably interwoven.[4] Moreover, the newly decolonised states themselves denied multiple identities and discriminated against minority groups, tribes or ethnic groups within their territory and whom they usually compelled to merge within the wholly artificial mould of the nation state.

But the phenomenon is a global one and involves all domestic societies, whichever they may be, the situations being legion and each of them being narrowly dependent on context. And so to speak of 'minorities', 'peoples' or 'ethnic groups' as subjects of recognition is an extremely difficult exercise since each country has its own minority groups or peoples and it attaches its own historical, legal and cultural references to these descriptions. Inevitably, the problem has its repercussions on an international level and on the legal instruments that address these questions when the concepts have to be defined.[5] In truth, the purpose here is not to return to this point at this stage of our reflection, but to indicate above all why and how there has progressively

[4] Jean-Loup Amselle, *Les logiques métissées* (Paris, Payot, 1990).
[5] See Francesco Capotorti, *Study on the Rights of Persons Belonging to Ethnic, Religious and Linguistic Minorities* (New York, UN Publications, 1979).

emerged in the international arena a specific process of legal recognition of certain groups or peoples through the attribution of rights that are specific to their members or to themselves as subjects of rights.

A Rights of Minorities

Apart from a few very special cases like the regime of capitulations in Ottoman lands or certain clauses in European treaties designed to protect Christian minorities in Protestant or Catholic lands, it was only very late on, with the end of the First World War, that Euro-American international society recognised the rights of minority groups so as to find a solution to the aspirations of the many European minorities to identity. The famous principle of nationalities, that crystallised these expectations, had emerged in nineteenth-century Europe, especially in the Balkans, with the problem being unresolved. After the 1914–1918 War, several peoples found themselves in the position of national minorities split among several states and this deeply unsatisfactory situation was to accelerate the recognition of certain rights in their favour. In his historic 1918 speech enshrining the principle of nationalities, US President Woodrow Wilson announced a system of freedom and equality for all 'nationalities' and seemed to embark upon a true change in international relations in favour of minorities and dominated peoples. He stated that it was henceforth necessary to recognise 'the principle of justice to all peoples and nationalities, and their right to live on equal terms of liberty and safety with one another, whether they be strong or weak'.[6]

And yet Wilson's address had already caused tremendous misunderstanding in that, contrary to what so generous a formula suggested, it was not universally applicable but addressed solely to the minorities of Central and Eastern Europe. Wilson was not speaking about colonised people at all. Accordingly, when, further to this address, the Egyptian nationalist leader Saad Zagloul wanted to voice the aspirations to autonomy of the colonised or semi-colonised peoples in the League of Nations, Great Britain not only scuppered the project but also exiled Saad Zagloul and part of the Egyptian delegation.[7] This was the sorry paradox of an international society that was to begin to recognise the rights of some in Europe while continuing to violate the identity of others outside Europe.

Further to the US President's address, the exercise of the right of peoples to self-determination and the protection and exercise of certain rights of European minorities began to be implemented with the five 'Minority Treaties' of 1919–1920 (Poland; Czechoslovakia; Kingdom of Serbs, Croats

[6] Woodrow Wilson, Address to Congress of 8 January 1918; wwi.lib.byu.edu/index.php/President_Wilson's_Fourteen_Points.

[7] Karoline Postel-Vinay, *L'Occident et sa bonne parole. Nos représentations du monde, de l'Europe coloniale à l'Amérique hégémonique* (Paris, Flammarion, 2005), 84 *ff*.

and Slovenes; Romania and Greece) and the peace treaties of Saint-Germain-en-Laye (1919, Austria), Neuilly (1919, Bulgaria) and Trianon (1919, Hungary). All these treaties were imposed by the victor states on the vanquished states and on the newly formed states of Eastern Europe after the collapse of the great pre-war empires. They were supplemented by several bilateral undertakings, a number of unilateral declarations made by certain states to the League of Nations (Finland, Albania and the three Baltic states) and by the creation in 1919 of a Commission within the League of Nations for the new states and for the protection of minorities. Any member could then bring before the League of Nations or the Permanent Court of International Justice a case of conflict between a minority and a state. The system was even extended to individuals in 1926. In terms of recognition, the system enabled not just the recognition of the identity of the minority as such – since its existence was accepted de facto (but not de jure as a subject of law) – and its right to national and international protection, but also the application of the principle of non-discrimination and the more specific recognition of certain rights granted to its members.[8] These rights usually included the right to use their own language freely (considered as the priority), the free exercise of their religion and the right to specific teaching, especially the right to set up schools and to teach in their mother tongue. All these were part of their culture and to be duly ensured and supervised as part of belonging to a protected minority. Even so, innovative as it was, this set of principles merely instituted an exceptional regime as it was only valid for the minorities situated in the territory of the vanquished or newly formed states. It did not apply to the minorities of the victorious states and to the vanquished minorities, nor, a fortiori, to the other minorities or peoples of the rest of the world.[9] Although the system worked well initially, the 1930s marked its decline with the resurgence of nationalism, the advent of fascism and the instrumentalisation of the question of minorities for imperialist purposes. The League of Nations system no longer imposed or controlled anything. A number of minorities were systematically oppressed or assimilated and Hitler's policy, consisting in annexing Germany's neighbours on the pretext of reuniting or liberating oppressed German-speaking minorities, led to the Second World War.[10] This regression explains that while the

[8] From the outset, the recognition of equal dignity (non-discrimination) was associated with the recognition of specific rights. This was very clearly stated by the Permanent Court of International Justice (PCIJ) in its Advisory Opinion of 6 April 1935 in *Minority Schools in Albania* PCIJ Collection, 1936, Series A/B64, 17.

[9] Nor did it apply to all categories of minority. The Treaty of Lausanne of 24 July 1923 required Turkey to observe the rights of non-Muslim minorities in its territory and Turkey therefore concluded that this did not concern the Kurds. Turkey still denies the minority status to the Kurdish population today. Similarly, Greece relied on the Treaty of Lausanne to recognise a Muslim but not Turkish minority. This was contested recently in the European Court of Human Rights. See ECHR, *Tourkiki Enosi Xanthis v Greece*, 27 March 2008, Req No 26698/05.

[10] See Carol Fink, *Defending the Rights of Others. The Great Powers, the Jews, and International Minority Protection, 1878–1938* (Cambridge, Cambridge University Press, 2004).

League of Nations had wagered on a first form of recognition of minority rights, things were different after the Second World War.

For European minority rights only, the massive transfer of minorities was contemplated at the end of the war as a radical and terribly brutal solution flouting the most elementary individual rights. In 1946, Winston Churchill declared 'Expulsion is the method which [. . .] will be the most satisfactory and lasting. There will be no mixture of populations to cause endless trouble . . . A clean sweep will be made.'[11]

Indeed many transfers were made, notably of German minorities under the terms of the 1945 Potsdam Conference in the worst of conditions and in the post-war atmosphere of settling old scores. The outcome was a significant reduction in the numbers of certain minorities in Europe but the underlying problem was still not settled. It was the UN Charter that was to put an end worldwide to the system of protection of minorities established by the League of Nations. It does not even contain the word minority, an omission which was obviously not an oversight since the appearance of human rights internationally coincided with the provisional disappearance of the special rights of minorities. Human rights, which were integrated for the first time into an international text with the UN Charter, were to transcend any reference to minority rights. They were considered a far more satisfactory alternative for international society because they are not based on the idea of membership of any particular minority but on the idea of human nature that is common to all. They therefore reflect a model of protection that does away with all the cultural, religious or linguistic differences that characterised minorities and that were perceived, in 1945, as engendering violent and nationalistic claims that were deeply destabilising for the integrity of European states and for the world. So human rights alone are included as an objective of the UN Charter and they alone were the subject of the Universal Declaration of Paris in 1948, while no mention was given to the rights of minorities. From 1945 to 1948, from Dumbarton Oaks to Paris by way of San Francisco, came a string of votes that set aside the question of minorities each time.[12] The debates preceding the adoption of the 1948 Universal Declaration are illuminating testimony to this sidelining. They reveal that an article on the rights of national, linguistic and religious minorities was proposed by the USSR but ultimately rejected with near general consent. There were two reasons for the rejection: the delegates feared that any specific provision in favour of minorities might

[11] Winston Churchill, Declaration to the House of Commons, 15 December 1944. Cited in Fabienne Rousso-Lenoir, *Minorités et droits de l'homme: l'Europe et son double* (Brussels and Paris, Bruylant and LGDJ, 1994) 45.

[12] See Josépha Laroche, 'Internationalisation des droits de l'homme et protection des minorités' in Alain Fenet and Gérard Soulier (eds), *Les minorités et leur droits depuis 1789* (Paris, L'Harmattan, 1989) 82 *ff* and Albert Verdoodt, 'Influence des structures ethniques et linguistiques des pays membres des Nations Unies sur la rédaction de la Déclaration universelle des droits de l'homme' in *René Cassin, Amicorum Discipulorumque liber (I), Problèmes de protection internationale des droits de l'homme* (Paris, Pedone, 1969) 405 *ff*.

revive nationalist passions and see the whole of the new international order implode; and more incidentally that a discriminatory category might be set up for minorities differentiating the case of their members from any other individual. The fact is that while members of minorities were denied any specific rights, the principle of non-discrimination was, by contrast, contained in Article 2 of the Declaration, expressly prohibiting any discrimination on the basis of language, religion, sex, race or 'other status', which implicitly and specifically meant the status of members belonging to minorities.[13]

From 1945 onwards, minority rights were therefore protected primarily in the name of two fundamental human rights which are closely correlated: in the name of the principle of non-discrimination and in the name of the principle of equal rights of members of minorities and the others members of the state. International law at the time did not grant special rights to minorities, but it did ensure the members of minority groups equal treatment with the members of majority or dominant groups and equal entitlement to the same rights. In point of fact, the principle of non-discrimination was already applied to minorities in the inter-war years and so did not come as a surprise, but while it had been a principle of the pre-war international law of minorities, it became a principle of the post-war international law of human rights. It was set out in Articles 1 and 55 of the UN Charter, Article 2 of the 1948 Declaration and the 1966 Covenants and again in Article 14 of the 1950 European Convention on Human Rights and Fundamental Freedoms, which had similarly excluded any direct consideration of the rights of minorities. However, recognising equal treatment of members of minorities and majorities was not enough to ensure the cultural identities of the minority groups, nor was it the stated aim. It might even be thought that most states hoped, on the contrary, to be done with minorities and their identity claims which were viewed as a threat. They hoped that, through human rights alone, it might be possible at last to resolve the problem of minorities by no longer aiming to maintain minorities as such, but by aiming rather at their successful assimilation into society as a whole. From this point of view, the post-1945 international law of human rights was a resounding failure, for not only did human rights and notably the principle of non-discrimination prove wholly inadequate in combatting discrimination and the de facto sidelining of many minorities, but the attempts to assimilate minorities merely intensified their self-segregation by way of reaction. Drawing on the lessons from this failure, states, on two occasions, re-orientated international law in favour of renewed recognition of special rights for members of minorities, thereby renewing with the foundational intuitions and the highly specific legal experience of the inter-war years.

[13] International law scholarship of the time confirms this very widely held post-war view. See for example Pablo de Azcarate, 'Protection of Minorities and Human Rights' (1946) 246 *Annals of the American Academy of Political and Social Science*, 127 *ff*.

The first re-orientation came with Article 27 of the 1966 UN Covenant on Civil and Political Rights. It was essential at the time since, for the first time since 1945, international law broke with the generalised distrust shown towards minorities and explicitly recognised specific rights for persons belonging to minorities and in particular the right for members of 'ethnic, religious or linguistic minorities' to be able 'in community with the other members of their group, to enjoy their own culture, to profess and practise their own religion, or to use their own language'. In fact, this provision is limited as it imposes a negative obligation on states not to deprive cultural minorities of their own cultural life without imposing any positive duty. But at least the provision was a sign that attitudes were gradually changing and it was to allow these issues to be brought before the Human Rights Committee, allowing the Committee to clarify the provision itself by prohibiting forcible assimilation policies and to see it was applied by the states parties to the Covenant. A new approach had been opened up, but it was only from the 1990s onwards that the existence of specific rights for minorities was fully reaffirmed in international law, by means of a particularly insightful interpretation of their aspirations.

The end of the Cold War saw a second and far more decisive re-orientation of international law in this direction, wherein the fundamental idea was to connect the recognition of specific rights for members of minorities to the preservation of their identity and their cultural difference. It was time to take stock and experience since 1945 showed that despite the principle of non-discrimination and Article 27 of the 1966 Covenant, the same types of difficulties arose and it had not always been possible to successfully preserve minorities, which remained particularly vulnerable and stigmatised groups. Each time, the majority of the state imposed its cultural model by marginalising minorities and exacerbating their identity claims by way of reaction. It is not surprising, therefore, that, in compliance with the new values granted to recognition, a reaction took shape after 1989, notably in Europe, but also worldwide. Several international legal instruments were adopted which, this time, enshrined specific and distinctive rights for members of minorities, rights which were therefore based on the explicit recognition of cultural identity. They vary in the degree to which they are binding and for the time being are mostly European texts. They include the 1990 Organisation for Security and Co-operation in Europe (OSCE) Copenhagen Document; the Declaration on the Rights of Persons Belonging to National or Ethnic, Religious and Linguistic Minorities, adopted by the UN General Assembly in 1992; the Copenhagen Criteria set by the EU in 1993 as conditions for the Eastern European countries to join the EU, which imposed the protection of minorities; and the Framework Convention for the Protection of National Minorities of 2 February 1995.

The 1992 UN Declaration, which was adopted thanks to the accession of the new Eastern European states to the UN, which were particularly concerned about managing this problem after the Cold War, remains the only text of general scope dealing exclusively with this issue.[14] As part of the post-Cold War recognition paradigm, the Resolution sets out the question of minorities immediately on the terrain of respect for their identity (Article 1), with states being compelled to protect and promote it. It sets out the specific rights to be granted to members of minorities in order to preserve their identity, including, exhumed from the inter-war years, the rights to use their language, to practise their religion and to enjoy their own culture (Article 2). In the wake of the Declaration, the General Assembly also conferred in 1993 on the Office of the High Commissioner for Human Rights the task of promoting and protecting the rights of minorities enshrined in the Declaration and to begin dialogue with states on this subject, while the Sub-Commission on the Prevention of Discrimination and the Protection of Minorities created a working group that has become a particularly active forum for dialogue and reflection on the issue. To this is added the action of the Human Rights Committee which developed an interpretation of Article 27 of the 1966 Covenant that has also evolved in this direction and supports the general movement that is thus being deployed worldwide.

Even so, most of the essential legal instruments were adopted at a European level.[15] The end of the Cold War recreated a situation in Europe reminiscent of the inter-war years. The break-up of the major Communist states, the USSR, Yugoslavia and Czechoslovakia, reshaped Central and Eastern Europe into 28 states, most of which have national minorities representing more than 10 per cent of their population, while new minorities have emerged like the Russian minorities outside Russia or Serb minorities outside Serbia.[16] Now, the post-Communist transition stirred up nationalist feeling among most majority peoples and secessionist temptations among certain minorities, with the result that it once again became urgent for Europe to re-think the question of minorities and to find an appropriate response to their desire for recognition and to the need for stability. Tying back in with the novel experiences of the inter-war years, the European states developed a whole battery of legal instruments in a decade by which they define specific rights for people belonging to their minorities. Summarising the essential points of the new paradigm centred on the recognition of identities, the 1995

[14] It was drafted in two weeks thanks to the new Eastern European states, while the UN had failed to come up with a common text for more than 14 years. It is very general, however, and the frequent use of conditional forms heightens its non-mandatory character. Resolution AG/47/135 (18 December 1992), Declaration on the Rights of Persons Belonging to National or Ethnic, Religious and Linguistic Minorities; www2.ohchr.org/english/law/minorities.htm.

[15] This does not mean that other states around the world do not try to protect their minorities or attribute specific rights to them. See, for example, Rita Manchanda, *The No Nonsense Guide to Minority Rights in South Asia* (New Delhi, Sage Publications, 2009) and Alan Axelrod, *Minority Rights in America* (Washington DC, CQ Press, 2002).

[16] See Hugh Miall (ed), *Minority Rights in Europe. Chatham House Papers* (London, Council on Foreign Relations Press, 1994).

Framework Convention for the Protection of National Minorities considers in its Preamble that:

> [A] pluralist and genuinely democratic society should not only respect the ethnic, cultural, linguistic and religious identity of each person belonging to a national minority, but also create appropriate conditions enabling them to express, preserve and develop this identity.[17]

As for the content of special rights of members of minorities, the Copenhagen Document, for example, was one of the first post-Cold War texts adopted in this domain and it indicated the main rights, which were often taken from binding texts.[18] In its Part IV, it recalls first of all the principle of non-discrimination as a human right to be applied to all people belonging to minorities. But it supplements the statement of this right by a whole series of specific rights that members of minorities were recognised as having and that states must observe. These rights included the right 'to express, preserve and develop their ethnic, cultural, linguistic or religious identity and to maintain and develop their culture in all its aspects' (Article 32), the right to use their mother tongue (Articles 32.1 and 32.3), the right 'to establish and maintain their own educational, cultural and religious institutions' (Article 32.3) and to seek public assistance to this end (Article 32.2) and the right 'to profess and practice their religion' (Article 32.3). To all these rights there corresponds a positive duty of the state to implement them and ensure them, which entails taking account of their economic and social aspects.

One should not underestimate the scope of such rights and the magnitude of the shifts they reflect in legal terms. First of all, the new international law of minorities ties in, as said, with the law of the inter-war years on minorities, but integrating it decisively in the new paradigm of recognition, for while the rights of minorities had been conceded after 1918, it was primarily because of the new distribution of territory which had been made at the time and not directly to protect any right to be different. This was a complete turnaround compared with 1945 and 1948. Contrary to what had been attempted after 1945 and was often prompted by an implicit will to assimilate minorities, the question is no longer one of preserving minorities through the same rights granted to all, without discrimination, but of protecting them, too, through specific rights conferred on persons belonging to minorities, and therefore precisely because they do belong to minorities. In response to the minorities' need for recognition, these rights ensure a minority's particular characteristics and therefore, more fundamentally still, the right for their members to be different and to live differently in accordance with their own culture. In other

[17] conventions.coe.int/Treaty/en/Treaties/Html/157.htm. However, the Framework Convention reduces the field of protection to national minorities whereas the 1992 Declaration covers ethnic, religious and linguistic minorities.

[18] Document of the Copenhagen Meeting of the Conference on the Human Dimension of the Conference on Security and Co-operation in Europe, 29 June 1990; www.osce.org/odihr/elections/14304.

words, it really is a question of officially bestowing a right to be different while being equal. While it was thought in 1945 and 1948 that the indiscriminate exercise of the individual rights of freedom of speech, thought, religion or assembly, which were also recognised as being enjoyed by all, would suffice for minorities to live as they saw fit, after 1989, there was a change in legal strategy and rights were adopted which, in addition to the formal freedoms recognised as being enjoyed by all, directly ensured the exercise of their cultural *difference* and therefore their identity. For example, although the same right to free speech may be applied without discrimination, experience shows that it does not answer the concern of linguistic minorities for the protection of their languages.[19] By contrast, the existence of a special right to teach and speak one's language will preserve it sustainably as it creates the condition for its effective use over time. In this respect, the 1992 European Charter for Regional or Minority Languages even affirms that the use of a regional or minority tongue in public and private life is an 'inalienable right' (Preamble).[20] It should be emphasised that these changes mean that the principle of non-discrimination has itself been the subject of new interpretations converging in this direction as these interpretations take far more account of the diversity of concrete cultural situations of individuals than was the case before, with the result that the aim is no longer to treat different people equally but to treat different people differently because they belong to a minority.[21] There probably remains the tricky question of how to find a satisfactory articulation between this principle of non-discrimination (always affirmed by way of priority) and the specific rights of minorities, because the question is never clearly defined and may raise particularly delicate problems of interpretation and application. But what makes the act of recognition both difficult and subtle is its capacity to express itself in this articulation, on a case-by-case basis, when it is no longer a matter of enclosing minorities within their cultural difference but of recognising them as being both 'equal and different'; and so ultimately strengthening their equal standing with 'majorities' by combatting the formalism of earlier law, which far from being neutral and non-discriminatory, invariably favoured majority groups.

And so it can be seen how, despite a path strewn with many obstacles, the rights of minorities have finally been duly recognised in international law, paving the way towards a new legal arrangement based on difference and which it is hard to imagine being ignored nowadays as it corresponds to such a deeply

[19] This is what the PCIJ had already concluded in the inter-war period, when specific rights of people belonging to minorities were at last recognised. See PCIJ, Advisory Opinion of 6 April 1935, *Case of Minority Schools in Albania* PCIJ Series A/B 17 *ff*.

[20] conventions.coe.int/Treaty/en/Treaties/html/148.htm.

[21] See Human Rights Committee, General Comment 23 (1994) on Article 27 (Rights of minorities) §6.2: 'positive measures by States may also be necessary to protect the identity of a minority and the rights of its members to enjoy and develop their culture and language and to practise their religion, in community with other members of the group'; www.unhchr.ch/tbs/doc.nsf/(Symbol)/fb7fb12c2fb8bb21c12563ed004df111?Opendocument.

rooted requirement of minorities but also of the times we live in. The scope of the changes that have come about since 1945 in this area should not hide a restriction of a general order that still prompts much discussion: the fact that the rights recognised are individual and not collective rights, that is, they are enjoyed by individuals insofar as they belong to a minority and not to the minority itself as a subject of law in its own right. The non-recognition of a collective right should not come as a surprise since it is in accordance with the very old and not groundless fear that such collective rights would open the floodgates to a desire for secession of the new subject of law formed by the minority. That is also why, a fortiori, the right to self-determination of minorities is never recognised nor the right to internal self-determination, except for very ancient national minorities. The international law of minorities has been constructed historically on the basis of a difficult balancing act between the observance of the sovereignty of states and the necessity to grant certain rights to the minorities in their territory, and this double foundation explains why the individuals alone are recognised as having rights. But some observers fear that this time the minority as a group might vanish in the end. While the problem remains a real one, especially for small minorities, individual rights may work in favour of maintaining the group: although the minority itself is not recognised as a subject of law, it is clear that the rights of members of minorities are no less dependent on the capacity of the minority to be able to protect its group identity and culture in the interest of all its members, with the result that the recognition of individual rights for the members of minorities entails the protection of the group as such and strengthens its status as a minority.[22]

B Rights of Indigenous Peoples

Testifying in turn to this new favour currently enjoyed by recognition, the actions undertaken for the rights of native peoples, perhaps more than the actions for minorities, enhanced awareness that some groups had been particularly stigmatised for hundreds of years and still were, and that such a situation was not only troubling but simply unacceptable in respect of the new contemporary values and the post-Cold War requirements of international social justice. Native peoples, who were weaker and more vulnerable than the subjected populations in exploitation colonies, were particularly hard hit with, in the space of four centuries, the almost complete despoliation of their lands and the disappearance of 85–90 per cent of their numbers.[23] As a result,

[22] The international law of minorities does, however, have its dark side. See Patrick Macklem, 'Les droits des minorités en droit international' in Hélène Ruiz-Fabri and Michel Rosenfeld (ed), *Repenser le constitutionnalisme à l'âge de la mondialisation et de la privatisation* (Paris, Société de législation comparée, 2001) 233–59.

[23] Even worse, some were not just exterminated but completely erased from memoires, like the Arawak of the Caribbean. See Elazar Barkan, 'Genocides of Indigenous Peoples. Rhetoric of Human Rights' in Robert Gellately and Ben Kiernan (eds), *The Specter of Genocide. Mass Murder in Historical Perspective* (Cambridge, Cambridge University Press, 2010) 117.

they now present themselves to the international community as 'survivors of history', as per the rallying cry of the Australian Aborigines at the time of the celebration of the bicentenary of British colonisation in 1988: 'We have survived!'[24] Even so, one must again measure the substantial changes that have come about in this respect which pertain to the same profound change in attitudes and behaviours in this area, but also to a particularly shocking situation of historical injustice.

Indigenous peoples have been defined as the descendants of those who inhabited a territory before the advent of settlement colonies, which then completely subjected them. They are numerous throughout the regions of the world, including in Africa where some particularly vulnerable groups like the pastoral and hunter-gatherer communities aspire to be recognised as indigenous peoples.[25] The communities with the highest media profiles, however, are the indigenous peoples of South America and those colonised by English-speaking populations. For a long time, however, international law debated only the fate and standing of colonised peoples outside the mother country and ignored indigenous peoples, who were considered to come within the strictly internal jurisdiction of states. While the former finally achieved their independence at the time of decolonisation in the 1950s and 1960s, the latter continued to directly suffer the discrimination and disregard of the majority group, and were very brutally subjected to cultural, political and economic domination. However, as early as 1947, Belgium had excoriated the different legal and political treatment of non-self-governing peoples depending on whether or not they were characterised as colonies.[26] Only territories that were separate from the mother country and inhabited by peoples with specific cultural and ethnic features were considered to be colonies and as such were entitled to the protection of the Charter. Conversely, other non-self-governing peoples, dwelling within sovereign states, enjoyed no internationally defined protection. But why, Belgium asked, was no obligation imposed on the former settlement colonies? Why did the UN not control the way in which India treated the Nagas, the United States the native North Americans, Canada the Eskimos or New Zealand the Maoris, when it supervised the way states acted with respect to the colonies and territories covered by Chapters XI and XII of the Charter? As a colonising country itself, Belgium was not acting without self-interest but its proposal did at least expose the cynicism of some states that took an anticolonial moral stance while continuing unabashed to completely dominate the native peoples whose land they

[24] Bouda Etemad, *Crimes et réparations. L'Occident face à son passé colonial* (Paris, Ed A Versailles, 2008) 119.

[25] See International Processes. Report of the Working Group of Experts of the African Commission on Human and Peoples' Rights/Indigenous Populations/Communities; www.iwgia.org/publications/search-pubs?publication_id=116.

[26] See Jean Salmon, 'De la thèse belge sur les peuples autochtones (1947–1960) à la Déclaration des Nations Unies sur les droits des peuples autochtones (2007)' in *Droit, liberté, paix développement: Mélanges en l'honneur de Madjid Benchick* (Paris, Pedone, 2011) 163 *ff*.

had colonised of old.[27] This attempt to impose the same protective regime on indigenous peoples proved to be in vain and it was only much later that things began to change.

Progressively from the 1980s onwards, awareness of the need for a special regime for indigenous peoples spread to the entire international community. The indigenous populations concerned were behind a whole series of actions and initiatives that have been termed the 'indigenous peoples' movement', which successfully drew media attention to their cause and promoted it within their respective states and then internationally. In 1982, Ecosoc set up a UN Working Group on Indigenous Populations which was to be the keystone to the promotion of the rights of indigenous peoples internationally. True, a Convention 107 had been adopted by the International Labour Organisation (ILO) in 1957 on indigenous peoples, but it provided for their straightforward political assimilation, which was broadly denounced. It was superseded by a new Convention 169 adopted by the ILO in June 1989 on tribal and indigenous peoples which, in keeping with the undercurrent that swept the post-Cold War world, sought to replace the integrating and paternalistic perspective of Convention 107 by a policy that respected the customs of native peoples and their cultural identities. The change in outlook between the 1957 and the 1989 Conventions in itself summarises the shift in attitudes towards groups and cultural identities and attests again to the advent of the recognition paradigm into the contemporary world from 1989. In the wake of Convention 169, under the decisive impetus of the Vienna World Conference, 1993 was declared International Year of the World's Indigenous People and a first International Decade of the World's Indigenous People was declared by the UN in 1995.

Like minorities, most indigenous peoples do not seek to escape completely from state tutelage but to secure recognition of their existence and of their trampled historical rights, to recover control over their natural resources and to put an end to the stigma and social disregard to which they are subject. They call for equal rights but also for the recognition of their collective identity and their cultural difference based on their social organisation, their relationship to the land, their ancestral customs and their traditional arts. Some of them, however, would also like to benefit from the right to self-determination and a lively debate has arisen over the legal characterisation of these groups either as 'peoples', and therefore as being capable of exercising the right of peoples' to self-determination, or as simple 'populations' with no such right.[28] In truth, they may be characterised as a people without that

[27] On the violence of this domination in North America on which the international community has been silent, see Ward Churchill, *Struggle for the Land. Indigenous Resistance to Genocide, Ecocide, and Expropriation in Contemporary North America* (Monroe, Common Courage Press, 1993).

[28] Indigenous Issues: Report of the Working Group Established in Accordance with Commission on Human Rights Resolution 1995/32, Document E/CN.4/1997/102, 10 December 1996.

necessarily leading them to the status of independent state, but to a very broad degree of internal autonomy as was done for the Inuit peoples of northern Canada in 1999. Finally, a Declaration on the Rights of Indigenous Peoples was adopted in September 2007 by the UN General Assembly reflecting this development.[29] It was largely approved, as 143 states voted for it. It recognises indigenous peoples' right to self-determination in relation to internal affairs and to freely determine their economic, social and cultural development (Articles 3 and 4), but no mention is made of self-determination in respect of external affairs.[30] However, it solemnly states that the rights recognised 'constitute the minimum standards for the survival, dignity and well-being of the indigenous peoples of the world' (Article 43) and although it has no directly binding value, it is very specific as to the content of the obligations it sets out, offering a sound legal basis for UN and state action in this domain. As the point of arrival of a long journey towards recognition for peoples who until then had been invisible internationally, the Resolution finally attests to the general legal movement towards the recognition of cultural identities and differences and sets itself explicitly on the ground of the right to difference. The Preamble to the Declaration affirms that 'indigenous peoples are equal to all other peoples, while recognizing the right of all peoples to be different, to consider themselves different, And to be respected as such'.[31]

Those lines capture the spirit of the contemporary process of recognition and of what is particularly fertile in it. The terms are emblematic of what might be the new formula for living together within international society, which has already been evoked for minorities, and that best expresses the quintessence of current aspirations: to live 'equal but different'. This concern for equality, while remaining different, is the mark of soft or hard international law that is concerned for recognition and from it flows, in the same way as for minorities, the adoption of specific rights for the members of indigenous peoples, on the basis of their belonging to an indigenous group, that does not concern the other members of the society. Again, we find the now familiar provisions about the right to protection and use of their language, their religion, their customs, their traditional arts, their knowledge, but also the exercise of their rights to maintain and strengthen their political and economic institutions (Article 5), 'the collective right to live in freedom, peace and security as distinct peoples' (Article 7.2) and very detailed rights about their ancestral land and the resources it contains (Articles 26–30), for it is known to what extent these resources and lands have been and still are

[29] General Assembly Resolution 61/295 (13 September 2007) UN Doc A/RES/61/295, UN Declaration on the Rights of Indigenous Peoples; www.un-documents.net/a61r295.htm. On the whole of the declaration, see Stephen Allen and Alexandra Xanthaki, *Reflections on the UN Declaration on the Rights of Indigenous Peoples* (Oxford, Hart Publishing, 2011).

[30] It can even be considered it is prohibited by Article 46 recalling the necessary respect for the state's territorial integrity.

[31] UN Declaration on the Rights of Indigenous Peoples, A/RES/61/295 (n 29).

plundered and their rights flouted by oil, mining and logging companies. In this respect, international and domestic texts tend to more readily recognise certain collective rights for indigenous peoples – rights that are conferred on the group as a whole as a subject of law. This point is emphasised in the Declaration. Despite the fear of thereby prompting growing autonomy of the group that might lead to secession, recognising this type of collective rights is here a necessity if there is to be any true recognition of their identity and culture. An example is their relationship to land. Most indigenous peoples have a fundamental tie to the land as it defines much of their identity. This relation to the land is both material and spiritual since, they claim, the land belongs to the group and the group belongs to the land.[32] Being compelled to adopt the legal discourse on rights to defend their land, they have finally claimed a right of collective and not individual ownership. They wish to secure full ownership of their ancestral land to ensure its protection but they do not wish any individual to enjoy that right. And so it is by taking account of this very strong cultural background which is so intrinsically related to their identity and to their very being that existing international texts recognise their collective territorial and internal administrative rights.[33]

That being so, the practical implementation of such rights is particularly limited and runs up against the ordinary provisions of the municipal law of the states concerned. This is illustrated by the celebrated Mabo decision by the High Court of Australia in 1992.[34] Through this case, which was a landmark decision for the future development of international law, the Court, in a revolutionary move, recognised the Aborigines' natural right over their ancestral land, but, at the same time, ruled out any form of retroactive compensation for spoliation before 1975 and required the Aborigines to prove uninterrupted ancestral occupation of the lands claimed in order for a tribal land title to be granted. That, of course, excluded the majority of existing Aborigines from the outset, who had been duly 'de-tribalised' and removed from their territories during previous centuries.[35]

II Cultural Rights

So far, we have evoked the recognition of identity rights through the protection of the rights of minorities and of indigenous peoples or, in other words, because persons belong to specific groups identified as forming minorities or indigenous peoples. But might it not be thought that a genuine inter-

[32] See Erica-Irene Daes, 'Final Report on Indigenous Peoples' Permanent Sovereignty over Natural Resources' E/CN.4/Sub.2/2004/30 and ILO Convention 169, Articles 17 and 18.

[33] See GIPTA, *Droits territoriaux des peuples autochtones* (Paris, L'Harmattan, 2005).

[34] *Mabo and Others v Queensland (No 2)* [1992] HCA 23; (1992) 175 CLR 1.

[35] Isabelle Merle, 'La Mabo Case. L'Australie face à son passé colonial' (1998) 2 *Annales, Historie, Sciences Sociales* 223 *ff.*

national legal policy of recognition presupposes that cultural rights should be declared and guaranteed more generally for any human being for the simple reason that he or she is a human being? It is clear that the rights of minorities or of indigenous peoples are attributed solely on a specifically sociological basis, that is, they are dependent upon membership of highly specific groups and therefore promote an ethnic and collective conception of culture.[36] Conversely, individual cultural rights granted without reference to any minority or people purport to be much more generally applicable because they are recognised regardless of any ethnic, anthropological, linguistic or religious reference. Unlike the rights of minorities and indigenous peoples, they are therefore an integral part of human rights which they supplement and deepen in cultural terms. Accordingly, these are rights that are given much emphasis by contemporary discussion, but they are not all the subject of the same consensus and they are not all legally defined as being rights, for their importance used to be underestimated by focusing on other rights, whereas their importance is nowadays often overestimated out of fear that they might justify excessive claims. In a shorter term perspective, they have also suffered from the recognition of the rights of minorities and of indigenous peoples which has indefinitely postponed the adoption of a general text on them. As subjects of controversy, and marginalised compared with other rights, they are no less an essential feature of the new paradigm of recognition and of the international law of recognition, and because of the questions they prompt, they invite a general reflection on the challenges and limits of the right to cultural difference.

Internally, cultural rights were already the forgotten aspect of human rights deriving from the French and American traditions. The singularity and particularity they suggested ran counter to the universality and abstraction of the first generation of rights, especially those proclaimed in the French Declaration of 1789. Internationally, the idea of cultural right was nonetheless introduced into the Universal Declaration of 1948. Article 27(1) reads: 'Everyone has the right to freely participate in the cultural life of the community, to enjoy the arts and to share in scientific advancement and its benefits'. This wording enshrined the right to participate in the cultural life of one's country, a fundamental right in respect to the historical context after the Second World War since it was drafted in reaction to the Nazi decrees that had prohibited Jews from participating in German cultural life. This right to culture was therefore a bare liberty to participate in, create and have access to culture, but not a right designed to safeguard the cultural identity of individuals, a concept that was very little used at the time. It was the same type of cultural right that was recognised some 20 years later with the 1996 Covenant II on Economic, Social and Cultural Rights. Although cultural

[36] See Mylène Bidault, *La protection internationale des droits culturels* (Brussels, Bruylant, 2009) 3 *ff*.

rights are mentioned in the title of the Covenant, which seems to bestow equal importance on them as for economic and social rights, they are, in fact, very much the poor relations. They are defined principally in Article 15, which takes up in more detail the principle of a right of access, production, creation and protection in cultural matters, but they continue to take the back seat behind economic and social rights. Besides, this very limited scope that was assigned to them is hardly surprising because the Covenants were adopted in the midst of the Cold War and culture was a point of constant contention between the two blocs and, furthermore, the Eastern countries often engaged in political oppression in cultural matters internally. This was compounded by the fact that cultural rights were to be bound up with economic and social rights alone, and not with civil and political rights, so that they were also to suffer from their attachment to rights which, requiring state intervention, were already considered as less directly restrictive for states. There is nothing surprising therefore that the question of cultural rights was little discussed at the time and that it was not until the end of the Cold War that they truly came under debate internationally in direct conjunction with the resurgence of identity and cultural claims and new expectations with regard to recognition.

The 1993 Vienna Declaration and Programme of Action that closed the first major world summit on human rights after the fall of the Berlin Wall set out the indivisible and interdependent character of all rights and therefore of cultural rights with regard to other human rights (Point 5).[37] The Declaration was also adamant that states should guarantee and protect the specific rights of members of minorities and of indigenous peoples (Points 19 and 20). However, there is no provision which nominally concerns cultural rights and even today there are no legal texts which deal specifically with them. References to cultural rights are therefore found scattered throughout the various instruments of international law on human rights and they therefore obey separate legal schemes and controls. At a world level, they are provided for in particular by the pre-cited Article 27 of the Universal Declaration of Human Rights and Article 15 of the International Covenant on Economic, Social and Cultural Rights, as well as by a few texts adopted by the United Nations Educational, Scientific and Cultural Organisation (UNESCO) such as the 1960 Convention on the Fight against Discrimination in Education, the 1980 Recommendation Concerning the Status of the Artist or the 2001 Universal Declaration on Cultural Diversity. They are also found in some form or another in texts on minorities and indigenous peoples and in the various world conventions on the rights of certain categories of persons such as women, children or migrant workers. The practice of various international bodies such as the UNESCO Committee on Conventions and

[37] Vienna Declaration and Programme of Action, adopted on 25 June 1993 by the World Conference on Human Rights. See A/CONF.157/23, 12 July 1993; www.unhchr.ch/huridocda/huridoca.nsf/(symbol)/a.conf.157.23.en.

Recommendations,[38] the UN Independent Expert in the Field of Cultural Rights and the UN Committee on Economic, Social and Cultural Rights have progressively specified their content, nature and scope, so making them as concrete as possible and making good the absence of any specific text about them. The convergent action of these bodies, and in particular that of a UN Independent Expert,[39] attests to the interest there has been in them internationally since the end of the Cold War. Regionally, cultural rights are recognised by all the legal instruments relating to human rights, in Article 13 of the Inter-American Declaration of Human Rights and Duties, Article 14 of the Additional Protocol to the American Convention on Human Rights in the Area of Economic, Social and Cultural Rights and Article 17 of the African Charter of Human and Peoples' Rights. The case law of the regional courts with jurisdiction for these instruments is also essential in this domain, especially the extraordinary case law construction of the Inter-American Court that cannot be developed here but which is truly pioneering in the way cultural rights are considered and interpreted to protect cultural identities.[40]

Yet, opinions about cultural rights are not always unanimous, as attested to by a 1998 collective UNESCO publication titled 'Cultural Rights and Wrongs'.[41] It has to be agreed that the very idea that there can be cultural rights specifically is not necessarily obvious since, depending on the conception one has, different issues and rationales are involved. The points of discussion relate to the definition of cultural rights as the extension of identity versus cultural rights defined as a freedom. Two visions thus come head to head that pertain to separate underlying logics but which can be shown are not necessarily incompatible and may cross over so that it is possible to recognise the values of freedom and identity that define a human being.

On the one side are the familiar rights that can apply in the area of culture and that include both pecuniary rights and social rights but also civil liberties of freedom of conscience, association, information, creation and expression. These are civil, economic and social rights with a cultural component where we find the rights of the Universal Declaration and of the 1966 Covenants. They are often considered to be related to the existence of a democratic regime and an organisation like UNESCO endeavours, in particular since the Agenda for Democratisation of the UN Secretary General in 1996, to

[38] Kishore Singh, 'UNESCO and Cultural Rights' in Halina Niec (ed), *Cultural Rights and Wrongs* (Paris, UNESCO, 1998).

[39] Human Rights Council, Resolution 10/23 of 26 March 2009, 'Independent Expert in the Field of Cultural Rights'. Under the Resolution, the Expert is tasked with promoting cultural rights, identifying obstacles to their application, facilitating their implementation in states and ensuring coordination with the other UN bodies; ap.ohchr.org/documents/alldocs.aspx?doc_id=16299.

[40] See Antonio Cancado-Trindade, 'The Right to Cultural Identity in the Evolving Jurisprudential Construction of the Inter-American Court of Human Rights' in Sienho Yee and Jacques Yvan Morin (eds), *Multiculturalism and International Law* (Leiden, Brill, 2009) 477–99.

[41] See Halina Niec (ed), *Cultural Rights and Wrongs* (Paris, UNESCO, 1998). The French version published in 2000 is entitled *Pour ou contre les droits culturels?*

promote democracy as creating the most favourable environment for the exercise of cultural rights. These rights include those relating to the participation in the cultural life of the state, including in particular the right of access and the right to participate in cultural life, freedom of expression and creation but also the economic right to protect interests relating to cultural works. In the broad sense, these cultural rights are those first recognised internationally and that overall, even if they have an economic and social dimension, are grounded primarily in the freedom of any human being to make choices in cultural matters.

On the other side, there are more specific rights to participate in a given culture, with its practices, its language, its customs or its arts. It is these rights that are of particular interest here as they are directly related to the cultural identity of human beings to the extent that there is a transition from rights related to culture in general to rights related to the protection of cultures and the cultural identities of individuals. Some of these rights have been defined in an extremely precise and innovative way by inter-American case law, as said, but reference might also be made to the Fribourg Declaration to get a better grasp of them as they are gathered together in a very short statement. This Declaration of Cultural Rights does not strictly have any legal scope as it emanates from civil society but, being the outcome of more than 20 years of work, it is particularly clear and well thought out and can better delineate the nature of cultural rights of this type and the issues arising from their recognition in what is still a very uncertain area.[42] It identifies, as cultural rights, the right for any human being 'to choose and to have one's cultural identity respected, in the variety of its different means of expression' (Article 3a), the right 'to have one's own culture respected' (Article 3b), the freedom 'to choose to identify or not to identify with one or several cultural communities' (Article 4a), 'the freedom to teach and to receive teaching of and in one's language and in other languages', and the freedom to establish institutions to this end (Article 6) and 'alone or in community with others' to participate in cultural policies (Article 8). It can be seen from reading these rights that they are cultural rights in the narrow sense envisaged through the prism of recognition in that this is no longer the register of civil, economic or social rights where culture is viewed primarily as creation or freedom of expression, but the register of rights where culture is viewed in connection with the construction of individual identities. Accordingly, they form a category apart

[42] A group of specialists known as the Fribourg Group, in collaboration with UNESCO, proposed a Declaration on Cultural Rights in 1998. A new, reworked version was published in 2007; www1.umn.edu/humanrts/instree/Fribourg%20Declaration.pdf. See also Patrice Meyer-Bisch (ed), *Les droits culturels. Projet de déclaration* (Paris, Ed UNESCO, undated) 24 *ff.* The Fribourg Group are from civil society; the group originated from work by the interdisciplinary institute of ethics and human rights at the University of Fribourg, directed by Patrice Meyer-Bisch. It then widened with the involvement of UNESCO and Council of Europe members and other members of civil society. It has presented its work and its Declaration on Cultural Rights to many regional and international bodies, helping to clarify the issues involved in cultural rights.

which is essential and which is neither that of civil and political rights nor that of economic and social rights, with which they are all too often associated, but which is characterised by a new and common understanding of the concept of cultural identity. This is why it is better to define them and articulate them coherently with cultural rights in the broad sense. Without going into a lengthy abstract development that would go beyond the framework of this study, it has to be shown briefly what they are akin to and distinct from the first category of cultural rights in the broad sense and induce us to supplement them by reference to identity.

These cultural rights in the narrow sense are defined in relation to the existence of 'cultural communities' that are identified very flexibly as constituting the social and cultural environment within which people flourish in keeping with their own values and cultural codes. The existence of such communities is so obvious for many countries that there is hardly any need to labour the point in order to attest to their importance and their reality, but it is sometimes denied by states, with France being among the frontrunners, which do not wish to recognise the existence of such cultural communities out of fear of seeing ghetto communities developing and of compartmentalising individuals. In truth, the argument relies on a strictly communitaristic definition of community, that one is certainly not forced to follow as it is so rudimentary and confined to a purely negative meaning from which negative effects are inevitably inferred. 'Cultural communities' may be perceived in quite a different way, as open, permeable sets that come in many forms, ranging from regions to occupational spheres, and therefore dismissing any communitaristic conception of community as contravening cultural rights themselves.[43] To this end, it is necessary even so to clarify the de jure relations between the individual and the community because they raise the most problematic aspect of the new category of cultural rights. The question is whether the individual is free with respect to his cultural community and the exact nature of the cultural rights connected with that community. In this legal debate, the Fribourg Declaration takes a position for a very liberal interpretation of these rights that raises questions. It formulates the right to cultural identity as a *freedom*, making it possible to *choose* both one's cultural identity (Article 3a) and whether or not one belongs to a community (Article 4a). Now, in point of fact, such a position, for which the underlying reasons and the cogency of the argument are understandable, seems excessive to me since it is not readily compatible with what is known about the constitution of identities. It is far from certain that one's cultural identity can be the result of an entirely free and deliberate choice in that it is the cultural contexts in which we live that form that identity. It is precisely in that that we connect identity and community, namely that our identities are not constructed in

[43] On the different possible conceptions of 'community', see Michael Sandel, *Liberalism and the Limits of Justice* (Cambridge, Cambridge University Press, 1982) 147 *ff*.

the abstract but principally in connection with groups, communities, cultural circles that may be manifold but that are already there and that must be recognised and protected by the state since they are the objective condition for the constitution and flourishing of the identity of each individual. That does not mean that the cultural rights to identity are collective, they are individual rights but they have the particularity of presupposing a cultural community that is recognised as a prior given to the constitution of a situated individual. And so, without subscribing to a communitarian standpoint, it is doubtful that we can really speak of freedom of choice for one's identity in the strong sense of the word.[44] Between those who consider that one can only discover one's identity, which is fully determined by cultural communities, and those who assert that identity is solely the outcome of a deliberate choice, there is, it seems to me, room for a less coarse perception by which the formation of identity is a construction that is done through pre-existing communities but which may then develop through discovery of and contact with other communities and cultures, or even in accordance with the policies which identity may serve.[45]

From this it can be seen, by contrast, that the Fribourg Declaration is quite right in suggesting that the identity of individuals is never fixed and unique but is constructed, plural and evolving. Postmodern critical theory has enabled us to understand that while identities are rooted in natural givens (ethnic groups) or a cultural heritage (religion, language), they are also, in part, constructions that vary over time depending on the context in which they develop and the strategies that drive them.[46] On their side, the social sciences have taught us that the individual tends to define himself by multiple forms of belonging, overlapping various communities or cultural spaces and it is only in the framework of totally closed or radically traditionalist communities that the human being defines himself regressively by membership of a single culture.[47] This entrenchment of identity, which is legitimately feared by all, would violate not just the plural dynamics of identity, but would also work to the detriment of the 'patriotic' or 'national' identity of the state, that is, to the detriment of the shared common values of the community. An essential right arises from this, which is invariably recalled for minorities and indigenous groups, which is the right of any person to leave his community and which shows as clearly as can be the ultimate value attributed to freedom within the scheme as a whole. A cultural community, a minority or an indigenous people cannot claim in international law, in the name of the protection of their common cultural identity, to impose on their members customs and usages that some no longer wish to accept and they must leave

[44] See Will Kymlicka, *Les théories de la justice* (Paris, La découverte, 1990) 226 *ff.*

[45] Joan W Scott, *Théorie critique de l'histoire. Identités, expériences, politiques* (Paris, Fayard, 2009) 129 *ff.*

[46] ibid 129.

[47] Sen, *Identity and Violence* (n 2) 1 *ff.*

them free to leave the community so that they may develop their identities as they wish.[48]

Contrary to what one might infer, this does not result in a depletion of cultural identities but, on the contrary, in a flourishing of these identities for freedom comes here to preserve the possibility of seeing one's identity develop. More generally, it can be seen that the two categories of cultural rights are mutually reinforcing because their effects converge. The first category of cultural rights, cultural rights in the broad sense, the freedom to create, freedom of conscience and freedom to protect one's work, are necessary to achieving cultural identity rights as they give concrete effect to the possibilities of protection but also of furthering one's identity and expressing it by leaving everyone the freedom to make their own cultural choices. The second category of rights, cultural rights in the narrow sense, allows the holders of these rights to positively protect the qualities that make their identity and their culture the thing that not only makes them flourish but increases their autonomy and therefore also their opportunities to make free personal choices corresponding to their true aspirations.

Those who call for a general recognition of cultural rights internationally, in a single legal instrument, in both the narrow and the broad sense, consider that such recognition would fill the gap in the international law of human rights in this area insofar as cultural rights have not yet sufficiently guaranteed what makes the singularity, particularity and difference of any human being. According to this perspective, cultural rights are not perceived as opposing human rights based on the equal dignity of people but, on the contrary, as an extension of them as they are something that furthers the equal dignity of human beings. So not recognising such cultural rights amounts to an infringement of this equal dignity, while by recognising them, it can be hoped that people will not feel disregarded and so turn in on themselves.[49] Far from leading to any self-segregation, cultural rights therefore arguably promote the integration of people into a given society. In addition, it is interesting to observe that the holders of these cultural rights take the exact opposite stance to those who reject them and emphasise that recognising specific rights relating to the cultural identity of any human being means that their equal dignity can be more readily respected and is not a source of potential conflict as it eases and fosters relations between people who, thanks to law, feel their identity and their cultural choices are respected. In truth, the danger of use for conservative or radical traditionalist purposes cannot

[48] This is generally termed the 'right to exit'. It is essential but not without difficulties if one reasons in terms of the survival of small communities. On minorities, see Patrick Thornberry, *Minorities and Human Rights Law* (Lenders, Minority Rights Group, 1991).

[49] As Emmanuel Decaux states, cultural rights are not part of 'closed societies' but, on the contrary, are part of 'open societies', open to the mixing of cultures and identities: Emmanuel Decaux, 'Preface' to Mylène Bidault, *La protection internationale des droits culturels* (Brussels, Bruylant, 2009) XI.

be ignored and is a dark side since identity is also a reconstruction that can serve diverse political interests and give rise to conflict-oriented usages which the legal recognition of rights cannot prevent, or may even enhance if it is diverted from its original purpose. This is a point that has been highlighted throughout this study, that is, what we call the dark side of law; in order to have a more clear-sighted understanding of the rules and practices which, in reflecting the demands of social justice, are sometimes themselves unfair in some of their effects and therefore constitute a problem at the same time as they offer a possible solution.

III Human Rights

The contemporary theme of recognition highlights 'the complexity of the modern idea of humanity'[50] as it is conveyed today in international law where an attempt is made to take account of the share of humanity that is common to all and of the culturally different identities of each individual. But from this standpoint, it also prompts the question again of a possible cultural imperialism of human rights and we again stumble upon one of the best known dilemmas of contemporary law.[51] Does the international law of human rights not deny cultural identities and the diversity of cultures by imposing a universal standard of Western origin that is not necessarily shared by all? Are the rights proclaimed in international texts really universally valid, extending beyond cultural divides and binding on all? Although the problem is not a new one, I would like to show how its current revival is directly related to the paradigm of recognition and to the emergence of a multipolar, postcolonial and post-Cold War international society that is progressively moving towards establishing cultural diversity and respect for identities as fundamental principles.

A Historical Development

The question of a possible cultural imperialism of rights was raised on the international stage in Paris in 1948 at the time the Universal Declaration of Human Rights was drafted. Human rights arose from the Euro-American Enlightenment tradition; they are the highpoint of that culture and of the history of European modernity. It was no chance matter, then, that, because of concerns of the still dominant European and American powers of the post-war years, they were to be recognised internationally. But the Human Rights Division tasked with preparing the Declaration was fully aware of the prob-

[50] Sylvie Mesure and Alain Renaut, *Alter ego. Les paradoxes de l'identité démocratique* (Paris, Flammarion, 1999) 17.

[51] See Emmanuelle Jouannet, 'Between Universalism and Imperialism: The True-False Paradox of International Law' (2007) 17 (3) *European Journal of International* Law 407–50.

lem of universalising rights derived from one specific culture and it had identified many questions bearing on this point. The American Anthropological Association (AAA) had filed a report asking that the Declaration should not be drawn up solely from the perspective of the dominant values of Western Europe and America and that it should not mean the automatic application of human rights to other cultures. At the same time, in 1947, UNESCO published a report in which its experts attempted to avoid this pitfall by trying to identify the common foundations of human rights across the many human cultures and civilisations. Space was also given to many non-Western thinkers who were consulted on their cultural traditions, with the Chinese delegate Peng Chun Chang advising the Secretariat to study Confucianism in much more depth so as to enhance its view of rights.

In point of fact, the Universal Declaration was only adopted because of very special circumstances: because it was just after the Second World War, it was a simple declaration without any binding force and because a common ideological minimum agreement was still possible between East and West. It was passed by the UN General Assembly on 10 December 1948. No state voted against it, but among the eight that abstained were South Africa in the days of apartheid, which refused non-discrimination between races, Saudi Arabia, which contested equality of the sexes, and the Soviet Union, Czechoslovakia, Yugoslavia and Poland because of the definition of the principle of universality of Article 2(1). Besides, there were only 56 states present in Paris since the colonised nations were absent. That in itself made it contentious and particularly indecent to make a declaration about 'recognition of the inherent dignity and of the equal and inalienable rights of all members of the human family' and to claim that the Declaration was 'a common standard of achievement for all peoples and all nations' (Preamble).[52] Even if the Declaration did call for the application of rights in territories under the jurisdiction of Member States (Preamble), even so it thereby legitimated colonisation in a particularly insidious and shocking way and therefore both the system of exploitation and the deep-seated discrimination between people that it implied.

However, one cannot reduce the 1948 Declaration to these historical circumstances and ignore its fundamental scope with respect to the processes of recognition that are of particular interest here. From this point of view, it is not difficult to understand that the particularly ponderous European context of the post-war period was decisive and transcended in part the cultural considerations and above all the ideological divides that opposed representatives from East and West.[53] In reaction to the Nazi atrocities of the Second World

[52] UN General Assembly Resolution 217 A (III) (10 December 1948). Text available at www.un.org/en/documents/udhr/.

[53] See Emmanuel Decaux, 'La genèse de la Déclaration universelle des droits de l'homme' (1989) 10 *Bulletin de l'Association René Cassin* 15 *ff* and for the entire Declaration and its context in depth, see Johannes Morsink, *The Universal Declaration of Human Rights: Origins, Drafting, and Intent* (Philadelphia, Pennsylvania University Press, 2000).

War, an entirely new process of international recognition was at work since human rights, which were finally proclaimed in 1948, reflect the legal recognition of a human identity common to all through an equal legal status. This was of substantial historical scope since for centuries and for many human societies, the idea had prevailed that humanity ended with their tribe, their region, their culture or their borders.[54] The Declaration affirmed from the outset 'recognition of the inherent dignity and of the equal and inalienable rights of all members of the human family' (Preamble, paragraph 1) and Article 1 provides that 'All human beings are born free and equal in dignity and rights'. The idea of 'dignity' is at the heart of this process as it becomes the mark of the part of humanity that deserves respect and recognition.[55] The little known discussions between the Lebanese and Chinese representatives, Charles Malik and Peng Chun Chang, are illuminating in this respect as they relate to the ideas of human being, dignity, and equality of rights and show the crucial importance that was henceforth attributed to them. They are to be rediscovered to understand the state of mind of the time. One can perceive a few compromises depending on cultures of which some articles bear the mark, but generally a spirit of consensus and universality prevailed, because of the circumstances of the post-war period but also because the representatives were all trained in Western culture. The 'international' declaration as a term was significantly superseded by 'universal' declaration and so marked the turning point towards the universality of rights. The consensus was secured above all thanks to the recognition of economic and social rights alongside civil and political ones, thus bringing about the coexistence of European liberal and social traditions of human rights. In the end, there was a tangible surge of optimism. The representative for Chile, Hernan Santa Cruz, observed:

> I had the very clear feeling that I was participating in an event truly unique in its scope in the course of which consensus was achieved on the supreme value of the human person, a value that did not originate in the decision of a power of this world [. . .] there was [. . .] an atmosphere of authentic solidarity and fraternity among men and women of all latitudes, an atmosphere I have never found again in any international instance.[56]

Indeed, it never was to be found again. The Cold War was already underway while decolonisation was to give rise to a Third World that had been almost absent in 1948, anxious to stand apart from the cultural hegemony

[54] See Claude Lévi-Strauss, *Structural Anthropology* (New York, Basic Books, 1963) 277 *ff.*

[55] For more on this and the policy of equal human dignity based on reciprocity as the first process of recognition, see Charles Taylor, *Multiculturalism. Examining the Politics of Recognition* (Princeton, Princeton University Press, 1994) 47 *ff.* The 1948 Declaration enshrines the original form of liberalism of human rights internationally, which is a liberalism of equal rights. On the concept of liberalism of human rights, see Emmanuelle Jouannet, *The Liberal-Welfarist Law of Nations. A History of International Law* (Cambridge, Cambridge University Press, 2012) 216 *ff.*

[56] Cited in Gérard Fellous, *Les droits de l'homme Une universalité menacée* (Paris, La documentation française, 2010) 204 (our translation).

of the former colonisers. While the Third World nations were to be divided over economic and social questions, they were never so much of one mind as when denouncing Western cultural imperialism. At Bandung in April 1955 they denounced, as a form of cultural oppression, the fact that fundamental rights could be imposed on them in a binding way. The final communiqué of the Bandung Conference recognises their indisputable value but states that 'the right of peoples and nations to self-determination' is 'a prerequisite of the full enjoyment of all fundamental Human rights' (C, 1).[57] Five years later, Resolution 1514 (XV) of 14 December 1960 on the granting of independence to colonial countries and peoples proclaimed that, to ensure 'universal respect for, and observance of, human rights', an end to colonialism must first be made.[58] However, while contesting the conditions of its application, the Third World countries rallied definitively to the legal discourse on human rights with the 1968 Teheran Proclamation and Resolution 32/130 of 16 December 1977 which both reaffirmed the interdependence of all rights. The Declaration was itself to inspire more than 70 treaties on human rights that have been very widely ratified.[59] Now, this worldwide rallying consecrated the beginning of a de jure generalisation of the international law of human rights and the general recognition of human beings as subjects of law, holders of equal rights to all other human beings, regardless of their sex, ethnic group, skin colour, religion or culture. This point is essential to recall even today since the adhesion of almost all of the world's states to the legal discourse on rights is attested to by their international commitments and is taken up by many international organisations. That does not call into question the fact that human rights are originally the product of a culture that imposed itself on the world because of Western hegemony and a combination of knowledge and power that it established for its own benefit. All the same, the adhesion of the countries of the South to this discourse marks a decisive step. The states of the North and South, East and West have thus legally committed themselves to a long-term process in which they are far from able to control all the aspects and from which they often try to escape, but, even so, this marks the contemporary tipping point that has been pointed out many times – of international law towards human beings and no longer towards the state. This phenomenon of recognition is now being extended by human rights, that is, where the continuous expansion of the sphere of application of those rights includes ever more areas and individuals because of ratifications of international texts and because of struggles for recognition conducted concretely on the ground in the face

[57] Asian-African Conference, Bandung, April 18]24, 1955; fds.oup.com/www.oup.co.uk/pdf/bt/cassese/cases/part3/ch18/1702.pdf.

[58] www.un.org/peace/etimor99/a1514xv.pdf.

[59] See Antonio Cançado Trindade, 'La déclaration universelle des droits de l'homme', United Nations Audovisual Library of International Law; untreaty.un.org/cod/avl/pdf/ha/udhr/udhr_e.pdf.

of experiences of exclusion, discrimination or oppression, struggles that may even take the form of revolutions like those of the Arab Spring.[60] The victories that have been won in these fights for recognition are reflected by self-respect, which lies at the heart of the feeling of rediscovered pride of which Paul Ricœur speaks so finely.[61]

That being so, as the works prior to the adoption of the 1948 Declaration announced, during the Cold War the debates about rights were not about culture. Opposition between West and East and North and South crystallised over civil and political rights and economic and social rights, without the question of their compatibility with different cultures of the planet really being addressed. While the Universal Declaration mixed both types of rights, the Eastern camp, followed by much of the decolonised Third World, was to invoke the priority for concrete freedoms (economic and social rights) rather than the formal freedoms (civil and political rights) defended by the West and was to consider achieving them as the prerequisite to the implementation of civil and political rights, which needed to be rethought in a communist context as they were considered to be bourgeois and backward. The West defended the exact opposite position by insisting on the establishment of civil and political rights as a priority. Economic and social rights were not considered fundamental and some even thought them unachievable. Hence the adoption in 1966 of two separate Covenants; the first on civil and political rights and the second on economic, social and cultural rights.[62] Cultural rights were added but in fact, as said before, they were of secondary importance.

The difficult reconciliation of rights with non-Western cultures was not ignored, though. As early as the 1960s, the resort to reservations and interpretative declarations was one of the leading legal techniques of states to allow them to ratify treaties on human rights while setting aside or interpreting provisions so as to allow their own cultural practices to prevail. The adoption of regional instruments on human rights in Europe (1950), America (1969) and Africa (1981) was one way not just of making the rights proclaimed at world level more effective but also of adapting them to a particular regional cultural environment. The 1950 European Convention on Human Rights explicitly situates the rights it guarantees as part of 'a common heritage of political traditions, ideals, freedom and the rule of law' (Preamble), while the African Charter of Human and Peoples' Rights affirms that 'the values of African civilisation which should inspire and characterise their [the African Union member states'] reflection on the concept of human and peoples' rights' (Preamble). Accordingly, the case law of the supervisory bodies for

[60] Ricœur, *Parcours de la reconnaissance* (n 1) 314.

[61] Ricœur citing Joel Feinberg, *Rights, Justice and the Bounds of Liberty, Essays in Social Philosophy* (NY, Princeton, 1980) in *Ricœur, Parcours de la reconnaissance* (n 1) 315.

[62] Some rights, such as the right of property, asylum or to not be deprived of one's nationality, although they were set out in the Universal Declaration, were deliberately omitted from the Covenants so that a consensus of opinion could be reached.

the Conventions was to draw on shared national traditions and regional cultural values in interpreting the common rights of the states parties.

But it is only since the end of the Cold War that the cultural question has truly emerged in the discourse on human rights. The line of confrontation over rights shifted very markedly after 1989 since the question of civil and political rights versus economic and social rights divides states far less nowadays than that of the place of culture and cultural specificities with regard to the universalism of human rights. This shift in concerns after 1989 in regards to human rights can be explained by the end of the ideological confrontation between East and West over social and political rights and the beginning of the era of recognition with respect to questions of identity and culture, the indisputable repercussions of which are plain to see. The end of the Cold War forcefully brought home the idea that human rights must necessarily take account of the values and cultures of each individual so as not to artificially promote what is considered an overly Western position unsuited to the climate in which the rights must apply. This requirement grew stronger during the second decade after the fall of the Berlin Wall, for, while initially the legal discourse of human rights was the subject of an incontrovertible re-enhancement and all-round consensus that had never existed before, it subsequently prompted strong criticism. As the post-Cold War consensus of opinion broke up, the criticism of the cultural imperialism of human rights surfaced again when they were invoked to condemn the cultural and traditional values of certain regions or non-Western states and, above all, to justify armed intervention or particularly selective and arbitrary condition-bound policies. This is what Bertrand Badie aptly summarises as international diplomacy of human rights wavering between 'ethics and the will to power' and is one of the most obvious dark sides of human rights.[63] Some have seen in this the establishment of a new Western neo-colonialism or imperialism, a vector for new 'civilising missions' conducted in the name of human rights and revealing a cultural ethnocentrism that for the time being remains specific to the West: setting up one's own values as universal values and claiming that what is good for the West is good for the World.[64] It is only when the populations concerned, like the Arab populations of Egypt, Tunisia or Libya, themselves seize hold of human rights that a non-hegemonic use of these rights is truly at work and they are endowed with their tremendous emancipatory power.

If one seeks to identify more specifically one of the significant moments of the post-Cold War emergence of the issue of human rights and cultures,

[63] Bertrand Badie, *La diplomatie des droits de l'homme. Entre éthique et volonté de puissance* (Paris, Fayard, 2002).

[64] See for example Vasuki Nesiah, 'From Berlin to Bonn to Baghdad. A Space for Infinite Justice' (2004) 17 *Harvard Human Rights Journal* 75–99 and Makua Mutua, 'Savages, Victims and Saviors. The Metaphor of Human Rights' (2001) 42 (1) *Harvard International Law Journal* 201–45.

mention can be made of the first great international conference on human rights organised in Vienna in 1993 as the event that incontrovertibly sparked the first real questions on this topic and, at the same time, was an occasion that celebrated re-found unity in this domain. Although they had been roughly handled by the adoption of the two separate Conventions in 1966, the indivisibility and interdependence of all rights were proclaimed with the adoption of the Conference Declaration and Programme of Action and they marked the end of the deadly ideological conflict between economic and social rights and civil and political rights. All rights were not to be treated 'on the same footing, and with the same emphasis' (Declaration, point 5), familiar wording that in the new context raised the hope that it would at last be applied. However, the UN Secretary-General, Boutros Boutros-Ghali, in his opening address to the Vienna Conference, warned states against cultural claims that had already been manifested and that, in his view, were a new challenge to human rights in a post-Cold War world. The primary objective of the Conference, he stated, should be clearly to assert an 'imperative of universality' against the cultural and religious relativism that was spreading around the world, by nonetheless taking account of 'the most challenging dialectical conflict ever: between "identity" and "otherness", between the "myself" and "others"'.[65]

In fact, the debate was only just beginning, for in the dialectic about identity and otherness which Boutros-Ghali spoke of in the Vienna address, otherness was hardly taken into account in the declaration adopted – other than through the rights of minorities and indigenous peoples – because the emphasis leaned so heavily on universality. But behind the proclamation of unity and universality displayed in the Final Declaration, there appeared already, as Boutros-Ghali had observed, numerous calls for human rights to make more allowances for all cultures and values. Some of the regional conferences held to prepare the Vienna Conference, and which were supposed to reflect the aspirations of the various regions of the world in this domain, had already proved to what extent cultural questions were beginning to be seen as essential, in particular the Bangkok Conference of Asian countries and the Tunis Conference for African states. They were concluded by final declarations fully reaffirming the principle of the universality of rights, but also asking that national and regional cultural peculiarities be better integrated into the definition and application of rights. Point 5 of the Tunis Declaration notably recalled that 'no ready-made model can be prescribed at the universal level since the historical and cultural realities of each nation and the traditions, standards and values of each people cannot be disregarded'.[66]

[65] Quoted in Fellous, *Les droits de l'homme. Une universalité menacée*, 87; www.ohchr.org/EN/NewsEvents/Pages/DisplayNews.aspx?NewsID=7906&LangID=E.

[66] Declaration of Tunis of 6 November 1992; www.ohchr.org/EN/ABOUTUS/Pages/ViennaWC.aspx.

In the wake of this, the movement continued and a far more aggressive policy has been in evidence in recent years which tends to seek to impose a vision of rights that is more relativist and more adaptable to each culture. Emerging countries like China and Russia and many Muslim countries are adopting unilateral, individual or collective declarations, looking to have a different interpretation of human rights prevail or even to combat rights in the name of observance of their traditions, their civilisation or their religion. Although very rare, some political, but not legal, declarations seek to defend an alternative version of rights and to dismiss rights as quite inappropriate for their own traditions and cultural values. We can cite the emblematic declaration of 1991 on Asian values of a few states of South-East Asia, which was over-publicised given the small group of leaders who rallied to it, but which is part of the fight against human rights conducted by certain non-Western politicians at the helm of authoritarian governments.[67] Many declarations by the Islamic Conference Organisation (ICO) might also be cited, such as the 2004 Declaration on Cultural Diversity or the 2009 Declaration on Health which, intentionally, make no mention of human rights but emphasise the obligations of all, pursuant to Islam, to look to the well-being of each person. Nonetheless, apart from these more or less head-on attacks, which remain very marginal, most declarations still fit in with the legal discourse on human rights and seek rather to promote a cultural interpretation of those rights which is consistent with the cultures and religions practised.

Beyond certain political and legal offensives that are instrumentalised by authoritarian and radical traditionalist powers, there has emerged much more generally a genuine and marked concern for the necessary cultural adaption of rights. This concern has asserted itself all the more plainly because the correlative demand for recognition by many non-Western states of greater respect for their cultures, which was materialised by the 2005 UNESCO Conference, could not fail to have repercussions on the way human rights are conceived and applied. Besides, it has always been known, although not taken into account, that Asian and African societies and the many indigenous South American communities generally reflect a community ideal that does not match Western individualistic values. They have another way of organising solidarity, considering the relationship to religious belief, assuming responsibility and expressing dignity. The result of this is that they relate observance of individual rights to respect for legal obligations towards the family, district, community, religion or state which are not alienating for individuals but, on the contrary, allow individuals to flourish.[68] Now, in the context of post-Cold War globalisation and the heightened fear of seeing

[67] For a good inside view and discussion on Asia, see Michael C Davis (ed), *Human Rights and Chinese Values. Legal, Philosophical and Political Perspectives* (Hong Kong, Oxford University Press, 1995).

[68] See for example Keba Mbaye, *Les droits de l'homme en Afrique* (Paris, Pedone, 2002).

cultures threatened, such an essential dimension could not be ignored and the fact is that this dimension is called for as something that should necessarily be integrated into the definition, interpretation and/or the application of rights.

B Discussions and Solutions

Highlighting these new requirements subjects the international law of human rights to a legal rationale that is now familiar to us as it characterises all of the international law of recognition. There is an undetected shift away from a process of recognition of persons based on the assertion of equal standing and equal dignity of each human being, regardless of cultural differences among individuals (1948 Declaration and 1966 Covenants), towards a new stage of recognition based on cultural differences. The rights recognised in 1948 and 1966 are supposed to be universally the same; they represent an identical set of rights for all which prohibits discrimination on the basis of the cultures and traditions of each people. Now, today, on the contrary, it is a matter of interpreting and adapting human rights to make them compatible with the cultural particularism of each people and to take them into account positively. In other words, with regard to rights themselves, an attempt is made to shift from a uniform definition or application of rights to a conception that is 'hospitable' to difference.[69] This leads to the contemporary, new stage of recognition with a transition from formal equality to differentiated equality. Were such a development to be confirmed, it would mark a very clear change of course in the liberal and universalist model of human rights in a multicultural and particularist direction.

The question remains, however, as to how far such expectations can be contemplated with respect to the original logic of rights that is encapsulated in international texts. To what extent can cultural difference of rights be recognised without giving in simply to 'force of prejudice'?[70] How can one manage, at the same time, the universalist affirmation of rights and the cultural and national particularities (Bangkok Declaration), or the idea of refusing a single model applicable to all (Tunis Declaration)? Without re-opening what is already a very copious case load,[71] I shall simply underscore a few possible implications for the current topic.

The first item of evidence to be adduced in this matter is to recall that, for the time being, international texts enshrine in the main the primacy of human rights over cultures and the cultural values of peoples, groups and individuals. This is the side on which all the international instruments on cultural

[69] To take up the term in Taylor, *Multiculturalism* (n 55) 61.

[70] Pierre-André Taguieff, *La force du préjugé. Essai sur le racisme et ses doubles* (Paris, Gallimard, 1987), *The Force of Prejudice. On Racism and its Doubles* (Minneapolis, University of Minnesota Press, 2001).

[71] For an overview of the abundant literature on this question, see Jack Donnelly, *Universal Human Rights in Theory and Practice* (Ithaca, Cornell University Press, 1989).

diversity, the rights of minorities or of indigenous peoples and cultural rights come down. Further to the UNESCO Declaration, the 2005 Convention on the Diversity of Cultural Expressions provides for this necessary compatibility with human rights, by considering that 'No one may invoke the provisions of this Convention in order to infringe human rights and fundamental freedoms as enshrined in the Universal Declaration of Human Rights or guaranteed by international law, or to limit the scope thereof' (Article 2). Article 46(1) of the 2007 Declaration of the Rights of Indigenous Peoples specifies that the (collective or individual) rights of indigenous peoples must be exercised with respect to human rights and fundamental freedoms. This primacy is recalled in the various instruments on the rights of minorities, and cultural rights themselves are considered as part of human rights and it is often specified that the respect for cultural identities and communities cannot be materialised unless communities and individuals themselves respect all human rights.

This, it will be agreed, does not a priori seem to leave much scope for taking on any new expectations in cultural matters, but above all it does not solve the problem in that asserting the primacy of human rights does not settle the question of their interpretation. For example, in response to the question asked above as to whether, out of respect for African or Islamic cultures, cultural practices like excision or stoning should be guaranteed, it has been seen that the answer seems to be decidedly not, as these are cultural practices which, it will be argued, are not compatible with, for example, the prohibition of inhuman and degrading treatment. However, the discussion can be pursued by recalling that it is all a matter of interpretation of what constitutes inhuman and degrading treatment and generally a matter of interpretation of fundamental rights themselves. Can anyone fail to see that the countries where stoning is practised claim its application as consistent with Sharia law, which itself guides the interpretation of the most fundamental rights? The Declaration of Human Rights in Islam, adopted in 1990 by the ICO Member States, asserts that 'The Islamic Shari'a is the only source of reference for the explanation or classification of any of the articles of this Declaration' (Article 25).[72] At a session of the Human Rights Council in June 2006, a representative of a non-governmental organisation who dared to denounce stoning was expelled and vehemently accused of Islamophobia by numerous Council delegates, including those of India and Pakistan. Should this position be taken for a valid interpretation of rights in line with the most eminent cultural values of the religious culture of those countries, or should it be considered that these are the 'cultural prejudices' denounced by the Vienna Declaration when they entail violence to persons (point 18)? It can be seen that in the inter-subjective and still decentralised condition in which international society still finds itself,

[72] Cairo Declaration on human rights in Islam, 5 August 1990; www.unhcr.org/refworld/publisher,ARAB,,,3ae6b3822c,0.html.

the impassable legal boundary formed by the most fundamental human rights may be meaningless in practice.[73]

At this stage, there may be complete opposition between a universalist conception of human rights and certain strictly culture-based interpretations. Some will rejoice in this as there is no longer any fear of a cultural imperialism of rights, but it must be admitted that the price to pay does seem particularly high in that such a development would mean a complete turnaround of the founding principles of human rights and in particular of the originating act of recognition from which they flow. The rationale behind such cultural interpretations leads to radical differentialism at state level which impedes any common interpretation of rights and therefore amounts, in fact, to introducing a subtle but particularly insidious negation of rights, which is usually the true but undeclared purpose of strictly culturalist positions. In this case, human rights are no longer rights that are recognised equally to all and shared by all, but they become particular rights that are no longer founded on anything but the recognition of the differences and cultures of all. It is no longer a matter of living equally and different but simply different, since people are only recognised because they belong to a culture and no longer because of their shared humanity. But was it not above all through the legal proclamation of the equal dignity of human beings, of their equal value, regardless of their differences, that human rights had been marked out in 1948? From shift to shift, a complete turnaround in the original rationale of human rights may occur, with the result that, replaced in the paradigm of recognition, such a development would call into question the gains of the first fundamental process of recognition that the 1948 Declaration had achieved and thereby fall back into a state of disregard of rights internationally which was the state that characterised international society before the Second World War. Or, in the dialectic of 'myself' and 'other' evoked by Boutros-Ghali in his 1993 Vienna Address, it is the 'other' who would win this time since, by a subtle subversion of the original spirit of rights, people would come to be defined legally in terms of their radical cultural heterogeneity. This would bring us back, by an irony of history, to the position of colonial international society when otherness and cultural differences trapped individuals and peoples alike in irreducibly different legal statuses.

It is hardly difficult, then, to show the dead-ends and even the negation of rights to which radical cultural interpretations are intentionally or unintentionally exposed with regard to human rights but, for all that, the question of the cultural adaptation of rights has still not been resolved and remains a

[73] Examples from countries of the North might be the execution of minors and the mentally disabled in the United States, which long justified this in the name of a cultural practice of criminal justice that many observers find incomprehensible (these practices were prohibited by the US Supreme Court in 2008); or the death penalty that 138 countries have abolished but that Japan, for example, maintains because of the profoundly different cultural context where the death penalty is considered an act of human dignity. See Mireille Delmas-Marty, *Vers une communauté de valeurs?* (Paris, Seuil, 2011) 245 *ff*.

real problem. From this standpoint, and so as to clarify the issues at stake, it seems necessary to understand that one can rightly not go with the 'strong' culturalist argument, which suggests strict differentialism, while going with a 'weak' culturalist argument which remains fully relevant if one no longer wishes to settle for a strictly liberal conception of human rights that would leave no room for the new post-Cold War cultural demands and would not seek to de-Westernise those demands in part for the benefit of true cultural pluralism.[74] It would also be to consider that human rights cannot claim to be entirely neutral, as some argue, even if they can be generalised to the whole world, and to accept that they remain marked by their Euro-American liberal cultural origin, with the result that it is necessary to integrate a 'hospitable variant'[75] of these rights that might include cultural differences. Just like the classical liberal international law of states, the classical international law of human rights is not neutral and through its formalism it favours a certain conception of rights that has imposed itself on the world historically. This is why we find for human rights in general what has been observed for the other domains of recognition; namely, that the recognition of the cultural specificities of any individual and of their membership to a particular culture may make it possible to go beyond the formalism of earlier law and contribute to furthering and rendering the principle of the equal dignity of human beings more effective by taking into account the cultural dimension of any human being.[76]

In other words, human rights and cultural specificities maintain complex relations as they are both antagonistic and complementary and this dialogic relationship[77] necessarily problematises any dogmatic position, whether universalist or relativist. It explains why quarrels over the issue are endless, with the result that we can at best, as Stuart Hall observes,[78] attenuate in practice

[74] Balakrishnan Rajagopal, 'From Resistance to Renewal. The Third World, Social Movements and the Expansion of International Institutions' (2000) 41 *Harvard international Law Journal* 416 ff.

[75] Taylor, *Multiculturalism* (n 55) 62. The distinctions he draws between two forms of liberalism are also relevant internationally. There is thus a shift from strictly liberal liberalism of human rights (liberalism 1) to a 'liberalism 2', allowing for cultural differences among peoples, but without questioning the foundations of equal dignity of individuals and equal rights. This liberalism 2 of the international law of human rights purportedly includes all the specific rights spoken of here but also the possibility, evoked here, of cultural definition/interpretation/application of rights that is more open to the inclusion of the cultures of all peoples.

[76] This presupposes a dialogic conception of the individual in the sense of Paul Ricœur, *Soi-même comme un autre* (Paris, Seuil 1990) 11 *ff*; *Oneself as Another* (Chicago, University of Chicago Press, 1992) who differentiates 'me' as 'identity' from 'me' as 'individuality'.

[77] As defined by Edgar Morin, *Introduction à la pensée complexe* (Paris, Ed ESF, 1990).

[78] Stuart Hall, *Identités et cultures. Politique des Cultural Studies* (Paris, Ed Amsterdam, 2008) 407 *ff*. This is to apply to human rights the 'comprehensive pluralism' approach defended by Michel Rosenfeld, *Just Interpretations: Law between Ethics and Politics* (Berkeley, University of California Press, 1998) 199 *ff*. See also the very original approach of Yasuaki Onuma, *A Transcivilizational Perspective on International Law: Questioning Prevalent Cognitive Frameworks in the Emerging Multi-Polar and Multi-civilizational World of the Twenty-First Century* (The Hague Academy of International Law, 2010).

the tension between the opposing principles by adopting concrete approaches on a case-by-case basis, depending on each context, and thus making fine but essential adjustments to rights to enable them to perform their double function of recognition. Obviously, the work of the courts is seen here as particularly significant, whether it be the European, Inter-American or African courts. Admittedly, the regional courts do not settle every human rights case that comes up, but their role is symbolically decisive in the interpretations they give to rights in terms of culturally shared references by the states parties to the regional system of protection of rights and in terms of their own cultural interpretation of rights. It is noteworthy that the European Court uses the 'national margin of appreciation' to allow each state to adapt rights to its own culture.[79] Worth noting too are certain decisions of the Inter-American Court of Human Rights where the Court has taken very close account of the values and traditions of indigenous communities in re-defining human rights in light of them, even including the right to cultural identity as an element of the right to life. It even took account of this in a particularly novel way when it determined that compensation should be paid to the widows of a polygamous man who was unlawfully killed or allowance for the 'indigenous cosmovision' between the living and the dead to return bodies and put a value on the specific character of the loss incurred.[80] In truth, the work of the courts remains very marginal on the international stage even today and many other concrete approaches are made empirically to attempt, without necessarily theorising their action as such, to root rights in each particular cultural soil and so attenuate the unresolved tension between universalist and culturalist principles. Here we can evoke the idea of conducting a 'grass roots' consultation in some countries, as advocated by Louise Arbour in 2007 when she was High Commissioner for Human Rights, whenever a potential reconciliation of cultures with the rights set out in international texts was to be discussed, not with the representatives of states but with the groups directly concerned by the application of rights, vulnerable persons, minorities, women and any individual whatsoever, so that they might express how they experienced this possible reconciliation. There is much to investigate further on this alternative path, since it is an approach that has the benefit of relying on reflection about deliberative spaces as the locus of construction of identity and on reflection about subaltern groups.

[79] This is examined at length in Mireille Delmas-Marty, *Le relatif et l'universel* (Paris, Seuil 2004) 64 *ff*. But it is a solution that is thought quite inadequate by some who wish to adopt declarations of human rights adapted to the cultural specificities of certain populations. This is a claim, for example, of the Catalans and the Scots. See Stephen Tierney, *Constitutional Law and National Pluralism* (Oxford, Oxford University Press, 2004) 329 *ff*.

[80] See a whole series of cases where the Court, ruling on the merits or on reparations, reconciled cultures and human rights: *Aloeboetoe versus Suriname* (1993); 'Street Children' (*Villagran Morales versus Guatemala*, 1999–2001); *Bamaca Velasquez versus Guatemala* (2000–2002); *Mayagna (Sumo) Awas Tingni Community versus Nicaragua* (2001); *Yakye Axa and Sawhoyamaxa indigenous communities versus Paraguay* (2006) and *Moiwana Community versus Suriname* (2005–2006).

IV Women's Rights

No one will be surprised that the situation of women has given rise to an international legal policy of recognition in that the sexism of every society in the world creates constant discrimination against women depending on whether they are excluded from certain activities or from the benefit of having certain rights that are culturally reserved to men or whether they are maintained de facto or de jure in a situation that is subordinate and unequal to that of men. With the fight against sexual discrimination affecting women, another type of claim has also emerged over the course of history, based on sexual identity or gender.[81] This was to give rise to several legal responses before and after the Cold War and nowadays constitutes a forceful challenge to the old classical liberal international law.

A The Principle of Equality and the Fight against Discrimination

Although claims relating to such discrimination are long-standing, they were not to be taken into account internationally until after the Second World War via a whole series of legal provisions and instruments that were to attribute growing scope to them within the international arrangements on human rights and were to confirm the recognition of equal dignity of women as subjects of law. Admittedly, before then certain international conventions pertaining to women had been adopted but for the sole purpose of protecting them as particularly vulnerable beings and not to treat them as subjects of law equal to men. Among them were the 1910 Paris Convention on the Suppression of the White Slave Traffic or the ILO Conventions of 1919 on female labour that saw women merely as specific objects of law, as mothers or as weaker and more vulnerable human beings than men, and who therefore required special measures of protection or specific treatment. Even if they made it possible to advance the cause of women,[82] those conventions in truth reflected a vision that was opposed to any idea of equal status between men and women, since the difference in sex served as justification for dealing with men and women differently. For its part, the League of Nations roused great enthusiasm among feminist associations who shared the new organisation's values and hoped to find in it the means to further their ideas internationally

[81] The UN is far more divided over the general question of sexual orientation and the totally discriminatory situation of homosexuals in particular. The Human Rights Council did manage to secure the adoption (albeit by a narrow majority) of the Resolution of 17 June 2011 on violence and discrimination based on sexual orientation and gender identity.

[82] See, on the decisive work of the ILO, Carol Riegelman Lubin and Anne Winslow, *Social Justice for Women. The International Labor Organization and Women* (Durham, Duke University Press, 1990).

and domestically.[83] Alongside the Peace Conference, a conference of suffragettes from allied countries and the United States was held, a delegation of which had filed a memorandum with the drafters of the Covenant summarising their claims. But while marking an important step in women's struggle, especially because of equal access of both sexes to positions in the organisation (Article 7 of the Covenant), the work accomplished in Geneva did not lead to the adoption of an international legal instrument along these lines. In addition, while the principle of equality between men and women was obviously already at the heart of the claims of feminists in the League of Nations, it was not until 1945 that such a principle was to be proclaimed internationally. This was because of the new post-war context marked by the entrance of human rights onto the international stage but also by the new position women had taken during the Second World War. This was compounded, more concretely, by the very active role played by certain feminists and the Inter-American Commission of Women which received the prominent support of Eleanor Roosevelt.

Somewhat surprisingly, the principle of equality between men and women is mentioned in the UN Charter from the outset, as early as the second paragraph of the Preamble. This inclusion is in a particularly prominent position in the Charter and all the more disconcerting as it is oddly adjacent to that of the equality of nations 'large and small'.[84] The principle of equality is reasserted indirectly next through several provisions of the Charter which prohibit any discrimination based on sex (Articles 1(3), 8, 13(1), 55c, 68 and 76c) and above all it was to lead concretely to the establishment in 1946 of the Commission on the Status of Women within the UN, a body that was to be crucial in the subsequent fight against sexual and gender discrimination. In the follow-up to the Charter, the states did not cease to reiterate and deepen their commitment to this end, through texts relating to human rights (Universal Declaration, Article 2 and the two Covenants, common Article 3), the major resolutions and programmes of action from the world conferences on women, but also through treaty instruments including the Convention on the Political Rights of Women of 20 December 1952, the ILO Conventions 100, 103 and 156, and, above all, the Convention on the Elimination of All Forms of Discrimination Towards Women of 18 December 1979 (CEDAW), which came into force in 1981.

Now, the path that opens up with regard to recognition through these various legal instruments, and especially CEDAW, occupies a novel position

[83] See Michel Marbeau, 'Les femmes de la Société des Nations (1919–1945). Genève, la clé de l'égalité ?' in Jean-Marc Delaunay and Yves Denéchère (eds), *Femmes et relations internationales au XXème siècle* (Paris, Presses Sorbonnne nouvelle, 2006) 163 *ff*.

[84] UN Charter Preamble: 'We the peoples of the United Nations determined [. . .] to reaffirm faith [in the equal rights of men and women and of nations large and small'. It is worth pointing out this strange analogy between humans and states and its implicitly gender-biased orientation where the parallel in the comparison between humans and nations means that men are associated with 'large' nations and women with 'small' ones.

among the different forms of recognition identified so far, as it is halfway between the form of abstract recognition of equal rights and that of a right to be different, grounded here on sex or gender. This in-between position is the end of an empirical search to make the principle of equality as effective as possible. However, it presents certain shortcomings that leave the door open to other forms of recognition and above all to shortcomings that have led feminists, in recent years, to call for far more general reflection on the entire international legal system.

The combat of women internationally has relied primarily on the principle of equality recognised in the UN Charter as a form of recognition of their equal dignity and of equal rights to men. The legal enshrinement of equal standing and the existence of equal rights between men and women is a first process of recognition that has already been seen at work as it can ensure that the conditions for mutual recognition are founded on equal respect for each other as subjects of law and therefore, a priori, it can end the denials of recognition and discrimination of which women are systematically the object. The principle of equality thus asserted seeks to thwart the former representations of a hierarchical relationship between women and men but also to see that the celebrated rights of man should also be the rights of woman and therefore be truly applied to all in a universal and undifferentiated manner. In other words, the whole objective at this stage is to blot out sex-related differences so as to secure uniform application of the same model of rights. When resituated in the humanist and European philosophy of human rights from where it originates, the principle of equality must be understood as a principle of equal freedom by virtue of which the same freedom of action must be enjoyed by women and men in public and private life. That is, behind the demand for equality, there is an equally essential demand for liberty that may be summarised as the right of everyone to enjoy the same fundamental freedoms.

However, this formal principle of equal liberty was to prove powerless in ending sexual discrimination and inequality which were to persist de facto because of a structure of male domination that underpinned all societies. The problem of formal equality, proclaimed abstractly and generally in the post-war texts on human rights, was that while it prohibited the adoption of rules that discriminated against women, it still left all the existing material discriminations and the demeaning cultural representations that accompanied such discrimination intact, with the result that despite the proclamation of the principle of equality, women did not always really accede to the same positions and could not always concretely exercise the same rights as men. The principle of formal equality was at play and still is at play in such a context that men are in the end clearly 'more equal' than women, as George Orwell might put it. Hence, the texts enshrining the principle of universal equality of men and women and of non-discrimination depending on sex were to be considered insufficient in ending the inequalities facing women and were subsequently to make necessary the 1979 CEDEW Convention which specifically endeavours to fight actively and no longer passively 'all forms of discrimination' to which women are subjected in matters of health, education, the family and employment.

The fruit of 30 years of labour by the Commission on the Status of Women, the Convention on the Elimination of All Forms of Discrimination towards Women, is still the most complete international legal instrument in this domain.[85] The Convention situates its object in the domain of the recognition of equal rights from the outset, the beacon and crucial point around which all the other provisions must revolve. It deplores that 'extensive discrimination against women continues to exist', that such discrimination 'violates the principles of equality of rights and respect for human dignity' and asks states parties to take all appropriate measures 'guaranteeing them [women] the exercise and enjoyment of human rights and fundamental freedoms on a basis of equality with men' (Article 3). From that departure point, the Convention sets out a programme of action for restoring equality and therefore conditions that allow women to actually enjoy their rights and freedoms. There are several provisions for the full enjoyment of civil and political rights (with the right to vote, Article 7), but also the opportunity to represent their governments on an international level (Article 8) or rights relating to nationality so that women are truly recognised as full subjects of law. Articles 10, 11, 13 and 16 affirm equal rights in education, employment and economic and social activity, marriage and family relations. To this is added another vital provision, even if it is often ignored, by which states are asked to take measures against cultural patterns that discriminate against women (Article 5(a)). In terms of denials of recognition and the negative cultural representations for which they are vectors, it is crucial to modify such representations if one is to truly counter discriminations and therefore combat, beyond legal statuses, the stereotypes and cultural prejudice of all kinds, derived from tradition or religion that trap women in a subaltern image from which it is particularly difficult to escape. The interpretation of the articles made subsequently by the Committee on the Convention clarified that specific measures of protection, guarantee or positive discrimination were not only possible, but also recommended so that states might really combat existing discriminations given that the elimination of legal impediments alone was insufficient to ensure equal rights between men and women.[86] These are the celebrated 'temporary special' measures provided for by Article 4(1). In a general recommendation in 2004, the Committee even considered that provided they were temporary, such measures were in fact an obligation and not a simple option for states, given the little progress observed in the fight

[85] On the conditions in which it was drawn up against a background of East/West and North/South division, see Vivianne Yen-Ching Weng, *Evolution de la problèmatique des droits des femmes dans le système de protection de l'ONU* (Paris, PhD thesis Paris 2, 2008).

[86] General Recommendation No 23, §15, 1997, 16th session; www.un.org/womenwatch/daw/cedaw/recommendations/recomm.htm#recom23.

against inequalities, authorising the text of the Convention to be bypassed in the hope of shifting the line a little.[87]

In this, there is a very clear shift in the way the questions of inequalities to which women are subjected is contemplated since the principle of non-discrimination here materialises the principle of equality which remains purely formal. According to a logic that is found to be operative whenever formal equality is opposed to real inequalities, it is a matter of only treating equally people who are in equal situations, in the case in point women, so as to equalise their statuses to give effect to the proclamation of their equal rights with men. In other words, there is a need, beyond the proclamation of the principle of equality, to adopt specific measures in favour of women to realise the principle of equality and to combat the material and social discrimination that women experience daily. This supplementary dimension of the principle of equality introduced by the CEDAW Convention is well known as it is commonly used in many internal societies where a distinction is drawn between the principle of equality *before* the law and the principle of equality *through* the law. In the first instance, states are asked to abide by the principle of equality and so not to introduce any discrimination against women through their legislation or regulation; to ensure that sex is not used in any way as an argument to introduce inequalities through the law and in the attribution and enjoyment of rights. But this first principle is supplemented by the principle of equality via the law, which implies special protection measures or positive discrimination (deliberately or inadvertently) – the temporary special measures of the Convention – concerning women alone so as to offset their actual unequal status with regard to education, health, public and political life or public and private sector employment. From which it can be seen that, by this means and through the temporary special measures, a second supplementary category of women's rights is now guaranteed, that are no longer existing human rights but rights that adapt to the specific condition of women by making it possible to lean towards genuine equality, such as the right to rely on one's identity as a woman in order to enjoy more protective or more beneficial preferential measures. The paradox is that doing this means necessarily taking account of sexual differences in order to adopt temporary measures where the aim is to dispense of them in the name of the principle of equality. The temporary special measures mean that women are treated differently precisely because they are women, trapping them within a condition from which they are attempting to free themselves. This may crystallise frustration and intensify the feeling of stigma.

These difficulties are inevitable but they are not decisive for the aim is not to constitute a set of permanent differentiated rights that confirm differences, as for minorities or indigenous peoples, insofar as we are primarily in

[87] General Recommendation No 25, §24; www.un.org/womenwatch/daw/cedaw/recommendations/General%20recommendation%2025%20(English).pdf.

a perspective of a principle of equality that can apply indifferently, regardless of people's sex.[88] This is precisely what differentiates the rights we have just evoked from a third category of women's rights which is explicitly based on their female identity and for which recognition acts here as recognition of a permanent right to difference based on their sex. In support of this option, we can cite the CEDAW Convention Article 4, paragraph 2 which provides that special maternity measures are not discriminatory measures. In its commentary, the Committee specifies that the non-identical treatment of women and men due to their biological differences means the specific measures will this time be permanent.[89] This new category of women's rights also includes specific rights for women, scattered through various legal instruments, such as those concerning maternity, abortion, rape or conjugal violence. Now, it is plain to see that this is a whole new perspective and new form of recognition, which is similar this time to that of the rights of minorities or of indigenous peoples as it is based on respect for what constitutes the specific sexual identity of women just as the recognition of the rights of minorities and of indigenous peoples was based on respect for their cultural identity. It reflects a transition from a claim to equality designed to wipe out sex-based discrimination and to ensure that women enjoy the same standards as men; towards an identity-based demand aimed at obtaining a special status, separate from that of men. Unsurprisingly, it prompts criticism and much debate over female identity. On one side, there are those who fear that highlighting a specific female identity might inadvertently naturalise or 'essentialise' women, that is, trap them, in essence, in a biological and sexually stereotyped way, whereas much of the contemporary effort of feminists has been to put an end to this type of reductionism that reproduces the errors of the past in another form.[90] On the other side are those who contest there can be any universalism of humankind and who may therefore be led to support the existence of rights based on sex differences between men and women and condemn any universalist claim of existing human rights or even condemn any policy based on the recognition of subjective rights, of any kind, that would supposedly be typical of a male conception of ethics and justice.[91]

[88] While accepted at international level through the Convention, this idea is far from unanimous internally and even among feminists. It is interesting to read the criticism of French feminists by those from the English-speaking world who claim they fail to take sufficient account of the relevance of a policy based on sexual difference. See especially Joan W Scott, *Only Paradoxes to Offer. French Feminists and the Rights of Man* (Boston, Harvard University Press, 1996).

[89] Permanent measures at least 'until such time as the scientific and technological knowledge referred to in article 11, paragraph 2, would warrant a review'. General Recommendation No 25 § 16; www.un.org/womenwatch/daw/cedaw/recommendations/General%20recommendation%2025%20(English).pdf.

[90] See for example Elizabeth Grosz, 'What is Feminist Theory?' in Carole Pateman and Elizabeth Grosz (eds), *Feminist Challenges: Social and Political Theory* (Sydney, Allen & Unwin, 1986) 335 *ff*.

[91] For example Carol Gilligan, *In a Different Voice. Psychological Theory and Women's Development* (Cambridge, Harvard University Press, 1982).

Although there is the subject matter for a vital debate concerning women, it should be observed that, with regard to international law, the existence of rights specific to women based on their sexual difference does not for the time being call into question in any way the international arrangement for the observance of human rights and the general outlook of a universalist policy of equal respect and non-discrimination between men and women. The 1995 Beijing Declaration, adopted unanimously by all the state representatives present, is particular evidence of this as it reaffirmed that women's rights were an integral part of human rights and that equality of the sexes was a universal question, awareness of which should be a priority for all.[92] Conversely, the invocation of sexual and biological differences as a basis for legal regimes or specific rights for women is raised in a more polemical way by those who do not wish to establish a principle of equality between men and women. The cultural argument addressed earlier is invoked again in this specific context to limit the effects of the principle of equality that many states recognise. While declaring that they accept the principle of equality, some states completely undermine its effects by arguing at the same time that the question of the status and role of women is a cultural fact that stems from tradition and religion and must therefore be observed like other cultural practices, expressions or facts. Any interpretation aimed at imposing a strict application of the principle of equality on them is denounced as amounting to imposing a Western cultural model to the detriment of their own model.[93] Some governments recognise women's rights, albeit in a limited way, and in the context of general inequality of status between men and women, where notably the idea of equal sexual rights and women's free disposition of their bodies are excoriated. The direct effects of this opposition can be seen in the many reservations over the ratification of the CEDAW Convention. It has the embarrassing privilege of being one of the international conventions that has been most widely ratified and which at the same time is the subject of the greatest number of reservations and interpretative declarations aimed at modifying its content and the scope of states' commitments under the treaty. It is particularly instructive to compare the 100 or so reservations to this Convention with the four fundamental reservations to the 1965 Convention on the Elimination of All Forms of Racial Discrimination, a comparison that shows how much the fight against racism has become a shared objective of states, but not the sexism of societies which remains one of the most universally tolerated throwbacks to the past. As an example, several of the reservations and declarations to the 1979 Convention come from Islamic countries

[92] Beijing Declaration of 15 September 1995 (point 8); www.un.org/womenwatch/daw/beijing/platform/declar.htm. Recalled also in the 1993 Vienna Declaration (point 18); www.unhchr.ch/huridocda/huridoca.nsf/(symbol)/a.conf.157.23.en.

[93] See Françoise Héritier, 'Les droits des femmes dans la controverse entre universalité des droits de l'homme et particularité des cultures' in Jean-Loup Amselle et al (eds), *Diversité culturelle et universalité des droits de l'homme* (Paris, Ed Cécile Défaut, 2010) 19 *ff*.

which consider that certain provisions of the Convention should be set aside or interpreted in line with Sharia, Sunnah or the Koran, with the result that while being parties to a text that combats discrimination, several states may in actual fact continue to confer on their female citizens a discriminatory and subordinate status based on the difference of sex, which is consistent with their religious convictions. There is hardly need to insist on this to understand that such a (strong) culturalist position amounts to making meaningless the very principle of equality between men and women and the entire philosophy of recognition and of equal respect that drives it, as well as the humanist perspective that underpins the scheme of international law that arose from human rights. Besides, several of these reservations are of more than dubious legal validity as they run directly counter to the object and purpose of the Convention.[94] One cannot for all that underestimate certain aspects of the problem that remain, for, beyond the manipulations of the cultural argument by conservative, male powers that maintain sexual inequality for their own benefit, the cultural specificities and the North/South divide resound on the issue of the recognition of women's rights and lead to the defence of a 'weak' culturalist position, which is perfectly legitimate. Third World feminists are thus in a situation that is particularly difficult to manage, where they need to arbitrate between the traditionalist values of their countries and what they consider to be a strictly Western model, to come up with formulas specific to the aspirations to equality of women in societies of the South.[95]

B Post-Cold War Developments: New Demands Relating to Gender and the Androcentric Character of International Law

The different legal responses given to sexual inequalities and to the denial of recognition of the equal dignity of women do not exhaust all the complexities of a subject that continues to fuel discussion, especially within feminist movements, about sex, gender and sexuality, and new finer and deeper calls for recognition have arisen in the last 20 years or so with the ending of the Cold War.[96] The Fourth World Conference on Women in Beijing in 1995 brought together more than 40 000 people and marked a turning point in the policy of recognition of equality between men and women because of the new world context. It is significant of the new post-Cold War concerns to see how the Declaration and Platform for Action adopted reinstate the

[94] See the 1997 Report of the Human Rights Committee UN Doc A/42/40, vol I, para 42.

[95] See, for example, Celestine Nyamu, 'How Should Human Rights and Development Respond to Cultural Hierarchy in Developing Countries?' (2000) 41 (2) *Harvard International Law Journal* 381–419; Carol Mohanty, 'Under Western Eyes: Feminist Scholarship and Colonial Discourse' (1988) 30 *Feminist Review* 61 *ff*; Chilla Bulbeck, 'Hearing the Difference: First and Third World Feminisms' *Women's Studies Conference* (University of Melbourne, September 1990) 3 *ff*.

[96] See Elsa Dorlin, *Sexe, genre et sexualités* (Paris, PUF, 2008).

fight against sex and gender inequality as a 'condition for social justice' and one of the pillars of what ought to be a 'fair' and 'equitable' international society.[97] Moreover, the feminist movements gathered in Beijing managed to develop awareness of the need to shift attention, which had been focused on the sexual identity of women, towards a broader context of gender or 'social sex'. Since the take-off of gender studies, there has been growing awareness of the importance of gender, that is, of the cultural and social roles that supposedly correspond to biological sex and to the fact it has an effect of domination and stigmatisation of women. So it was necessary in Beijing to combat on the international stage not just the discriminations relating to biological sex but also the discriminations relating to gender and so to act on the social structure of societies as a whole and on the dominant cultural patterns insofar as they too perpetuate very deep-seated inequalities in male/female relations. Since Beijing, the reference to gender discrimination and to gender mainstreaming has supplemented the sex-specific approach that has become ubiquitous in the discourse of the major international and regional organisations.[98]

In order to escape from such traps, a final series of criticisms have developed internationally, which this time are far more radical and challenge all classical liberal international law. The deconstructions of gender and of its pernicious effects bring about a realisation that the recognition of the equal dignity of women, of their equal rights and gender mainstreaming cannot be fully effective unless they are part of a world where, on a global scale, mental, cultural and symbolic representations that make women inferior and marginalised will disappear. These overall patterns of representation form a deep cultural structure which, like the neoliberal economy in the face of international development law or cultural diversity, biases the effects of the international law of women's rights. The policies of equal respect but also of gender mainstreaming even become lures if they are part of an international legal system that itself continues to be entirely sex-based or generically

[97] Declaration and Programme of Action of 15 September 1995; /www.un.org/womenwatch/daw/beijing/platform/.

[98] The sex-specific approach was initiated by the Vienna Programme for Action (§37) which asks that allowance be made systematically in all areas of UN action of the male/female question. See for example 'Review and appraisal of the system-wide implementation of the Economic and Social Council's agreed conclusions 1997/2 on mainstreaming the gender perspective into all policies and programmes in the United Nations system', Report of the Secretary-General, UN Ecosoc, Substantive Session 2004, UN Doc E/2004/59 (2004). Some contemporary English-speaking feminists go even further, calling not only for the elimination of gender, and therefore of any gender-based identity, but also for the deconstruction of biological sex, as in the works of Judith Butler, *Gender Trouble, Feminism and the Subversion of Identity* (New York and London, Routledge, 1990) which defends the idea of sexual and gender dis-identification. But this highly sophisticated work opens up perspectives that would have difficulty finding their place internationally where the fact that one is on a world scale, encompassing the diversity of all present-day societies, means that claims essentially take the form of aspiration to the recognition of equal status and rights and the fight against discrimination based on gender and sex.

orientated for the benefit of men.[99] From this perspective, the international law of women's rights is therefore considered rather inefficient or even as having exhausted its possibilities and needing to be extended by legal reflection of a far more general order.[100] Feminists have highlighted perfectly the many limits of women's rights, including

(1) The fact that defining women's rights in specific instruments leads to them being excluded from the main agenda on human rights and to their cause being marginalised.[101]
(2) The fact that they make women simple individual subjects with individual rights, but who are then largely disadvantaged compared with other subjects of law in a male-dominated system.
(3) The fact that certain rights have been defined without taking sufficient account of the specific interests of women, such as rights protecting the family and private life whereas these may be at the heart of violence and subjection for women, or the freedom of religion which may have particularly insidious effects if it leads to the observance of precepts that contravene women's fundamental freedoms.
(4) Finally, the fact that they usually mask economic, social and cultural rights concerning women although they are equally decisive for women.[102]

The outcome is that the recognition that should be granted to women on an equal footing with men requires primarily, for some, a double challenge: a global challenge to classical international law which, far from being neutral, is itself an androcentric instrument and a vehicle for male hegemony, and a challenge to ways of thinking and analysing international law, since it is only on the condition that their categories and discriminating effects against women can be deconstructed that it will be possible to truly take into consideration concerns about women and their vision of international relations and of law.[103]

Without being able to develop any more subtle analyses here, it should be recalled first, as feminists do, that the history of international law is a history made by men and for men. Men have developed the political and legal

[99] For forceful feminist criticism of UN gender mainstreaming, see Hilary Charlesworth, 'Gender Mainstreaming' (2005) *Harvard Human Rights Journal*; cigj.anu.edu.au/cigj/people/staff/charlesworth.php#full.

[100] Carol Smart, *Feminism and the Power of Law* (London and New York, Routledge, 1989) 138 *ff*.

[101] Hilary Charlesworth, 'Alienating Oscar: Feminist Analysis of International Law' in Dorinda Dallmeyer (ed), *Reconceiving Reality: Women and International Law* (Washington DC, American Society of International Law, 1993) and Roseline Letterton, 'Les droits des femmes entre égalité et apartheid' in *Mélanges Hubert Thierry. L'évolution du droit international* (Paris, Pedone, 1998) 292 *ff*.

[102] Maurice Cranston, 'Are There Any Human Rights?' (1983) 4 *Daedalus* 1 *ff*.

[103] Hilary Charlesworth, Christine Chinkin and Shelley Wright, 'Feminist Approaches to International Law' (1991) 85 *American Journal of International Law* 613–45.

structures internationally in line with their own values and interests and that, in addition, if this liberal law was challenged after decolonisation by the new developing countries which had been excluded from it until then, it was never seriously questioned in regards to its complete obliviousness to women. The structures of classical international law rely on states and international organisations in which women do not figure. They are constantly under-represented and left in subaltern positions within states but also in an international institutional world where it is the criteria of geographical or civilisational distribution that is required and not the integration of female representatives of half of the world's population.[104] For evidence of this, one need only look at the quite derisory number of women who hold positions in bodies as important as the International Court of Justice, the International Law Commission or the UN Security Council. The domination of this male elite, which can be traced back to the division of labour within states, means that the norms and practices of international law primarily reflect male concerns, interests and ways of thinking. By way of consequence, even though the international rules do not try to establish discrimination against women, they have been shaped in such a way that they are gender-biased; that is, orientated in an underlying way for the benefit of men. As an example, a major part of the edifice of international law still reproduces the distinction of public law and private law, that is internal to states, and thereby perpetuates the exclusion of women, their concerns and their way of thinking, whether with respect to armed conflict,[105] the law on the use of armed force,[106] development law,[107] environment law,[108] international responsibility[109] or human rights.[110] So the recommended solution no longer lies just in the recognition of equal status with men nor a right to difference based on sexual or gender identity, but also in the concrete possibility for women to have equal power to men so as to fully reformulate the norms of the old classical liberal international law by flushing out the underlying gender prejudices first of all.

[104] Despite the progress made thanks to Article 8 of the UN Charter, which has followed on from Article 7 of the Covenant of the League of Nations. See Muriel Ubeda-Saillard, 'Commentaire Article 8' in Jean-Pierre Cot, Alain Pellet and Mathias Forteau (eds), *La Charte des Nations Unies. Commentaires article par article* (Paris, Economica, 2005) V.I, 603 *ff.*

[105] Judith Gardam, 'The Law of Armed Conflict: A Gendered Regime?' in Dallmeyer (ed), *Reconceiving Reality* (n 100) 171.

[106] Christine Chinkin, 'Peace and Force in International Law' in Dallmeyer (ed), *Reconceiving Reality* (n 100) 203.

[107] Hilary Charlesworth, 'The Public/Private Distinction and the Right to Development in International Law' (1992) 12 *Australian Yearbook of International Law* 190 *ff.*

[108] Lorraine Elliott, 'Gender, Feminism and the Environment' Presentation to the Annual Conference of the Australian Political Studies Association, Monash University, 29 September–1 October 1993.

[109] Hilary Charlesworth, 'Worlds Apart: Public/Private Distinctions in International Law in Margaret Thornton (ed), *Public and Private: Feminist Legal Debates* (Oxford, Oxford University Press, 1995) 243–60.

[110] Margaret Thornton, 'Feminism and the Contradictions of Law Reform' (1991) 19 *International Journal of the Sociology of Law* 453 *ff.*

The real issue here is that the feminist critique of international law invites a thoroughgoing deconstruction/reconstruction of the language, modes of analysis and legal categories of international law in a far more radical way than any of the Third World critiques of international law that had contributed to maintaining the pillars of classical international law. While the path charted raises many perfectly legitimate questions and while it seems impossible to embark upon it as it upsets the most firmly rooted certainties of international law circles, it does suggest that the ideal synthesis that is now sought in international law between universal rights and individual women's rights will inevitably run up against some form of sexism which, for now, remains intrinsically tied to all existing normative and institutional international law. In the search for a fair international society based on the recognition and reparation of injuries done to identities, the expectations of women are liable to be persistently marginalised compared with what are considered more essential issues by a world that is still dominated by men. In addition, a sort of unhealthy implicit competition may even give rise to old prejudices in this domain, as attested to by the declaration of an Indian delegate to the Tenth World Conference on Women in 1980 in Copenhagen, who remarked that 'since he had experienced colonialism, he knew that it could not be equated with sexism'.[111]

[111] Quoted in Hilary Charlesworth, 'The Sex of the State in International Law' in Ngaire Nafine and Rosemary Owen (eds), *Sexing the Subject of Law* (Sydney, Law Book Company, 1997) 251–68.

8

Reparations for Historical Wrongs: The Lessons of Durban

IT IS UNDENIABLE that the injuries to women caused by the sexism that is ubiquitous in all the world's societies are not considered by states to be as serious as the wrongs arising from racism or colonialism. It is in the name of the latter that another type of contemporary claim based on recognition has arisen in the form of calls for the reparation of historical crimes committed because of racism, colonialism or imperialism. Does not recognition of the Other within postcolonial society involve acceptance of a shared history that sheds light on centuries of denial of the Other and the need for reparations for historically inflicted losses?

These claims were made by the Third World upon independence, including in the context of the New International Economic Order, but it cannot be denied that since the end of the Cold War they have become far more pressing. One need only look how these calls for recognition have become more numerous and more diverse in line with the historical prejudices invoked. They range from new calls for compensation for the victims of German Nazism in Eastern Europe and Japanese imperialism in Asia to claims from indigenous peoples such as the New Zealand Maoris or the Australian Aborigines, not forgetting the demands from Africans because of slavery, the slave trade and colonisation of the past. Whereas history seemed to have accepted that what was done was done with regard to these destructions and enslavements, people have organised and now want states to face up to their responsibility for historical crimes committed against them and to make reparation.

But what scope can really be attributed to these calls for reparation where the crimes of the past resurface with their sadly countless lines of victims and their descendants in search of recognition? Can one repair history, Antoine Garapon asked.[1] And is there an international law of reparation of historical losses, or even a right to reparation nowadays? To these questions, which are really decisive in that they raise the problem of the actual possibility of reparation for history and for wounded identities, the 2001 Durban Conference (and the review in Geneva in 2009) attempted to provide political and legal answers to provide an understanding of the essential issues in this type of

[1] Antoine Garapon, *Peut-on réparer l'histoire? Colonisation, esclavage, Shoah* (Paris, O Jacob, 2008).

claim with regard to recognition and the aporias and limits to which it is open when resorting to international law. Obviously, it is just one example from among the many disputes over reparation that are underway today, but at least it can be emphasised that the purpose of the Durban talks is probably one of the most relevant for our analysis of postcolonial/post-Cold War global society and at the same time is exemplary of the more general debates about the reparation of past historical wrongs.

I Durban's Failures, Breakthrough and Questions

A The Background

In September 2001, the UN organised an international conference against racism, racial discrimination, xenophobia and intolerance in Durban. It was to be an opportunity not just to review the contemporary manifestations of racism and the means to confront it, but also an opportunity to face the past together through the historical forms of racism and xenophobia related to slavery, the slave trade and colonialism. It is this last aspect in particular that interests us more here since the problem of reparation of historical wrongs has arisen through it.

Organised in South Africa, which had managed to achieve reconciliation and pardon for the crimes of Apartheid, Durban was to be the world conference that cleared the accounts of the colonial past of post-Cold War world society. In a common message of 21 March 2001, Mary Robinson, the then UN High Commissioner for Human Rights and Nelson Mandela, the President of South Africa, had set out the objectives of the future conference. They underscored that in addition to the discrimination of which Roms, African descendants, indigenous peoples and women were victims, it was the irrational fear of what was different and the inability to recognise and express regret for the serious injuries inflicted in the past, that were the main sources of racism in the contemporary world.[2] They went on to assert the need to learn the lessons of the past so that humanity could put an end to the all too long and tragic history of racism.

The result was plainly not guaranteed given the passions related to this past, but when in 1996 the UN contemplated this new conference, it seemed convinced that there would be no repetition of the failures of the first two conferences against racism of 1978 and 1983 which had focused on the question of the Near East. It was a time of great optimism marked by the end of the Cold War, a Near East that was engaged in the peace process and the implementation of legal instruments with 'conciliatory' aims like South Africa's Truth and Reconciliation Commission, the many declarations of repentance

[2] www.un.org/WCAR/e-kit/vision.htm.

made by the West, the new calls for compensation by the victims of history, but also the international criminal courts. But this optimism was short-lived. After a long preparatory process, the Conference was held from 31 August to 7 September, in the presence of thousands of non-governmental organisations (NGOs). Now, under the influence of several African and Arab NGOs, the NGO forum witnessed a wave of anti-Semitic declarations and an incredible outburst of violence against Jews, going as far as calls to murder. The United States and Israel then left the Conference which was to be dominated by intolerance and to serve in part an entirely different purpose from that for which it had been established, which resulted in a Declaration (and Programme of Action), paragraphs 32 and 68 of which insisted on incriminating Israel by name. From this point of view it was a dismal failure, since it was a long way short of the ideal of a reconciled international community. So it was by a cruel but perfectly understandable irony that at the Review Conference in Geneva in 2009 (Durban II), the new final declaration was rushed through by the second day of the Conference out of fear that many countries might leave the Conference further to the hateful anti-Semitic diatribe by Iran's President Mahmoud Ahmadinejad. The final declaration of 2009 which was adopted *in extremis* was a priori a compromise that sought to gloss over the subjects of disagreement of 2001, that is, all the anti-Israeli aspects of the first declaration and a much denounced paragraph on the defamation of religions, but it was no less equivocal in that it reaffirmed at the same time its support for the 2001 Declaration and Programme of Action which stigmatised the State of Israel alone for racism against Palestinians.

The Durban and Geneva texts are without binding force and the 2001 Declaration expressly sets out that the states concerned are under a moral but not a legal obligation to take appropriate measures to terminate the detrimental consequences of past practices of colonialism and slavery. They provide an understanding of the direction given by a majority of states on these questions and the possible legal channels that may be opened up for most of the claims made at the time referred to the violation of norms of international law and so one needs to look at the state of existing international law in this domain to appraise the orientations given at Durban in the context of future dispute settlement. The matter currently before the High Court in London opposing four Kenyans to the UK is interesting in this respect. The plaintiffs allege they were tortured in 1957 at the time of the Mau-Mau rebellion and have asked the UK for an official apology and compensation fund for the victims (over 70 000 were imprisoned in camps and 12 000 allegedly died there, with only 1400 still alive today). The UK dismisses any legal liability for its colonial past but the case continues and plainly there is a fear that its outcome might inspire other former members of the Empire, whether in Cyprus, Malaysia, Nigeria or former Rhodesia.[3] The same applies, of course,

[3] *Le Monde*, 7 April 2011.

to all other former colonial powers. The fact is that the reparations granted to indigenous peoples by former settlement colonisers for the wrongs they suffered in the past (confiscation of land, natural resources, forced assimilation) are more frequent and similarly raise the question of the responsibility of the state or of private companies for the historical wrong caused. All these cases therefore confirm what is inescapable about the calls for recognition expressed in Durban, but they remain problematic for they give rise to questions that are legally unresolved and therefore to the need for renewed thinking on these matters.

B Questions on Compensation for Historical Losses

Instead of attesting to a rediscovered understanding among states, the Durban Conference demonstrated the inability of states to share a common history of colonialism and slavery and to agree on the way to remedy the faults of the past. True, at the end of the preparatory process before the 2001 Conference, everyone seemed agreed to identify slavery, the slave trade and colonialism as wrongful acts that had massively destructive effects. But the specific legal characterisation of such practices and the more specific determination of their consequences in terms of liability and compensation were to crystallise antagonism during the Conference. During the talks, opposing views were quick to arise, especially between African and European countries but also among African countries since some peoples once reduced their neighbours to slavery and some African states still practise slavery today. The concepts of 'crime against humanity' but also of 'regrets', 'apologies' or 'reparations' were the subject of intense debate and fierce opposition.[4]

Several principles included in the Final Declaration of 2001 deserve notice, especially three principles that were stated further to the multiple compromises which attest to some advance in this domain:

(1) The principle that 'slavery and the slave trade are a crime against humanity and should always have been so' (point 13).
(2) The official recognition that 'these historical injustices [slavery and colonisation] have undeniably contributed to the poverty, underdevelopment, marginalization, social exclusion, economic disparities, instability and insecurity that affect many people in different parts of the world, in particular in developing countries' (Programme of Action, point 158).
(3) The principle that the 'States concerned' should 'honour the memory of the victims of past tragedies' (point 99).

In this respect the Declaration notes that 'some States have taken the initiative to apologize and have paid reparation, where appropriate, for grave and

[4] However, some states like Germany recognised their guilt. See Nadja Vuckovic, 'Qui demande des réparations et pour quels crimes?' in Marc Ferro (ed), *Le livre noir du colonialisme* (Paris, Hachette, 2004) 1044 ff.

massive violations committed' (point 100) and invites 'those who have not yet contributed to restoring the dignity of the victims to find appropriate ways to do so' (point 101).[5]

But this was only the beginning and the compromise raised many questions that have still not been specifically answered, especially with regard to the possible liability of the state giving rise to reparation.[6] The Conference organisers did not themselves contemplate actions in liability but the recognition of the crimes committed, official apologies and possibly the principle of voluntary reparations. In other words, it was primarily a question of seeking 'reconciliation and healing' (point 101) and basically of transposing to world society the process of the Truth and Reconciliation Commission that had worked so well for South Africa after Apartheid. Durban was an attempt at implementing transitional justice on a world scale to recognise the crimes of the past so as to move into a postcolonial and post-Cold War world which is both appeased and does not repeat the mistakes of the past. The ultimate challenge was to see the descendants of the former colonial society live together in the same postcolonial world society and to bring about a transition to enable such co-existence to be organised. But as Pierre Hazan has shown so well,[7] this transposition proved impossible at an international conference of some 200 states and thousands of NGOs. Instead of creating the conditions for an appeased dialogue and a process of recognition of historical crimes, the UN inadvertently created the conditions for a generalised confrontation, caused by a series of identity-based reactions and amplified the dangers that await any process of this kind, such as victims attempting to outdo each other and the clash of memories. Extremely strong tensions arose from a policy of reconciliation transposed to world level where states squared up to one another, defending state interests. Finally, Durban leads us to question the exact role that international law can play in such cases.

The first question is whether the slavery of past centuries can be characterised as a crime or even a crime against humanity when it was perfectly consistent with the international law and national systems of law at the time; and so whether states can be held answerable on this basis. The same obviously applies to the colonial system which Euro-American international law considered lawful for centuries. This is a question of the inter-temporal application of law which gives rise to the classical answer in international law that a new law is not retroactive. Therefore there is no retroactive responsibility. A state's behaviour only constitutes an unlawful act entailing its international

[5] www.un.org/WCAR/durban.pdf.

[6] See Jean-François Quéguiner and Santiago Villalpando, 'La réparation des crimes de l'histoire: Etat et perspectives du droit international public contemporain' in Laurence Boisson de Chazournes, Jean-François Quéguiner and Santiago Villalpando (eds), *Crimes de l'histoire et réparations: les réponses du droit et de la justice* (Brussels, Bruylant, 2004) 42 and Vuckovic, 'Qui demande des réparations et pour quels crimes?' (n 4).

[7] Pierre Hazan, *Juger la guerre, juger l'histoire. Du bon usage des commissions Vérité et de la justice internationale* (Paris, PUF, 2007) 95 *ff*.

responsibility if it constitutes a failure to fulfil an international obligation that existed at the time it occurred. Hence the compromise adopted in the 2001 Declaration that 'slavery and the slave trade are a crime against humanity and *should always have been so*' (point 13). Article 13 of the latest Report on State Responsibility (2001) confirms this existing state of law and the fact that there would only be a breach of an international obligation if a state was bound by that obligation at the time the act occurred. In its commentary on Article 13, the International Law Commission (ILC) specifies that even when a new norm of *jus cogens* arises (to which the prohibition of slavery and perhaps colonialism can be likened), there cannot be any retroactive effect even so.[8] Nor is this provided for by the 1948 Convention for the Prevention and Punishment of the Crime of Genocide. In truth, while the argument itself is incontrovertible from a formal point of view, it should not be forgotten that the principle of non-retroactivity, which is well established in international law, has already suffered memorable exceptions with the examples of the Nuremberg and Tokyo Tribunals and certain present-day international criminal tribunals.[9]

The only possibility accepted today is that the state voluntarily consents to admit its responsibility retroactively for 'conduct which was not at the time a breach of any international obligation in force for that State' (Article 13 ILC Report, 2001).[10] International legal acts may establish the voluntary recognition of past crimes and grant reparation, as for example a bilateral treaty between the former coloniser and the former colonised country. This was the case in the friendship treaty between Italy and Libya of 30 August 2008, which for the time being is unique at inter-state level. It is also the case in the historical dispute settlement between the Sioux and the US Government and the 70 agreements concluded by Canada's provincial governments, the Federal Government and the representatives of the indigenous populations over the recognition of past spoliation and the assertion of a new status for those populations.

Another question is how such responsibility can be invoked and for what kind of prejudice? As presented in Durban, there were multiple acts which caused the loss: death, slavery, forced labour, plunder of natural resources, confiscation of land, destruction of cultures and ways of life, and contemporary underdevelopment. But the legal characterisation is not established even so. Following the general tendencies and the Final Declaration, a double

[8] ILC, Draft articles on Responsibility of States for Internationally Wrongful Acts with commentaries, 2001, Art 13, para 5, 58; untreaty.un.org/ilc/texts/instruments/english/commentaries/9_6_2001.pdf.

[9] Danilo Zolo, *La justice des vainqueurs. De Nuremberg à Bagdad* (Paris, Actes Sud, 2009) 188 *ff*. Certain atrocities committed in the past are comparable to genocides or crimes against humanity with the advent of the modern world. See Robert Gellately and Ben Kiernan (eds), *The Specter of Genocide. Mass Murder in Historical Perspective* (Cambridge, Cambridge University Press, 2003).

[10] ILC 2001 (n 8) para 6, 58.

prejudice can be identified. A moral prejudice exists, resulting from centuries of humiliation and denial of recognition for so many populations. This moral prejudice goes along with a material loss related to the plunder of resources, the system of enslavement, the colonial system of exploitation and the spoliation of land which allegedly account for the current state of underdevelopment of formerly colonised countries but also of indigenous peoples. The Declaration states that colonisation has engendered not only past injuries but also 'lasting social and economic inequalities in many parts of the world today' (point 14). There results, therefore, a current prejudice that is intrinsically related to the past prejudice. However, several difficulties occur at this stage. How can one evaluate the extent to which the current prejudice may be related to past prejudice? And how can this be proved? For example, the underdevelopment of certain countries is presented as a consequence of past colonisation; but does it not also result from several factors involving the responsibility of the postcolonial countries? The difficulty increases when the past prejudice must be defined: how can it be proved, for slavery and colonisation in particular, the existence of specific acts directly attributable to the state when these were generalised systems of exploitation of great scope with multiple causes and involving many actors? True, these are still questions that pertain to strictly formalist arguments, but they are no less relevant and plainly complicate the principle of seeking liability for the crimes of history.

The arrangements for reparation raise associated difficulties. What kind of reparation should be awarded? How can one identify the current successors in title down the course of generations? In Durban the problem was simplified as it was the responsibility of one state towards another that was called into question, so the beneficiary was simply the formerly colonised state and the debtor the former colonising state. In the case of indigenous peoples, it is also usually the people that are considered the beneficiaries of reparation and the state as being bound to make reparation. However, the question may prove far more intricate if the author of the prejudice was a private company, say, and if the plaintiffs are simple individuals who claim to be the descendants of despoiled and discriminated generations. Moreover, with regard to the form of reparation, the international law of responsibility provides several possibilities: restitution in kind, financial compensation and satisfaction. All have been invoked, whether within the Durban framework or in the context of specific actions. For restitution in kind, one thinks notably of actions for the return of stolen cultural property, sometimes mummified human remains, which have occurred in some instances.[11] Under a special statute of 6 March 2002, France thus returned to the Khoi Khoi people of South Africa the remains of Saartje Baartman, known as the Hottentot Venus, and

[11] Such reparation in the form of restitution is expressly set out in Article 11(2) of the UN Declaration on the Rights of Indigenous Peoples; www.un.org/esa/socdev/unpfii/documents/DRIPS_en.pdf. The discussion focused essentially on the return of cultural property, with the creation of an intergovernmental committee within UNESCO for that purpose.

she was finally buried in May 2002 in accordance with the traditional rites of her people. The multiplication of this type of claim for human remains kept in Western museums is an additional indication, were any needed, of the spectacular rise in demand for recognition of identities wounded by history, based both on equal respect for every human being and the acceptance of their differences.

However, it is usually other forms of reparation that are invoked. Compensation is the most common form. It must correspond to the economic loss resulting from the wrongful act but also, possibly, the moral harm for the injuries done to persons. The Abuja Declaration on colonialism, adopted by many African heads of state in 1993, includes for example a requirement for 'full monetary payment of repayments through capital transfer and debt cancellation'.[12] Sao Paolo University's Centre for Black Consciousness is demanding payment from the United States of US $100 000 for each of the 60 million descendants of slaves. In 2003, President Jean-Bertrand Aristide considered that France ought to repay Haiti the celebrated debt of independence paid by Haiti to France between 1825 and 1887, the equivalent of 90 million gold francs. As these examples show, the question remains of the amount of compensation that should be attributed, which varies with the valuation of the loss. But how can adequate financial reparation be evaluated when the wrong results from several centuries of economic exploitation and denial? How can it be evaluated when the wrong is considered to persist over time because of underdevelopment? The difficulties are enormous and the most realistic idea is probably to reach a negotiated settlement on greater development aid. This was achieved by the 2008 treaty mentioned earlier between Italy and Libya, in which Italy apologised for 30 years of colonisation and undertook to pay $5 billion in damages in the form of investments over the following 25 years. In this case the financial measures are considered to be reparation for the historical prejudice incurred, which is wholly different from a symbolic (and legal) point of view from the aid that former colonising states now grant through unilateral or multilateral commitments. This means agreeing to include financial aid in a perspective of recognition of responsibility for historical wrongs committed with the result that such aid counts symbolically as a form of reparation for the injured identities that may thus find their place in the repaired fabric of history.[13]

Besides, financial compensation may be seen as insufficient or wholly inadequate with regard to the type of historical prejudice invoked and some states and victims refuse any form of financial compensation. Some African

[12] www.ncobra.org/resources/pdf/TheAbujaProclamation.pdf.

[13] This is why the first compensation process established by the King of Morocco, Mohammed VI, in 1999, for the victims of torture and 'disappearance' did not really work. It provided for 'straight' compensation for the crimes of the regime but without recognising them as crimes. A second more satisfactory process had to be established. See Garapon, *Peut-on réparer l'histoire?* (n 1) 214–17.

states have vilified the idea of receiving monetary payment as reparation for the slave trade and colonialism and this is also true of the case of the Lakotas Indians who refused the compensation proposed in 1980 by the US Government for the unlawful possession of the Black Hills, since to accept, they argued, would be to accept the theft of their sacred land. In fact, if it is wanted, financial compensation may help to close and repair the historical wrong done to identities but provided that, as said, it is accompanied by a discourse that makes the compensation meaningful by tying it in with a 'discourse of justice'[14] and the recognition of the massive denial of identity. It is evident that satisfaction as a form of reparation may appear to be the most suitable when dealing with immaterial losses of such seriousness and such a nature because satisfaction is aimed directly at symbolic reparation of the wrong. It may take on extremely varied forms including, say, the recognition of responsibility, the expression of regret, formal apologies, or asking forgiveness. In a memorable case, Virginia was the first American state to publicly apologise and express its 'profound regret' for the enslavement of blacks and the exploitation of Indians, as well as the violation of their most fundamental rights. Similarly, Germany officially apologised in Durban for its colonial policy. Much like what the Inter-American Court ordered in several cases involving the indigenous peoples of Latin America, less ordinary but probably more effective measures can be adopted such as the organisation of cultural events, the creation of foundations, commemorative stones, memorial days or memorial museums or the establishment of aid associations for indigenous populations.[15]

II The Paradigm of Recognition and the Limits of Resort to Law

As can be seen, the thing which casts light on the mechanisms behind such claims and which may illuminate the most appropriate response to them is the fact that those claims are part of the contemporary paradigm of recognition. This paradigm explains why all the history-related claims are so pressing today whereas at one time they were usually settled by silence and the passage of time. In a now famous speech made in 1992, the Australian Prime Minister expressed this new attitude towards the Aborigines:

> And, as I say, the starting point might be to recognise that the problem starts with us non-Aboriginal Australians. It begins, I think with that act of recognition.

[14] Garapon, *Peut-on réparer l'histoire?* (n 1) 219.

[15] This is also recommended by Resolution 2002/5 of the Sub-Commission for the Protection and Promotion of Human Rights (point 6): Recognition of responsibility for massive and flagrant violations of human rights which constitute crimes against humanity and which took place during the period of slavery, colonialism and wars of conquest; www.unhchr.ch/Huridocda/Huridoca.nsf/(Symbol)/E.CN.4.SUB.2.RES.2002.5.En?Opendocument.

> Recognition that it was we who did the dispossessing. We took the traditional lands and smashed the traditional way of life. We brought the diseases. The alcohol. We committed the murders. We took the children from their mothers. We practised discrimination and exclusion. It was our ignorance and our prejudice. [16]

Admittedly, the demand for recognition of historical crimes is not entirely new; there are examples of this from the past.[17] There are obviously other explanations for the current enthusiasm for this type of action, in particular the extension of the human rights discourse and the will to punish crimes that are in the category of what is unjustifiable and for which there is no statute of limitations.[18] But the demand for recognition of historical crimes has been substantially intensified by the new perception of the identities of peoples, groups and individuals and by the new way in which they perceive themselves nowadays through history and the passing of time. They define themselves not just through their present status and culture, but also through the history and memories of their group, state or community.[19] For Ricœur, these are individual identities that are forged collectively in a temporal dimension that includes what may be centuries-old discriminations against these groups.[20] The temporal dimensions of the identity of individuals and groups means that not only are they their own history but that history is not limited to the narrative account of their existence, it is also woven from the histories inherited from the past and the common memory that has been handed down from one generation to the next. And so individuals, groups and peoples experience the present effects of the crimes of the past, based on the denial of individuals, by internalising an image of themselves that is depreciatory or demeaning and so suffering a deep-seated denial of recognition which is handed down the generations and is not repaired in any way.[21] Now, the awareness of this denial that still weighs on the victims or their descendants is transformed today into a demand for justice, that is, into an implication of the state's responsibility and a call for reparation of the crimes committed, which then serves as a process of recognition of the Other. The recognition of responsibility and reparation should put an end to the general feeling of devaluation and stigma that has lasted over time by designating the guilty party, by exposing the scale of the crimes committed, by honouring the

[16] Declaration for reconciliation. Draft text adopted in 1999 by the Council for Aboriginal Reconciliation. Quoted in Martine Piquet, *Australie plurielle. Gestion de la diversité éthnique en Australie de 1788 à nos jours* (Paris, L'Harmattan, 2004) 215–16; www.antar.org.au/issues_and_campaigns/self-determination/paul_keating_redfern_speech.

[17] See Bouda Etemad, *Crimes et réparations. L'Occident face à son passé colonial* (Paris, A Versaille, 2008) 25 *ff*.

[18] Paul Ricœur, *La mémoire, l'histoire et l'oubli* (Paris, Seuil, 2000) 609.

[19] The connection between identity and memory is an idea that is now investigated as much by philosophers as by sociologists or anthropologists. See Michel Wieviorka, *La différence. Identités culturelles : enjeux, débats et politiques* (Paris, L'aube, 2005) 163 and Joël Candau, *Mémoire et Identité* (Paris, PUF, 1998).

[20] Paul Ricœur, *Parcours de la reconnaissance* (Paris, Gallimard, 2004) 331.

[21] ibid 332.

memory of the victims and by rehabilitating people both in terms of their equal dignity and of respect for their ethnical or cultural difference.

The Durban Conference was part of this new context. It was aimed not so much at the violence directed against individuals and peoples through slavery and colonialism but the total disregard for individuals which meant they could be treated as things, as chattels or that their property could be seized as if it did not belong to anyone. In particular, the 2001 Declaration emphasised the 'negation of the essence of the victims' by their enslavement and the racism that went with it. It is this denial, along with the economic exploitation which is still the kernel of actions for reparation and that shows the connection with the paradigm of recognition. The very deep wound inflicted on identities, being passed on over several generations until the present day, gives rise to expectations about the recognition of the crimes committed and their reparation, with recognition not only being perceived as a final rehabilitation of the dignity of the victims and of all those who were stigmatised, but also of the entire history of a people or community.

This explains the big difference between a dispute over reparations further to an ordinary armed conflict, however destructive it may be, and a dispute over acts of denial of the other affecting identities.[22] In this situation, the treaties or the various legal instruments by which the culpable states have sought to shirk their responsibility and the issues of reparation are simply intolerable for the individuals or communities that suffered such acts. For example, Japan shelters behind a 1965 treaty on the normalisation of diplomatic relations between Japan and South Korea to escape any subsequent implication for crimes relating to its policy of imperialistic conquest. The treaty provides for South Korea's waiving of the right to claims from the Korean people against Japan in exchange for new economic cooperation and the recognition of the Korean Government in office as the only legitimate one. But since the 1980s, Korean women, who were subjected to sexual enslavement by the Japanese military, have been challenging the validity of this treaty by which one state is exempted from its responsibility for violating fundamental rights, accusing the Korean state of having abandoned actions in (domestic and international) responsibility against the Japanese state and fighting to obtain reparation both for the suffering they were subjected to and the stigma of being seen as 'soiled women'.[23]

Finally, this is why Africans and indigenous peoples are taking the lead with these claims internationally. Some observers have pointed out that neither

[22] The case of the peace treaty between Japan and the United States ending the Second World War waiving any action related to the destruction of Hiroshima and Nagasaki is an interesting limiting case since, through its massive and indiscriminate force, nuclear power is another fundamental denial of individuals.

[23] The validity of this type of treaty is highly debatable. See Luigi Condorelli, 'Conclusions générales' in Boisson de Chazournes, Quéguinier and Villalpando (eds), *Crimes de l'histoire et réparations* (n 6) 300–01.

India, nor Indonesia, nor former Indo-China (Vietnam, Laos, Cambodia) have claimed reparations, and that the Africans are in a marginal position. But this would be to pretend not to see that, like indigenous peoples who were sometimes decimated, Africans are the ones who have suffered most from contempt, racism, humiliation and de-humanisation both through the slave trade and colonisation, which are two systems of massive exploitation that wrought their effects over several centuries. Taking up one of the major themes of the 1993 Abuja Conference, the Independent Commission on Africa published a Report in 2002 entitled 'Winning the War against Humiliation'. The Report explains how the main task of contemporary Africa is to win that war because of a global system of negation of Africans that dates back to the slave trade and is perpetuated with the latest episode of globalisation.[24] According to the Report, centuries of domination and humiliation are an extremely burdensome legacy for present-day populations as they have led to a generalised lack of self-esteem and a feeling of devaluation that is still deeply ingrained.[25] It is in this that, in addition to underdevelopment, the historical crimes associated with slavery and colonialism are incontrovertibly considered to have effects that are still felt by individuals, peoples and communities.

There is no possible way of going back on these issues. The entry of our era into the recognition paradigm means that we can no longer be rid of the question of historical wrongs related to mass crimes based on the denial of the identities of individuals that still affects the present. Can France, for example, long continue to deny its responsibility and not recognise the great wrong it did to Algeria and to its former colonised territories?[26] How can successive governments fail to see, beyond the ethical act, the interest they have in acknowledging the faults of the past so as to be able to really move forward today; how can they fail to see how their discourse, by being oblivious to the past, is what prevents people from forgetting and how it unfailingly postpones the time when people will want to move forward together? Likewise, Algeria, too, should recognise the crimes of the time of the national liberation, for this absence of mutual and reciprocal recognition prevents people from honouring the memory of the victims and from learning the lessons of

[24] Albert Tevoedjre, *Winning the War against Humiliation. Report of the Independent Commission on Africa and the Challenges of the Third Millennium* (Benin, Centre Panafrican de prospective social, 2002).

[25] ibid. Albert Memmi and Frantz Fanon were among the first to highlight this phenomenon, that is, the way the coloniser imposed a negative self-image on the colonised. They showed that the colonised would not be freed until they could get rid of this debasing self-representation. See Albert Memmi, *The Colonizer and the Colonized* (Boston, Beacon Press, 1965) and Fanon, *The Wretched of the Earth* (New York, Grove Press, 1963).

[26] When President Sarkozy during a 2010 visit to Algiers said he had come to 'talk business', Algeria's President Boueflicka replied that 'memory comes before business' (quoted by Philippe Marchesin, 'La revanche pour le Sud' *Le Monde,* 30 October 2010, 19. See also Nicolas Bancel and Pascal Blanchard, 'La colonisation: du débat sur la guerre d'Algérie au discours de Dakar' in Pascal Blanchard and Isabelle Veyrat-Masson (eds), *Les guerres de mémoire. La France et son histoire* (Paris, La découverte, 2010) 141 *ff.*

the past.[27] This would result in a state of 'positive mutual debt' as Jacques Godbout terms it, which would at last make a new start possible.[28] Some states and governments still fail to see that this requirement for historical recognition has become unavoidable because of the new paradigmatic values of our age and the circumstances of post-Cold War justice. Even though, it can be readily admitted, there is no easy solution. Durban is indeed an example of this. Can one contemplate, as the conference organisers hoped, a transitional justice at world level that would allow a transition to a postcolonial world society that is at peace with the past and the shift from a racist and colonised society to a truly decolonised, multicultural international society that is reconciled with its history? Transitional justice corresponds to a mixed set of legal institutions that aim to bring about a transition from non-democratic to democratic societies and from societies at war to societies at peace, by responding to the acts committed by the former oppressor regime so as to move towards a new society having righted the injustice of the past. But is this feasible on a world scale?

Today, it is easy to understand that setting excessive objectives of this type for a single international conference was probably a mistake and that it is better to opt for other arrangements at national bilateral and regional level. It all depends on the context and the scale of the wrongs caused; and also on the way in which the infringement of identity and the reparation of immaterial wrongs are handled through the responses given. One can also and foremost see the limits of what international law can offer when recognition pertains not just to the order of justice and law but to the order of love, social esteem, education and morals. This is a decisive aspect to identify after this review of the various domains where the right of recognition has manifested itself. The concept of recognition is aimed at an expectation that law and justice can never fully meet because it involves acceptance of the Other for what he or she is and cannot be calculated by nor measured by law alone.[29] This is compounded by the fact that, for the major historical crimes at issue here, they are of such political, moral and historical importance that the law alone cannot from this point of view be the only appropriate response to expectations as to recognition. For historical crimes, the solution is not only legal but also social, political, educational and cultural. Apart from justice for a specific case relating to a specific historical crime or apart from what law can contribute through a formal instrument on the general recognition of responsibility, both of which inevitably remain limited, only education, or the

[27] Notably with regard to the crimes against the Harkis, troops of Algerian origin supporting France's presence in Algeria, tens of thousands of whom were massacred by the National Liberation Front (and abandoned by France, which eventually acknowledge its wrongdoing to them).

[28] Jacques Godbout, *L'esprit du don* (Paris, La découverte, 2007) 168.

[29] Both Honneth and Ricœur show, through a threefold arrangement of order of intersubjective recognition, that there are structures of recognition that anticipate or go beyond legal matters. See, for example, Ricœur, *Parcours de la reconnaissance* (n 20) 295.

creation of new institutions can enable the next generations of ex-colonised and ex-colonisers to learn the lessons of the mistakes and crimes of the past by helping to deconstruct the political and moral structures, and the underlying cultural representations that enabled those crimes and to pinpoint any continuation of stigmatising rules, practices and institutions. At this stage, a distinction must be made between the discourse of international law containing official recognition, relating to a decision of justice or an act of repentance or responsibility, and the historical, educational and cultural work of deconstruction/rehabilitation that cannot take the form of a legal text or judicial decision.[30]

More generally, it is the goal of a global postcolonial reconciliation among all states and peoples that should be definitively deconstructed because of the illusions and therefore the frustrations that such an objective may engender, since dreaming of a world that has completely settled the accounts of the past and balanced off its historical legacy is just as dangerous an illusion as not wanting to face up to that past or to try to repair wounded identities. The idea of making a fresh start and returning to some state of original innocence, which never existed anyway, must give way to the idea of a world that confronts its past but accepts the fact that all crimes are not reparable and all visions of history must have their place.[31] And if the return to history is essential in this domain, since it is at the heart of the approach involving recognition of the historical wrong committed, such a return cannot consist of serving up a single historical version – whichever it may be – of past international history, a sort of great re-founding myth that would supersede classical official history, which had justified colonisation, and that would be enacted in a new international instrument ratifying the reconciliation of postcolonial society. One cannot legally enact a new official world history which would count as definitive global recognition of what has happened, through a common declaration in international law, as the Secretary-General of the Durban Conference wished in advocating the writing of such a history.[32] Nor can one settle for producing a Western counter-narrative as a substitute to the former narrative. In its 2001 Report, the Independent Commission on Africa called for some 'mechanism' to 're-establish the truth' about the slave trade and colonisation.[33] The 2001 Durban Declaration emphasised 'the importance and necessity of teaching about the facts and truth of the history of humankind from antiquity to the recent past' (Point 98). But all these formulations are troublesome as they seem to suggest that there is

[30] Conditional upon the limits related to revisionism of these mass crimes, although those reservations are also contested. See Johann Michel, *Gouverner les mémoires. Les politiques mémorielles en France* (Paris, PUF, 2010) 135 *ff*. See the parallel with the international criminal courts in Martti Koskenniemi, *The Politics of International Law* (Oxford, Hart Publishing, 2011).

[31] Garapon, *Peut-on réparer l'histoire?* (n 1) 247 *ff*.

[32] Conversation between Mary Robinson and Pierre Hazan in the daily newspaper *Libération*, 25 August 2001.

[33] 2001 Cotonou Report cited in *Winning the War against Humiliation* (n 24).

only one 'truth of the history of humankind' and so inadvertently highlight the difficulty of the exercise. However necessary it might be, resorting to history cannot reveal any universal truth about historical crimes, a truth which would ideally be shared by all and would settle the accounts of the past, as this would be a deeply mistaken conception of history that has been sufficiently deconstructed by postmodern scholars and would only prompt new claims, expectations or denials of recognition.[34] To resort to history in this way would be to claim to be able to reconstruct the past afresh. This is intellectually impossible and, in addition, always and inevitably leads to bias, as it is done principally in line with present concerns and usually, as its purpose, lends legitimacy to the powers-that-be and more specifically here to officially institute a new vision of world society and its international institutions for the postcolonial and post-Cold War world.

[34] Mark Osiel, *Mass Atrocity, Collective Memory, and the Law* (New Brunswick and London, Transaction Publishers, 1999).

9

The Law of Recognition versus International Development Law and International Economic Law

THE LAW RELATING to recognition is new. It reflects the need to recognise the importance of culture, diversity and identity in international law in order to respect what it is that imparts meaning to the lives and history of individuals, women, groups and peoples and in order to put an end to the countless denials of recognition to which they are subject. The law of recognition makes it possible therefore to take account of demands made in symbolic and cultural terms and no longer in terms of rationally defined material interests as is the case for most of development law, thereby suggesting that a major redistribution of the demands for justice has come about over the last 20 years.[1] It must be observed, even so, that the distinctions between development and recognition have been simplified with respect to what is a far more complex reality.[2] In differentiating between them in this way for the needs of analysis, I have deliberately ignored the way in which they are intertwined and have therefore provisionally left aside an aspect that ought to be developed as it is essential to understanding all of these changes. I would like to give a glimpse of how, far from being separate entities, the situations relating to development and recognition are often intimately bound together in such a way that claims about them very often overlap. This intermeshing cannot fail to have repercussions on the interplay of the rules and practices of the law pertaining to recognition with the rules and practices of development law. But the relationship between the law of recognition and international economic law must also be examined insofar as, as with development law, international economic law may restrict many of the effects of the law of recognition.

[1] Alain Caillé, 'Introduction' to Alain Caillé (ed), *La quête de la reconnaissance. Nouveau phénomène social total* (Paris, La découverte, 2007) 5.

[2] See Fraser, *Qu'est-ce que la justice sociale?Reconnaissance et Distribution* (Paris, La découverte, 2005) 18 *ff*.

I Intersecting Situations and Demands

We probably need to look back briefly to understand why the question of cultural identity ousted the questions of development and economic redistribution from centre stage. The new post-Cold War paradigm of recognition developed internationally because it met requirements that had until then been secondary to development needs. During the Cold War, it was economic issues that were the focus of attention for international political actors and that crystallised opposition between East and West and between North and South, prompting controversy over economic and social rights, over the New International Economic Order and over classical development law. After the Cold War, with the triumph of globalisation and liberalism, new expectations relating to identity and culture superimposed themselves on the expectations of development. As Fraser emphasises, the new perception based on the concepts of identity, difference and cultural domination stole a march on the old socialist perception, which was largely discredited after 1989, and on all the interpretative schemas involving economic exploitation and oppression.[3] The struggle for redistribution also yielded to the struggle for recognition, including internationally. Culture and identity thus became the key explanations to post-Cold War conflicts and collective frustrations on a worldwide scale. This tendency was further nurtured by the general disappointment arising from failed development policies that arose at the same time and by the fact that the expectations of the first Development Decades sank into disillusion and that it was left to the interplay of neoliberal rules of international economic law to settle development issues. Questions relating to respect, culture and identity gained in importance internationally, pretty much in proportion to the failure of development solutions and to the declining interest in them.

But the significance attributed to culture was in turn challenged by various strands of thought. Some liberal observers criticised the very principle of cultural identity, the sociological weight of cultures and the idea that they might have a decisive role in the lives of individuals and groups, which, it can readily be agreed, makes it pointless to have a body of law designed to protect cultures or identities.[4] Some postmodern commentators have vigorously opposed these principles and deconstructed the new dichotomies they introduce, while some Neo-Marxists have denounced the shift towards culture that has supposedly come about at the expense of arguments about economic exploitation, notably for the countries of the South, and that has

[3] ibid 14.

[4] For examples of this criticism, which is directed above all at multicultural policies, see Seyla Benhabib, *The Claims of Culture. Equality and Diversity in the Global Era* (Princeton, Princeton University Press, 2002) and Brian Barry, *Culture and Equality: An Egalitarian Critique of Multiculturalism* (Cambridge, Polity Press, 2000).

allegedly contributed to them being overshadowed.[5] This has given rise, for example, to subaltern studies which, unlike postcolonial studies with their focus on cultural issues, seek to let the oppressed make their voice heard.[6] In other words, if the question of the economic and social development of Third World states long evinced the struggle for recognition of historical and cultural identity, conversely, the highlighting of questions of culture or of self-esteem may be used so as to no longer really address economic and social matters or to impose true 'identity dictatorships'[7] that reject any idea of economic and social development. One of the risks associated with the emergence of legal practices of recognition is that demands for symbolic recognition may be given precedence over economic and social development processes and over the defence of a fair international order. There is a readiness to grant symbolic acts, to recognise suffering and past and present humiliation, but without looking into the causes of suffering and humiliation that are very often related to economic and social causes and which therefore call for remedies involving economic and social justice.

The multiplicity of criticism is evidence that the question of cultural identity touches on a particularly sensitive area and many of these analyses rightly denounce the limits of the new discourse when it hypostatises culture or identity in a way that proves that it is not just mistaken but also particularly dangerous with regard to the possible manipulations to which they may give rise. It must be observed even so that, embarrassing as they are, such criticisms cannot constitute a definitive objection and they often have their own limits, like mirror images of the theories of recognition, hypostatising the primacy of human freedom or of economics to the detriment of culture. This is probably why it came to be realised in recent years that the analysis of the existing situation could not be reduced to one or other of these explanatory factors, but that they were inseparable and so had to be addressed together. A concrete examination of the various situations evoked throughout this book shows that those which are socially and economically least favoured are also the most stigmatised culturally and therefore that socio-economic injustices are related to injustices as to culture or identity. The circumstances of minorities in Europe, of indigenous peoples in Africa, Asia or America, and of the 48 'least advanced' countries, that is, the poorest in the world, 33 of which are African, are typical of this intersection of situations in which the state of poverty or extreme poverty of these groups and states is duplicated by their

[5] For an association of the struggle between class and identity see John S Saul, *Development after Globalization. Theory and Practice for the Embattled South in a New Imperial Age* (London and New York, Zed Books Ltd, 2006) especially 95 *ff*.

[6] Gayatri Chakravorty Spivak and Ranajit Guha, *Selected Subaltern Studies* (Oxford, Oxford University Press, 1988) and Vinayak Chaturvedi, *Mapping Subaltern Studies and the Postcolonial* (London and New York, Verso Books, 2000).

[7] Sophie Bessis, *L'Occident et les autres. Histoire d'une suprématie* (Paris, La découverte, 2003) 314.

intense social and cultural marginalisation.[8] Beyond the situations of groups and peoples, the same is true of certain categories of persons, especially women, who are exposed to the most numerous and most constant forms of economic domination and cultural discrimination. In a recent book, Martha Nussbaum evokes many concrete examples of these multiple discriminations against women economically and socially, as well as culturally and symbolically and therefore the fact that women are less well fed, less well educated and less well cared for because they are less well considered than men.[9] Women thus incur double economic and cultural discrimination, which is constant and pursues them throughout their lives.[10] In short, the overlap of these different situations shows that economic and cultural factors act together and reinforce each other to become even more detrimental to states, groups and individuals.

Now, if economic and cultural circumstances are usually intertwined, it is not surprising to observe that current demands are themselves very often interrelated and always have been, even if things were not put this way because the question of recognition was blotted out.[11] The desire to secure recognition of one's dignity and cultural identity and to put an end to the denials of recognition is closely wound up with the desire for a better life. Thus, the demands for recognition are not only demands for recognition of a right to equal dignity or a right to be different, but also social aspirations to greater actual equality and to a better standard of living. The Durban Conference amply illustrated this on a world scale for states and peoples. The denunciation of the unequal socio-economic conditions of states and of the world economic system was constantly associated with the feeling of marginalisation and of social and cultural exclusion. As seen above, African states are among the socio-political groups that experience the most serious economic and financial difficulties and the most intense feelings of belittlement. The same is true of the claims of minorities, indigenous peoples and women, although those claims cannot be examined here. It is not difficult to understand, though, that those claims combine aspirations to greater material well-being and to respect for their equal dignity and identity.

[8] See, for example, General Recommendation No 23, 1993, of the Committee on the Elimination of Racial Discrimination (CERD) on indigenous peoples in CERD Annual Report, Doc A/52/18 (1997) annex V and General Recommendation No 27 on discrimination against Roms in CERD Annual Report, Doc A/55/18 (2000) annex VC.

[9] Martha C Nussbaum, *Women and Human Development, The Capabilities Approach* (Cambridge, Cambridge University Press, 2000). See also Partha Chatterjee and Pradeep Jeganathan (eds), *Community, Gender and Violence, Subaltern Studies XI* (New York, Columbia University Press, 2000).

[10] Just like minorities or indigenous peoples, they may also suffer from other forms of discrimination linked to race, say, or language and religion. See Fareda Banda and Christine Chinkin, *Gender, Minorities and Indigenous Peoples* (London, Minority Rights Group, 2004) 1 *ff*.

[11] The use of the expression 'Third World' in itself expresses this tangle of meanings as it refers to a set of states that are economically exploited and culturally stigmatised with respect to the dominant blocs.

II The Law of Recognition and Development Law

From what has gone before, the need arises to understand the paired effects of the international law of recognition and the international law of development and to examine how they fit together.

First of all, it can be observed that some legal rules or practices have a dual effect in the areas of development and of recognition. This is the case, for example, of all the procedural rules that might restore equity in negotiation, information and decision making among states for the benefit of the least favoured of them within international economic and financial institutions. Not only would such rules allow negotiation, on an equal footing, of basic rules that would be more favourable to the least favoured nations in matters of development, but they would help to enhance the identity of marginalised states. Similarly, it has been seen that the principle of development aid may be a form of recognition if it has a symbolic meaning and entails the donor state's acceptance of its past responsibility for historical crimes committed against others. The rules on the protection and promotion of cultures may contribute to eradicating material and social inequalities because of the extremely positive and enhancing role of culture, and because of the legal protection that such rules may offer states or groups that are otherwise economically dominated. Another example is the protection of the rights of marginalised peoples over their forests, for such rights secure respect for their cultural identity (relationship with the forest) and ensure the conservation of their economic resources so as to protect their livelihoods.[12] As for forms of discrimination affecting women, they are so numerous and intertwined that any legal rule guaranteeing women's rights may have effects on development and vice versa.[13] This is a connection that is directly affirmed by the proclamation of the rule of *recognition* of equality between men and women as one of the eight Millennium Development Goals.

In actual fact, the reverse effect may equally well be obtained. Rules protecting the cultural rights of minorities or indigenous peoples and imposing positive measures for the establishment of schools, language centres or media may be perceived as creating economic and social advantages that are unwarranted in the view of the majority population and engender resentment and a feeling of injustice.[14] The reparation of historical wrongs may also induce negative effects. By way of reparation of the wrong done to the Maoris, New Zealand awarded them more generous social aid than for the rest of

[12] See the Rome meeting of 15 July 2011 under the aegis of the Food and Agriculture Organisation of the United Nations (FAO) on reforming forest tenure systems; www.fao.org/news/story/en/item/81870/icode/.

[13] See the 1995 Beijing platform for action (ch III, point F); www.un.org/womenwatch/daw/beijing/pdf/BDPfA%20E.pdf.

[14] Banda and Chinkin, *Gender, Minorities and Indigenous Peoples* (n 10) 5 *ff.*

the population, which prompted a very intense feeling of injustice from the less well-off and exacerbated their racism.[15] Contrariwise, rules on development may be detrimental to cultures or may harm identities. For example, the unilateral or treaty-based legal practices of development law that impose selective and arbitrary conditions on the beneficiaries of economic aid may be perceived as stigmatising by those who are forced to accept them. Development rules may therefore harm recognition and perpetuate a lack of self-esteem that affects an entire people. Besides, the whole of development law may be considered as stigmatising in itself through the distinctions it posits between states, which can be seen as a continuation of the dichotomies of the colonial period.[16] It is based entirely on a structure of cultural evaluation of world society that is thrust upon 'developing' or 'less developed' nations even if these expressions attempt to avoid the negativity of the former categorisations of 'underdeveloped' or 'backward'. One need only see, by contrast, the feeling of pride that nations feel when they are characterised as 'emerging'. For Philippe Marchesin, apart from considerations specific to development, one of the factors in understanding the awakening of the South has two elements to it: the desire to re-tie the strands of history that were severed by foreign domination and the desire to repair the humiliation incurred as former colonised nations.[17] The fact that this challenge is situated in the fields of economics and technology is all the more important for these countries of the South as these were the means that, for centuries, formed the basis of Western supremacy over the rest of the world. The arms of the former powers have therefore been turned against them. The deep colonial wound is thus the impetus for a longing for revenge and it is certain that once achieved, the economic and social development of states is this time the most effective instrument for re-enhancing their identity by putting an end to past feelings of inferiority. This explains the declaration of Brazil's President Lula upon his country being chosen to organise the 2016 Olympic Games: 'Because we were colonised, we have a chip on our shoulder about being small. Today, that is all over! This is our time.'[18]

This is why, far from challenging the cultural evaluation structure underpinning development law, the emerging countries adapt to it because they derive from it a feeling of pride at reaching the top of the ladder. And although it is an unfair structure of cultural evaluation, it has still got a lot of life left in it and will continue to stigmatise countries depending on whether they move up or down the development ladder. It raises a dilemma about the development/recognition relationship; a dilemma concerning all of development law which

[15] Bouda Etemad, *Crimes et Réparations. L'Occident face à son passé colonial* (Paris, Ed A Versaille, 2008), 130.

[16] See Firouzeh Nahavandi, *Du développement à la globalisation. Histoire d'une stigmatisation* (Brussels, Bruylant, 2002) especially 27 *ff*.

[17] Philippe Marchesin, 'La revanche pour le Sud' *Le Monde* 30 October 2010, 19.

[18] ibid (our translation).

is introduced so as to erase the material differences between states but which operates by taking notice of a difference to which a stigma is attached.[19] The only solution can be a fair and sustainable system that breaks with any idea of a belittling comparative scale, which sets all states on an equal footing and so makes development law effective in restoring equal dignity among states and peoples.

Secondly, a well thought out and effective arrangement of rules and practices for recognition and development needs to be devised. If the situations and demands are intertwined, if the challenges are closely bound together, then the remedies must be designed so as to act jointly or in a complementary fashion, that is, they must act at the same time on the development model and on the cultural models of representation of individuals, women, groups and states so as to address these questions in their totality. Who could believe that the problems of postcolonial society between the ex-colonised and the ex-colonisers could be solved by material prosperity alone, when the logics of racism and contempt and therefore of resentment are still present? Who could think that the expectations of women, indigenous people or minorities might be met just by the recognition of their rights without them being accompanied by the legal tools to improve their economic and social circumstances so as to make those circumstances fair compared with others?

It remains then for this necessary articulation between the two bodies of law to be thought out. In this respect, there is an interesting tendency that aims to associate culture and development more closely in the international area and therefore to bring together concerns that development law and the law of recognition usually address separately. The example can be taken of two types of connections that are easy to understand. First, the idea of a cultural dimension to development was launched several decades ago, when it was realised that there were limits and de-structuring effects for identities and cultures from the imposition of the Western model of economic development on societies alien to this culture.[20] Reconciling culture and development emerged as a priority and in 1988 the United Nations Educational, Scientific and Cultural Organisation (UNESCO) proclaimed a Cultural Development Decade. It then set up a World Commission on Culture and Development for the purpose of 'placing culture at the heart of development' thereby holding out new hope, which Javier Perez de Cuellar expressed in particularly emphatic terms in 1994: 'If culture becomes development's guiding star, if

[19] Another example of this is highlighted by Akhil Gupta; underdevelopment itself has become a form of identity for some Third World populations; See Akhil Gupta, *Postcolonial Developments: Agriculture in the Making of Modern India* (Durham, Duke University Press, 1998) 338 *ff*.

[20] See the Development and Culture Forum of the Inter-American Development Bank in 1996 in Paris; www.minefe.gouv.fr/fonds_documentaire/notes_bleues/nbb/nbb155/banque.htm. See also Alain Pellet and Jean-Marc Sorel (eds), *Le droit international du développement social et culturel* (Paris, L'Hermès, 1997) and Marc Poncelet, *Une utopie post-tiers-mondiste. La dimension culturelle du développement* (Paris, L'Harmattan, 1994).

it ranks first among the priorities of the national and international agenda, we will have protected the only untouched heritage of humankind: the virgin land of the future.'[21]

In fact, the idea was not really new since not only had the concept of cultural development existed since the earliest UN resolutions, but everyone had also very quickly gauged the relevance of such a step. In the 1980s, the big development agencies had begun to rehabilitate culture by looking to make local populations the main actors of their own development so as to give them prominence, to respect their cultural identity and, in so doing, make development more effective.[22] The introduction of a cultural dimension was designed to promote cultural adaptations of the development model by taking account of the cultural practices and historical and traditional contexts in which the model was to be put in place. Nonetheless, one can only observe that the actual achievement of this new form of development was very limited and remains so, which is all the more unsatisfactory because the relevance of the principle is reinforced by the few very fine successes achieved locally, which certainly attests to the fact that the only models that can work are those that respect the cultures in which they are to be introduced and the identity of the people who are to be the beneficiaries.[23] It is highly significant in this respect that it was the Asian countries, with the oldest traditions and most resilient cultures that achieved spectacular economic development and not the countries that were subject to the diktats of the International Monetary Fund and the World Bank. At the same time, it cannot be overlooked that, as development itself is a concept of Western origin, it is intrinsically a vector of Western principles and practices that partly slant the project and quickly show up the limits of the exercise.[24]

Secondly, cultural rights have been explicitly attached to the new face of development in its 'human' aspect. In 2004, a United Nations Development Programme (UNDP) report showed that cultural freedom is a decisive factor for human development.[25] The idea is that human beings cannot experience real development, and therefore truly choose the ends that make them flourish, unless they can fully live out their cultural preferences and those of their communities. As Patrice Meyer-Bisch so clearly expounds it, the violation of cultural rights is an aggravating factor of poverty, whereas, conversely, cultural rights may help to combat poverty and promote the

[21] *Le Monde*, 25 February 1994 (our translation).

[22] See for example Guy Hermet, *Développement et culture* (Paris, Sciences Po, 2000). With regard to South America and Africa, see Essé Amouzou, *L'influence de la culture sur le développement en Afrique noire* (Paris, L'Harmattan, 2009).

[23] See the UNESCO culture and development website.

[24] See the criticism by Suzanne Schech and Jane Haggis, *Culture and Development: A Critical Introduction* (Oxford, Blackwell Publishers, 2000) and in another way Gilbert Rist (ed), *La culture, otage du développement?* (Paris, L'Harmattan, 1994).

[25] UNDP 2004 Report, 'Cultural Liberty in Today's Diverse World'; hdr.undp.org/en/reports/global/hdr2004/.

human development of individuals.[26] Cultural rights can improve the capabilities of individuals and their opportunities to make life choices that allow them to thrive. They can be an irreplaceable factor in integration while, conversely, the denial of such rights depletes individuals, reduces their life choices and worsens their state of poverty or of economic and social exclusion. Obviously, what holds for cultural rights also holds for women's rights, the rights of minorities and of indigenous peoples. They are essential to the improvement of the economic and social circumstances of categories of vulnerable and stigmatised persons in the same way as economic and social rights are the necessary corollary of specific rights ensuring the protection of their identity and culture.

Starting with these few examples drawn from actual practice, it can be seen that what is at play here, on a particularly crucial point, is the possibility of fitting together the legal responses given at the international level to the two most characteristic types of injustice of present-day international society so that these responses may reinforce one another without impeding one another; and this analysis needs to be taken much further than it has been here to identify other possible areas where the two bodies of law might fit together. Even then, not everything would have been said, for it must be understood that this question leads on to a far more general basic legal problem that goes beyond the question of the articulation between the law of recognition and the law of development. The recognition of the equal dignity of cultures and the restoration of wounded identities must go hand in hand with the reinsertion of stigmatised countries, peoples and human beings into a world economy in which the rules of the game are equitable and do not counter their effects. This brings us back once again to the existing legal and economic order.

III The Law of Recognition and International Economic Law

Here we come back to what was said at the end of Part one of this book, namely that international economic law remains the decisive component of all these legal practices. It has already been seen how the neoliberal rules of international economic law could influence all classical and new international law on development, often making development law sound like some beguiling discourse that no longer fooled anyone. Exactly the same may apply to the rules of recognition. International economic law is essential in making them viable since any cultural rule requires some material backing and fits

[26] Patrice Meyer-Bisch, 'Les violations des droits culturels, facteur d'appauvrissement durable: pour une observation des pauvretés culturelles' in Emmanuel Decaux and Alice Yotopoulou-Marangopoulos (eds), *La pauvreté, un défi pour les droits de l'homme* (Paris, Pedone, 2009) 185 *ff*. He develops arguments in Joseph Wresinski, *Culture et grande pauvreté* (Paris, Ed Quart monde, 2004).

into an economy; but international economic law can then, by this means, neutralise their impact if it imposes the rules of market capitalism, financial deregulation and ever greater free trade.

Let us take the example of cultural diversity. What might the rules of the 2005 Convention be worth if they fail to provide for their primacy over or at least their compatibility with the commercial rules of the World Trade Organisation (WTO)? What becomes of the principle of the diversity of cultural expressions adopted in 2005 at UNESCO if at the WTO the only legal system applicable is the far more restrictive system of cultural exception? And what if the world's leading economic power, the United States, uses the legal technique of bilateral agreements to systematically circumvent the rules so as to benefit free trade? Since the Convention was adopted, the United States has got around the principle of diversity by a series of bilateral agreements entered into with Third World states through which it makes the attribution of economic advantages conditional upon those states abandoning internal measures for the protection and promotion of national cultures provided for in the Convention. The cynicism of this policy destroys everything that was so symbolically decisive in the 2005 Convention in terms of cultural recognition and respect of identities. Let us take another example: what do the rights of minorities and indigenous peoples, the protection of their heritage, of their traditional arts, their forests and their ancestral lands count for if the national and transnational interplay of private economic actors, oil companies, mining and logging companies can quite lawfully impose itself on them, notably through investment contracts that are excessively favourable to the investor?[27] In Latin America, for example, several enterprises have seen new markets open up to them thanks to globalisation and the neoliberal system that favours the deregulation of investments but it is also to the obvious detriment of the rights of indigenous peoples.[28] On these grounds, accusations have been made against several enterprises such as Glamis Gold and Montana in Guatemala, Repsol in Bolivia and Peru and Texaco in Ecuador, but without there being anything in employment law, the rights of indigenous peoples or human rights to legally counter activities which are otherwise made lawful by international investment law.

The problematic relationship between these separate systems was notably discussed during negotiations on the 2005 Convention on the Protection and Promotion of the Diversity of Cultural Expressions. The negotiators knew perfectly well that the principle of diversity of cultural expressions would only be window dressing because of the imbalance of North–South, and now South–South, economic power if competition law took precedence over

[27] See Frédéric Deroche and Julian Burger, *Les peuples autochtones et leur relation à la terre: un questionnement pour l'ordre mondial* (Paris, L'Harmattan, 2008).

[28] See, for example, Janet Warden-Fernandez, 'Indigenous Companies' Rights and Mineral Development' (2005) 23 (4) *Journal of Energy and Natural Resources Law* 417 *ff.*

the law of cultural diversity.[29] They then tried to take account of the difference in the level of development of states but also to square the rules of the Convention with international economic law. There is a whole series of issues about development. They introduce the principles of cooperation, preferential treatment and the creation of a support fund for developing countries (Article 2(4) and Articles 13–18). However, the fund is only very moderately supplied for the time being and, moreover, as Hélène Ruiz-Fabri points out,[30] while the provisions on cooperation are used conditionally by rich countries so as to weigh on the cultural orientations of developing countries, those provisions may serve as an underhanded way of reinstating a new form of cultural imperialism. The new body of law may therefore itself have ambivalent effects and be used as a new constraint on poor countries. Moreover, the Convention makes provision for relations with the other treaty-based instruments of the states parties (Articles 20 and 21) including their economic and financial commitments. Article 20 provides that there should be three elements to the relationship: 'mutual supportiveness, complementarity and non-subordination'. Because of 'non-subordination', states parties cannot subordinate the 2005 Convention to other treaties and neither can they use the Convention as an argument to modify their other treaty commitments. This is a classical application of treaty law. That leaves only 'mutual supportiveness' or 'complementarity' and the hypothesis of some solution involving compatibility between the provisions of the Convention. Now, while the compatibility of rules – and of actions of the relevant institutions – may make it possible to come up with a common economic solution to give effect to the legal principle of diversity, it has to be observed that, at this stage, there is nothing to indicate how, in fact, the relation between the rules protecting and promoting cultural diversity will square with the rules of international economic law. And, for now, all the signs are that the WTO's international economic law will prevail as it does in other domains.

Through this we are led back, unsurprisingly, to the problems addressed with international development law because the international law of recognition may well prove to have very little effect in some of its branches and may largely fail to reform the violations of cultures and identities unless it can put an end to the economic and cultural domination that is an impediment to the diversity of cultures and the flourishing of identities. In this case, it would have a particularly worrying dark side, a highly rhetorical aspect that might even reinforce scepticism about all these legal developments because

[29] See Elsa Comby, 'Quel type de coopération peut être engagé entre pays du Nord et pays du Sud?' in Hélène Ruiz-Fabri, *La convention de l'UNESCO sur la promotion et la protection de la diversité des expressions culturelles. Premier bilan et défis juridiques* (Paris, Société de législation comparée, 2010) 255–66.

[30] Hélène Ruiz-Fabri, 'Conclusion à deux voix', *La convention de l'UNESCO sur la promotion et la protection de la diversité des expressions culturelles. Premier bilan et défis juridiques* (Paris, Société de législation comparée, 2010) 276.

this law of recognition might be seen as a roundabout way to further subject individuals, states, groups and marginalised individuals to a dominant neo-liberal world order that has no real concern for their identities and cultures, but merely gives the impression that they are respected.[31] The inevitable result is that everything that was said at the end of Part one of this book about the re-casting of the existing legal and economic system for more equitable development is applicable here; that is, ultimately everything involves the modification of international economic law, as set out above, but also the way in which international economic law can or cannot fit together with the other branches of international law. This final aspect of the question deserves attention as this enquiry is brought to its close, since there has not so far been any opportunity to evoke it and to say why it is so problematic because of the specific characteristics of the international legal order.[32]

Unlike domestic legal orders that are all hierarchical in some way or other, the present-day international legal order is characterised by the relative fragmentation of its regimes and the absence of any hierarchical order in its rules. It simply juxtaposes the general principles of law, international custom and the legal regimes engendered by bilateral and multilateral international treaties. The basic classical principle behind this is that of the normative equivalence between any norm and any source of international law. This means that the most insignificant bilateral treaty has the same legal value as the most fundamental of general customs. True, there are rules about the succession of norms and rules of minimum compatibility as to the interpretation of treaties, but they are of limited application. It is also true that there is a change afoot towards some degree of rank ordering of the norms of international law with the existence of a few common formal and material principles, but the international legal order still remains weakly coordinated even so.[33] With the latest phase of globalisation, it may be thought that international law is even more de-structured because of an ever more complex tangle of international, transnational and private normative spaces obeying their own principles of coherence.[34] And so this very particular state of the international legal order would seem to explain the juxtaposition of legal regimes without any connection between them, such as the regimes on human rights, environment law and therefore also economic law and the law of recognition. The international

[31] In line with a self-image consistent with what society expects which acts as an incentive to voluntary submission. This is an 'ideological' form of recognition that must be distinguished from these 'justified forms'. See Axel Honneth, 'La reconnaissance comme idéologie' in *La société du mépris. Vers une nouvelle théorie critique* (Paris, La découverte, 2006).

[32] I speak here of legal order in the weak sense of the term, without getting into the discussion of whether it forms a 'system' in the strong sense or merely a 'space'.

[33] See Pierre-Marie Dupuy, 'L'unité de l'ordre juridique international, Cours général de droit international public' (2002) *Recueil des Cours de l'Academie de Droit International* 297 and especially on the inclusion of commercial law in the international order, 450 *ff*.

[34] See Neil Walker, 'Beyond Boundary Disputes and Basic Grids: Mapping the Global Disorder of Normative Orders' (2008) 6 (3-4) *International Journal of Constitutional Law* 373–96.

legal order may at one and the same time, and without any express solution as to compatibility, include neoliberal international economic law and legal norms like those of recognition and development that involve escaping in part from that economic law, with each new regime being created to suit the needs of states and other actors of international society without them worrying unduly about any contradictory effects. In other words, the incoherent, limited or contradictory aspect of the different regimes of the international legal order is a logical consequence of its partially disordered character and of the insufficient rules of compatibility or the absence of any rank order among its norms. This rapid presentation simplifies in the extreme a phenomenon that has many ramifications, since two other factors should be taken into account:

(1) The fact that the functional regimes we have evoked (law of development, recognition, international economic law, etc), which co-exist without any hierarchical order, are compounded by regional regimes (European, American, African law, etc) and transnational regimes (*lex mercatoria*, *electronica*, *sportiva*, etc), making relations between norms and sources of the international legal order and the perception one may have of it highly complex.
(2) The fact that this relative fragmentation of the international order into separate functional, regional, transnational regimes stands alongside a dispersion of power bases (public and private) within international society that also particularly aggravates the phenomenon.[35]

From this it can finally be seen, at this stage, that, such as they are integrated into this legal order, the international law of recognition and international development law can at best correct but not transform the existing order[36] because they leave in place the deep-seated cultural and economic structures that underpin this order, that is, the dichotomous cultural patterns of representation inherited from the colonial/postcolonial period (and other patterns of representation for the other debased identities) and the market capitalist and financial system which both constantly reproduce economic and cultural inequalities. The law of recognition and the law of development do not deconstruct these structures but aim merely to correct their negative effects, aiming at greater fairness in the case of international development law and at greater valuing of culture in the case of the international law of recognition. However, if one were to adopt transformational solutions, these would have to address the basic structures of the economy and of culture and take, say, the form of economic de-growth and cultural de-construction. This would be to advocate a shift away from liberal international law, the end of international development law and of current international economic law, and a

[35] See Mireille Delmas-Marty, *Les forces imaginantes du droit (III) La refondation des pouvoirs* (Paris, Seuil, 2007).

[36] In the sense of the distinctions posited by Fraser, *Qu'est-ce que la justice sociale* 32 *ff* (n 2), who recommends transformational remedies.

move towards an international law of de-growth. It would also be to advocate the end of the international law of recognition and its replacement by an international law of cultural de-construction where all the dichotomies and differences would be abolished and replaced by a flexible network of multiple cultural references. I shall not venture to develop the implications of this here, but these are other viewpoints that exist and that are found in particular among post-developmentalists, de-constructivists, postmodernists or certain feminist movements.

Conclusion

I An Equitable and Decent International Society?

THE EVOLUTION OF international law between development and recognition was not a chance occurrence; it occurred in two stages corresponding to the appearance of two paradigms that have ended up intersecting, two intellectual and social matrices that dominate ways of thinking and behaving in international law and that have taken hold in two specific contexts. The development paradigm imposed itself after 1945 and was to reach its high point with decolonisation, while the paradigm of recognition was the product of the ending of the Cold War in 1989. The resulting international law relating to development and recognition has been formed by heterogeneous sets of practices, rules and discourses that have in some instances been abandoned, in others transformed or re-evaluated and in others, introduced in a new way. The two bodies of law are not perfectly autonomous and individualised branches of the law, nor are they collections of formalised rules, which matters little anyway. What matters above all, at this stage, has been to show that they may correspond to one of the most important reformulations of classical liberal international law and of its principle of formal justice. The principle of formal equality which is the basis of classical inter-state international law emerges with two twists, so as to allow for material inequalities and cultural differences. Admittedly, international law remains a liberal law in the political and economic sense, insofar as the liberties of sovereign states and of natural persons and legal entities are still paramount in this legal order and as the neoliberal model entirely dominates international economic law. But international law is beset by a double dynamic that tends to go somewhat beyond its original formalism and abstraction and that reflects the bounds such law comes up against when it is based solely on the principle of the equal sovereign freedom of states and on the individualism and artificial character of its legal constructions. It is in this way that the law of development aims primarily to restore a greater real equality among states whereas the law of recognition aims to ensure a differentiated form of equality, that is, a form of equality that combines equal respect for all with the entitlement to cultural difference.[1]

[1] A phenomenon occurs that is reminiscent in part of the dynamics of equality within certain present-day democratic societies where, in keeping with Tocqueville's analyses, equality extends to all areas of social life (Dominique Schnapper, *La démocratie providentielle. Essai sur l'égalité contemporaine* (Paris, Gallimard, 2002) 18 *ff*). Because of the changes in the objective and subjective conditions of international society, we are today seeing an extension of the principle

And yet we cannot overlook the darker sides of this evolution. The three main ones are pointed out here, without systematically going over the difficulties highlighted throughout the book. The first dark side is the de facto (but not de jure) subordination of these two bodies of law to international economic law, which means that the transition to more concrete and more differentiated equality does not, for the time being, counteract the rules which continue to support the economic and cultural domination of the powers-that-be and the major private economic operators especially. Accordingly, the two bodies of law remain partially ineffective legal instruments and sometimes even serve as convenient screens behind which the same all-out market logic is deployed as is enshrined in current international economic law. There may be a complete shift in what was assumed to be the original purpose of these legal instruments and a paradoxical turnaround whereby the promises of development and recognition actually serve to promote 'forms of voluntary submission' to the existing order rather than realigning and reshaping that order as they are supposed to.[2] And at the very least they now have ambivalent effects since, as they are taken up by international economic institutions, they provide tools for correcting the existing model while contributing to legitimate it. The second dark side is that the two bodies of law usually operate separately and not enough thought has been put into how they affect one another. This is how development law in itself comes to produce stigmatising effects and how the law of recognition can contribute to eclipsing questions relating to the economic exploitation of poor countries, individuals, women or vulnerable minorities. The third dark side arises from the fact that these two bodies of law are the fruit of dominant paradigms. They posit principles and dichotomies that these paradigms have themselves raised and it is therefore very difficult to go beyond these paradigms because we lose sight of them as paradigms, perceiving them instead as objective reality. Therefore, they inevitably restrict our knowledge of the facts and our interpretation of them. They also entrap the actors in a language game which they are forced to play in order to advance their claims, at the risk of losing their identity. Indigenous peoples, who are fighting for recognition, have been compelled to comply with the language of the dominant form of law and have described themselves as 'peoples' who hold 'rights' and wish to recover their 'sovereignty' over their 'natural resources'. However, these terms may not describe their circumstances correctly, which they might formulate differently in their own language. Feminists argue that the current legal language cannot do them justice as it is formulated completely in terms of male hegemony. Some peoples, who would like to develop autonomous forms of economies, are forced to present their demands in the only legal

of equality and its effects, and we can speak of a degree of 'democratisation' related to these phenomena.

[2] For recognition, see the approach and warnings of Axel Honneth, *La société du mépris. Vers une nouvelle théorie critique* (Paris, La découverte, 2006) 245 *ff* and 286 *ff*.

language available in terms of economic, human or sustainable 'development', which places them in a situation, and at a level of development, from which they might want to escape and which inevitably distorts their way of seeing things. The two bodies of development law and the law of recognition thus show that, through them, we endorse the socio-cultural presuppositions about well-being and self-esteem that are the product of the dominant values of our times, which we take to be morally superior to the past and which must therefore be imposed all round.[3] This is inevitable and does not in itself discredit them, but it does demonstrate that although the changes observed throughout this book are particularly noteworthy, they are nonetheless problematic and invite us to maintain a constantly critical perspective on things.

The critical approach is all the more important as we are dealing with bodies of law that address requirements of social justice. These legal evolutions may be interpreted as heralding a certain form of international justice. As I have tried to show, we may be seeing the barest outline of what could be social justice on a world scale, where the world itself becomes a context of justice. True, the two bodies of law on development and recognition are not the outcome of any deliberate ethical project; true, they are imperfect and raise real difficulties because of their ambiguity and their darker sides; they may even sporadically engender injustice; but they are nonetheless the outcome of certain specific circumstances that have seen the advent of a postcolonial and post-Cold War world which has given rise to new expectations in regards to justice.[4] So, they may be interpreted as ushering in a fairer international society that is both equitable (in response to socio-economic injustice) and decent (in response to cultural injustice) and one which is ordered around legal norms, practices and discourses that are based on both equity and respect.

The principles of equitable and decent justice that I have tried to highlight here are based on the simple empirical observation of the legal practices of existing international law. Those principles are the contingent product of a given historical period that brought together the particular circumstances of justice, and the question of their possible rational foundation remains open. They form a two-dimensional justice which upholds the demands of the paradigm of development and of recognition without either dimension prevailing over the other and in such a way that they are both complementary and

[3] ibid 249 *ff.*

[4] On the notion of 'circumstances of justice' inherited from Hume and so frequently used and discussed in contemporary theory, see Michael Sandel, *Liberalism and the Limits of Justice* (Cambridge, Cambridge University Press, 1982, 1998) 28 and Stéphane Chauvier, *Justice et droits à l'échelle globale* (Paris, Vrin, 2006) 91 *ff.* See also the remarkable work by Alain Renaut which directly inspired me to identify the circumstances relating to the postcolonial and post-Cold War world, but which he takes to be 'circumstances of diversity': Renaut, *Un humanisme de la diversité. Essai sur la décolonisation des identités* (Paris, Flammarion, 2009) especially 73 *ff.* I do not believe we have moved from a paradigm of identity to one of diversity since, as I have tried to show, the two are inseparably bound together.

irreducible to the other.[5] These principles integrate the features of distributive and corrective or even reparatory justice, which are already considered to have been transposed to the international level, contrary to what certain contemporary theories of justice sometimes suggest in seeming to ignore the actual facts of law and international society. To this is added, although not all its implications have been developed at this stage, the radical new principle of intergenerational equity related to sustainable development. These are principles that form what might more correctly be termed global rather than international justice, as not only does it include subjects and actors other than states, such as peoples, minorities, natural persons and legal entities, but it also reflects the gradual shift of international law in favour of the human person and away from the state, which inevitably leads to a reshuffling of the cards of international justice insofar as the consideration of the human person and of his or her fundamental rights tends to impose itself everywhere and to mark the boundaries of all other legal practices of recognition and development. It is this global justice which prevents development being brought about for the selfish benefit of states alone, which prevents recognition from switching into radical identity-based claims.[6] Now, if it were to prove definitive, this major contemporary switch would signal the ultimate transition from the old classical liberal inter-state law to an international law centred on the human being and the advent of a global justice no longer of states but of human beings.[7]

[5] This is the two-dimensional justice analysed by Nancy Fraser but modified due to being transposed to international level.

[6] See Charles Jones, *Global Justice. Defending Cosmopolitanism* (Oxford, Oxford University Press, 2004) and Thomas W Pogge (ed), *Global Justice* (Oxford, Blackwell Publishing, 2001). On the contemporary debates that followed Rawls's *Law of Peoples*, which completely disregards global justice, see Cécile Fabre, *Justice in a Changing World* (Cambridge, Polity Press, 2007) 95 *ff*. The very idea of global justice, or even of international justice, remains controversial. See Thomas Nagel, 'The Problem of Global Justice' (2005) 33 *Philosophy and Public Affairs* 113–47.

[7] See Antonio A Trindade-Cançado, *International Law for Humankind. Towards a New Jus Gentium* (The Hague, M Nijhoff, 2010). An examination of the origin of this major change and of its international effects will be the subject of my next book.

Index